The Book of
NYNEHEAD

A Village on the River Tone

Nynehead & District Local History Society

HALSGROVE

First published in Great Britain in 2003.

Copyright © 2003 Nynehead & District Local History Society.

British Library Cataloguing-in-Publication Data.
A CIP record for this title is available from the British Library.

ISBN 1 84114 248 4

HALSGROVE

Halsgrove House
Lower Moor Way
Tiverton, Devon EX16 6SS
Tel: 01884 243242
Fax: 01884 243325
email: sales@halsgrove.com
website: www.halsgrove.com

Frontispiece photograph: *The River Tone, looking upstream from the canal aqueduct, May 2003.*

Printed and bound by Bookcraft Ltd, Midsomer Norton.

Contents

Acknowledgements & Sources

This book has been a team effort, involving many people within and outside Nynehead. The work has been guided by a steering group of the Local History Society – Tony and Cynthia Lock, David Manners, David Rabson and Denis Dodd.

Written material has been contributed by Bridget Clarke, Joy Darby, Denis Dodd, Alan Ketley, Cynthia Lock, Tony Lock, David Manners, Geraldine Orr, David Rabson, Sheila Rabson, Alastair Riley, William Sanford and Neville Upham. There is not space to acknowledge everyone who has contributed memories, photographs and other material, but particular mention must be made of John Sparks, together with Jim Lake, Doug Lentell, Edgar Poole and Joy Stone. Thanks are also due to past members of the Local History Society who carried out research over the years and others no longer with us who have contributed unknowingly.

The photographic work has been co-ordinated by David Manners, Tim Manners has produced original maps and Tony Haskell has provided drawings specially for the book. The Grand Western Canal Trust has kindly allowed the use of drawings by Michael Blackmore. David Rabson has co-ordinated the Society's work on the book and edited the text. The copyright of illustrative material used remains with those who provided it.

The book would not have been possible without the wealth of material about Nynehead held in the Somerset Studies Library, the Somerset Record Office and the Somerset Environmental Records Centre, and thanks are due to their staff for their help. In particular access to the papers of the Sanford family in the Record Office has been essential and the help given by William Sanford of Chipley has been greatly appreciated. Reports of village activities in the *Wellington Weekly News* have also been invaluable. We have consciously not included detailed references or bibliographies in the hope that anyone interested in following up the story of Nynehead will make use of the resources available in the Studies Library and the Record Office. Material acquired during the research is being deposited in the County Record Office for future reference.

Finally, the financial support given by a National Lottery 'Awards for All' grant is gratefully acknowledged.

Recording memories of Nynehead – Jim Lake and John Sparks reminiscing.

Introduction

Nynehead lies on the River Tone about seven miles upstream of Somerset's county town of Taunton. In the 1780s it was described as being 'pleasantly situated in a country well wooded and watrd, and agreeably interspersd with small hills and vales', and first impressions today might be of a pleasant if unexceptional small village typical of south-west Somerset. As in all villages everyday life has changed fundamentally over the past 200 years, but there is much that remains special about Nynehead – the River Tone, Nynehead Court and its gardens, the fine Parish Church, a lost parkland, distinctive rural buildings, the Grand Western Canal, and the enigma of the Nynehead 'Hollow' – combined with the influence of the Sanford family for more than three centuries and the contribution to the wider world of people with Nynehead connections.

In 1971, when Nynehead hosted the World Ploughing Championships, local people put on an exhibition to tell visitors about the village. This led to the formation of the Nynehead & District Local History Society, with the aim of promoting research about the village. Thirty-two years later the Society continues to flourish, with members drawn from Nynehead, Wellington and nearby villages.

This book brings together the results of the Society's research along with new material. Over the years the investigations have led to other places in England and even as far as Australia! However, the book is not the final word on Nynehead's past and it is hoped that readers will be encouraged to explore further the history of this fascinating village.

Notes for readers

Most of the places referred to in the book can be seen from public roads and footpaths but there are some where the landowner's consent would be required. Public rights of way are shown on the OS 1:25000 Explorer Map no. 128 (Taunton and Blackdown Hills).

For clarity the part of the parish around Nynehead Court is referred to as 'Lower' Nynehead, although this name is not 'official'.

The spelling of local place names varies between sources and over the centuries. Normally consistent spelling has been used but this has not always been possible.

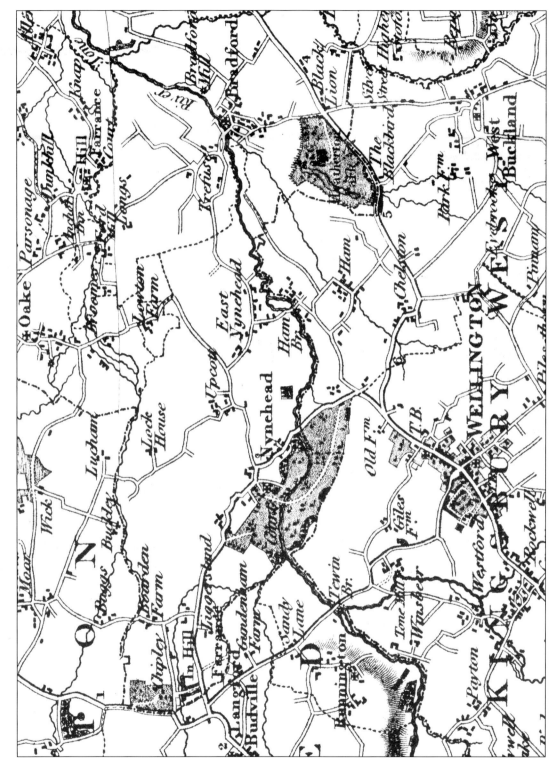

Nynehead in its setting. An extract from Greenwood's Map of Somerset, 1822.

Chapter One

SETTING THE SCENE

Nynehead lies in the heart of the rich and fertile Vale of Taunton Deane. Its setting can best be appreciated from the edge of the Blackdowns escarpment above West Buckland, four miles to the south. The view is stunning. Behind lies the plateau of the Blackdowns extending south to the English Channel, while in front is the vale bounded by the Brendon Hills 12 miles to the north-west (rising to 1,283 feet at Elworthy Barrows) and the hills of Mid Devon to the west. The long ridge of the Quantocks, rising to 1,261 feet at Wills Neck, extends to the Bristol Channel and on a clear day one can see the hills of South Wales 60 miles away to the north.

In the foreground the land drops away sharply through a patchwork of small fields and woods to the M5 motorway. The town of Wellington lies to the left while in the distance to the right is Taunton. The recent commercial development at Chelston and Poole is in the middle distance, while beyond is the undulating farming landscape in which Nynehead lies.

The Vale has long been recognised as a rich agricultural area and was largely under the control of the Bishop of Winchester's estates during the Middle Ages. In 1798 John Billingsley, in *A General View of the Agriculture of the County of Somerset*, described the Vale in a way that would have remained apt over many centuries:

The agricultural practices of this division of the county merit the attention of all travellers. The climate, particularly of that part which is called the Vale of Taunton Deane, is peculiarly mild and serene; and the soil highly fertile and productive. The eye is agreeably relieved by a judicious mixture of arable, and pasture; and if it be contrasted with some parts of the Northern District, it may emphatically be called the Land of Canaan.

The parish of Nynehead is roughly egg-shaped, about three miles from east to west and one and a half miles from north to south. The ancient parish, before it was extended, consisted of about 1,400 acres between the River Tone on the south and the smaller Luckham stream, which rises on Langford Common, flows into the Hillfarrance Brook and eventually joins the Tone at Hele, two miles downstream of East Nynehead.

The parish is set on a long ridge of land descending from the north-west to the south-east. The highest point (about 300 feet above sea level) lies to the north-west of Chipley on the boundary with the parish of Milverton. The best impression of the landscape is gained by following the road from Langford Budville – a gradual descent with the land falling away on each side of the road until one reaches Lower Nynehead, about 150 feet above sea level. From here the road rises sharply through the Hollow to Higher Nynehead (about 200 feet) before dropping to about 100 feet where the River Tone leaves the eastern end of the parish. Two high points break the pattern: the clump of trees known as the Burrows with extensive views over the Tone valley towards Wellington and the Blackdowns, and the Knapp, on the road to Oake, looking north towards the Brendons and the Quantocks.

Away from the houses and beyond the roadside hedges the landscape has a generally open appearance – this is probably relatively recent. The 1888 Ordnance Survey map shows many roadside and hedgerow trees, perhaps lost since 1945 as a result of agricultural improvements and Dutch elm disease. This openness contrasts with the enclosed wooded feeling, especially around the Court and at East Nynehead and Chipley.

The ancient settlements (Lower Nynehead, East Nynehead and Chipley) are sited in sheltered positions, avoiding both the prevailing winds to which the parish is exposed and the flood plain of the River Tone. Lower Nynehead lies in a dip to the east of the Court, which itself is set just to the north-east of a ridge looking west towards Wellington. East Nynehead and Chipley lie on south-facing slopes, while two of the outlying farms – Hornshay and Clavengers – are sited just above the Tone flood plain. In the flatter northern parts of the parish lies Heywood Farm (formerly Haywood), while Blockhouse Farm and the former settlement of Pixton sit on a low ridge overlooking the Luckham stream. Higher Nynehead is somewhat different. Originally called Upcott, after the farm on the Milverton road, it now consists of largely twentieth-century houses right on the ridge and exposed on all sides.

GEOLOGY AND SOILS

The view north from the Blackdowns looks across rocks of several geological ages from the Cretaceous

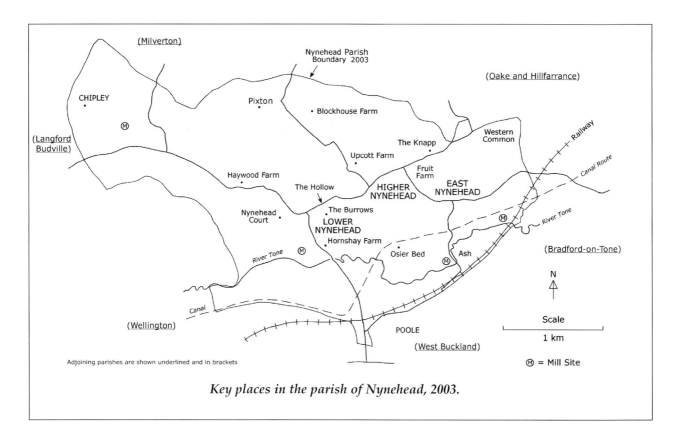

Key places in the parish of Nynehead, 2003.

series of the Blackdowns to the Devonian sandstones of the Brendons and Quantocks. In between the hills the Vale is distinguished by a long outcrop of Permian and Triassic rocks running north to south, giving the soils of the area their characteristic red appearance. In effect Nynehead lies on the Exe–Tees line which divides 'lowland' from 'highland' Britain.

The geology of the parish of Nynehead is relatively simple, the rocks being divided into two areas. The eastern half of the parish, from the top of the Hollow, is based on mudstones, while to the west otter sandstone predominates. This sandstone extends as far south as the estuary of the River Otter at Budleigh Salterton, hence its name. The rocks are thought to have been laid down in water in semi-arid conditions about 250 million years ago, leading to the patterns in the sandstone which can be seen clearly in the walls of the Hollow. The rock is variable in quality but has nevertheless been extensively used for building. The soils are fertile but heavy in places and are often washed away in heavy rain.

EARTHQUAKES

Compared with other parts of the world England is relatively stable with only about 200 earthquakes a year. Most are very minor, but occasionally a more serious event happens which hits the headlines. At about 3.30a.m. on 6 October 1863 the whole of the western side of the country from Liverpool to Tiverton experienced a major shock, but many people did not recognise it as an earthquake. Some believed that a burglar had entered the house while others attributed it to strong winds. William Sanford at Nynehead Court was quick to reach the right conclusion, as he informed the *Wellington Weekly News*:

We had a short shock of an earthquake last night at 3.30 a.m. It was so strong that it awoke me, and the room trembled so strongly that I thought some parts of the room were falling. I got up and examined it carefully but not finding anything I went to bed and heard this morning that the earthquake was felt at Bathealton at about the same time, so I have no doubt of the cause. The shock was followed or rather accompanied by a loud rushing noise like the falling of a wall or chimney, and the noise appeared to be on the north of the house.

(The paper felt moved to note that at Manila in the Philippines the previous June an earthquake had killed 4–5,000 people.)

SOME NOTABLE EVENTS IN THE HISTORY OF NYNEHEAD

c.737	First known reference to Nynehead.
1086	Domesday survey: a brief reference to Nynehead.
1091	Manor and church granted to the Fleury family – whence the name of Nynehead Florey for the area by the church and Court.
c.1300	John de Wyke becomes Lord of the Manor.
1292	First reference to a vicar of Nynehead.
1347–50	The Black Death. Nynehead has three vicars in three years.
c.1380	Nynehead Court rebuilt in stone.
1590	Martin Sanford buys the Court.
mid-1600s	The English Civil War.
1675	Nynehead Court rebuilt by John Sanford.
1680	A collection taken in the village for sailors taken captive by the Turks (i.e. Barbary pirates) raises £3.18s.0d.
1685	The Monmouth Rebellion.
Late 1600s	The philosopher John Locke a frequent visitor to the Clarkes of Chipley.
1700s	Nynehead relatively quiet.
1779	William Ayshford Sanford inherits the Court.
1789	The French Revolution.
1801	353 people lived in Nynehead.
1817	The three-arch bridge near the Court built. Building of Wellington Monument starts.
c.1818	Nynehead school opened.
1833	Avenue and coach road formed from the Poole Road to the Court.
1838	Grand Western Canal opened.
1843	Bristol and Exeter Railway reaches Beam Bridge.
1840s	Chipley House demolished by Edward Sanford.
mid-1800s	The Hollow created.
1867	Grand Western Canal closed.
1869	All Saints' Church enlarged.
1873	Ash Mill destroyed by fire.
1894	Nynehead Parish Council established.
1901	289 people live in Nynehead.
1912	Hornshay Bridge rebuilt.
1914–18	The First World War: six men of Nynehead died on active service.
1926	First houses in Farthings Close built.
1939–45	The Second World War: no Nynehead men killed in service.
1940	The Court and the estate sold by the Sanfords to Kleinwort Benson/ Bolnore Estates.
1948	Last resident vicar of Nynehead leaves.
1949	Outlying farms sold by the Bolnore Estates.
1950	Memorial Hall built.
1960s	The Avenue felled.
1967	Hornshay and Heywood Farms sold by Bolnore Estates.
1977	Jubilee Playing Field opened.
1991	354 people live in Nynehead.
1998	Nynehead cut off by floods (yet again!) in January.
2000	Golden jubilee of the Memorial Hall.
2003	Nynehead's first pantomime a great success.

*The footway across Hornshay Weir as built in 1882/3.
Compare the superstructure with that in 2003 (below).*

*Hornshay Weir in spate, 2003. River levels respond quickly following prolonged periods of heavy rain.
The silt-laden waters of rich orange-brown cause the river banks to change constantly.*

Chapter Two

THE RIVER TONE

The River Tone is not a large river but is one of great and varied attraction. Over the centuries it has played an important role in the lives of the villages in its valley, draining the land and providing a source of energy, water, food and recreation. It rises at a height of about 1,200 feet above sea level on the Brendon Hills and flows first south then eastwards before entering the parish of Nynehead just east of the Wellington sewage works.

By the time the Tone reaches Nynehead it has developed into a lowland river meandering across a flood plain over 300 yards wide. The rocks in its catchment on the Brendon Hills are relatively impermeable, which has two implications for the areas downstream. The river rises quickly after heavy rain (and falls quickly as well), while in dry weather its flow can reduce rapidly. When in flood it carries a great amount of reddish-brown sediment that is readily deposited when the flow decreases. The river in spate at Hornshay Weir is a dramatic sight. The alluvium in the flood plain consists of fine red material, but at low water a layer of shingle can be seen, deposited by flood water from melting of the permafrost on the hills at the end of the Ice Age some 10,000 years ago.

As a lowland river the Tone continually alters its course. There are many traces of former meanders but the best and most recent is immediately upstream of the bridge carrying the Grand Western Canal over the river. Here is a superb example of a cut-off meander or ox-bow lake, created in January 2001. The neck of the meander had narrowed over a number of years until the river finally broke through and deposited silt, blocking access to the meander.

Despite its importance to the communities through which it passes the Upper Tone has rarely been seen as a significant river. In about 1880 a contributor to the *Somerset County Gazette* railed strongly against the lack of interest in the river:

In my opinion, the inhabitants of West Somerset in general, and those of Taunton in particular, have been culpably negligent of their duty in regard to this fairly presentable river of theirs. True, it is not a very magnificent stream: it has no mouth of its own, and can boast of very few feeders, but it is, nevertheless, the river of the district, and ought to be made the most of.

Nevertheless, use of the river and its flood plain have been central to the lives of the people in the area. In the Middle Ages the flood plain would have been largely used for grazing, while the tithe maps of the early-nineteenth century show that most of the flood plain was under meadow or pasture. Today, however, much of the land is under grass and maize in rotation.

The River Tone, looking upstream from the canal aqueduct, May 2003. Hornshay Farm is in the middle distance and the Burrows top right. Cow parsley can be seen in the foreground with overhanging foliage in a haven for wildlife.

FLOODS AND FLOODING

Annual rainfall in East Nynehead between 1971 and 1997 varied from 19.5 inches (in the drought year of 1976) to 35 inches (1984), but in the upper catchment around Clatworthy can be 50 inches. It is not surprising that flooding has always been a problem for the village, which is cut off two or three times a year. The roads at Hornshay and Ash are most affected, but roads into the village – from Bradford, Oake, Milverton and Langford Budville – are often impassable.

Attempts to control flooding have been made but are unlikely to succeed. In 1830 it was claimed that the enlargement of the river to form a lake in the 1810s was an attempt to control flooding, but clearly this did not work, at least in the long term. The flooding has an effect on farmland along the river and after a flood one can see the newly deposited red silt. In 1889 Stephen Bailey, the tenant of Hornshay

The upper weir/cascade in the early-twentieth century.

Farm, requested reconsideration of his rent because of the damage to his best riverside pastures caused by flooding and pollution.

In 1897 William Sanford had to forcibly reject the District Council's claim that recent flooding of the Hornshay road had been caused by the rebuilding of the weir 15 years before. The weir had been in existence for over 80 years, and in any case, there had always been winter flooding 'in the old days'. He said he could do work which would mitigate the problem (but does not appear to have done any). A long 90 years later the river authority rebuilt Hornshay Weir, but floods continue to affect the village. Some people claim that flooding is getting worse, because of the greater rainfall in winter (global warming?) and changes in farming methods.

USE OF THE RIVER

In common with other rivers the course of the Tone has been used and modified in many ways so that in some respects it can no longer be considered entirely 'natural'. Three examples stand out. To the south of Nynehead Court the main channel was moved in the 1810s from the southern to the northern side of the flood plain, as part of William Sanford's scheme to create a new parkland for the Court. To the west of Ash Lane the river follows the southern edge of the flood plain for about 850 yards, joining the present river at the pool above Ash Bridge. Much of the former course has been ploughed out but filled-in meanders can be seen in the field adjoining Ash Lane. This can be identified on old maps as it was the ancient boundary between Nynehead and West Buckland. It is not known when the new course was cut or whether it was a side channel, but it might have been done to ensure a satisfactory flow of water for Ash Mill.

Finally, between Ash Lane and Pickings Mill an earlier meandering course is clearly shown on the Tithe Survey and other maps. It was replaced at some time by a straighter stream parallel to it to the north that might have been dug or improved for the benefit of Pickings Mill. The former course was still present until the late 1990s, when it was filled in by the landowner.

WATER-MILLS

From early-medieval times the Tone provided power for mills serving local communities. Although now largely redundant for this purpose there is still an impact on the landscape made by the remains of mill buildings and the mill leats running parallel to the river for much of its course between Clatworthy and Taunton. At the beginning of the nineteenth century Nynehead had three mills on the Tone, but by the 1880s they had all disappeared.

Nynehead Mills (always in the plural) were on the river below Nynehead Court as shown on a 1794 survey for the Grand Western Canal. They are mentioned frequently in early documents. In 1760 the miller was John Williams, whose indenture from William Sanford shows that with 'All those Water Grist Mills' went a house, orchard, meadow and pasture totalling about ten acres. Clearly the miller did more than run the mill. At the end of century the then miller Thomas Bond did other work on the Nynehead Court estate. In 1798 he was paid for drawing timber and bricks, while in 1803 he received £18.0s.2d. for grinding and drawing bricks and lime for the ice house at the Court. His wife also played her part in the business, providing yeast, eggs and butter for the Court (she was paid 4s.6d. for 4lb of butter in March 1802).

Repair bills refer to three mills, or three sets of millstones on the same site. This implies a considerable flow and head of water, presumably from a leat, although there is no obvious evidence of this on the ground. Repairs were frequently needed, such as in 1768 when Matthew Warrin of Culmstock and his sons were paid £3.5s.6d. for:

... putting up of the millbed nix the house and working of the nu stone and pouting of him and bringing of it to work and gouging and runing of the same mill and marking a nu pare of heeds for the Great mill and gouging and runging of the same mill and tourning of brases to all three mills and putting in of chouckes and sitting of Gougings and with considerable other work don.

In 1815 the millwright Mr Jos Station received 8s.6d. for the estimate he had made in 1809 for repairing the mills. These repairs were probably never carried out as the mills disappeared in the parkland scheme during the 1810s. Today nothing remains apart from undulations in the ground marked by two oak trees in the field just downstream of the three-arch bridge over the Tone.

A little more remains of Ash Mill – a few stone walls and the leat, now blocked off from the river. The mill was a corn-mill on which the estate spent a considerable amount of money in the early part of the nineteenth century, perhaps to compensate for the demolition of the Nynehead Mills. Ash Mill is notable because its demise on 20 October 1873 was recorded in a letter to William Sanford from his agent Stephen Bailey at Hornshay Farm:

I fully intended sending you particulars of roofing for Blockhouse this evening, but am sorry to say that I have been obliged to go to Ash Mills in consequence of a fire there this afternoon. The whole building is burnt down, with the machinery. The fire seems to have originated in the dwellinghouse, through the boarded roof to the mill loft which was full of straw. Consequently there was no chance of saving any thing. I have just come home to write you this and am going down again to see after the people, as they have scarcely any thing left.

The miller was James Kiddle (aged 49) who was also a farmer in a small way, owning 14 acres of land including an orchard and employing one labourer. He lived with his wife Harriet (52) and on the day of the 1871 Census his nephew (9) and niece (1) were also present in the house. They also had a servant, 22-year-old Mary Stuckley.

The difficulty of dealing quickly with fires in pre-telephone days is shown by a report in the *Wellington Weekly News*:

On Monday afternoon a destructive fire ravaged the tenement and premises known as Ash Mills, in the parish of West Buckland, the outbreak in the roof being first discovered by a man in the employ of Mr. Burch, the neighbouring occupier. The mill and house, which belong to WA Sanford esq. were in the occupation of Mr. Kiddle, who happened to be from home at the time, and his household were in the orchard picking apples. Information being speedily given, an attempt was made to save part of the furniture in the upper rooms, but this was impossible as the flames had already taken a firm hold of this part of the house, and thence the fire soon communicated with the remainder of the premises. A messenger was speedily dispatched to Wellington, and the fire engine and brigade were soon on the spot and at work, pouring copious volumes of water on the burning mass. Owing to the firm hold the fire had taken on the buildings – in the structure of which a large amount of timber had been used – it was impossible to do more than prevent further damage to surrounding property,

therefore every effort was made to secure the safety of some valuable ricks close by, towards which the wind was blowing, and the endeavours of the brigade were successful in this direction. It appears the fire originated in a flue. The mill contained a large amount of corn, much of which belonged to the poorer classes resident in the neighbourhood. The premises were reduced to a total wreck in the course of a couple of hours, but at 10.30 p.m. when the brigade left no further danger was to be apprehended. We understand that Mr. Kiddle had not insured his property, but that the premises were insured in the Sun Fire office. The damage is roughly estimated at between £400 and £500.

The fire was the first attended by the new Wellington Fire Brigade and its fire-engine, purchased through public subscription in June 1873. Rebuilding of the mill appeared to be out of the question and no buildings are shown on the 1888 Ordnance Survey map.

Pickings Mill is the furthest downstream on the Tone, being about 700 yards below Ash Bridge. By 1774 it was already in a poor way. A lease of a messuage and tenement called 'Piggons' to William Collard includes the 'toft of a Decayed Mill'. It had ceased functioning as a mill by 1837 when it was described in the Tithe Survey as 'cottage, garden and orchard'. Perhaps its end was caused by changes to its water-supply resulting from the building nearby of the canal and railway. Pickings, also called 'Pidgeons' or 'Pickenses', was later divided into two cottages. One was occupied in the three Census years 1851, '61 and '71 by agricultural labourer Robert Turner and his wife (a dressmaker in 1851). The other was occupied in 1861 by James Totterdell and his family – wife, three sons (15, 11 and 2 months), three daughters (7, 5, and 2) and his mother-in-law. They had moved on by 1871. The cottage fell out of use but remains could be seen as late as 1970 and the leat and the intake from the river can still be traced.

Away from the Tone was the mill at Chipley, on the upper part of the Luckham stream. While there was an earlier mill here (there are references in 1675 and 1769), this was superseded by an estate sawmill built in 1859 by the Sanfords and later converted to a house.

BRIDGES

Today there are five bridges across the River Tone. Below Nynehead Court is Thomas Lee's elegant three-arch bridge, built in 1817 as part of the parkland scheme and replacing an earlier bridge on the old route from Nynehead to Wellington. The bridge which preceded it was itself relatively new, as in the winter of 1797/98 railings were cut for the 'new bridge at Courtfields' and for the 'new bridge by the mill', suggesting a wooden bridge on stone abutments and piers.

A crane lifting the new footbridge into position at Hornshay Weir in 1987.

Hornshay Bridge before rebuilding in 1912. Note that the arch had to be supported to prevent the collapse of the bridge.

Hornshay Bridge in 2003.

There are records of a bridge at Hornshay from the seventeenth century when the churchwardens of Nynehead contributed towards its repair. It was always something of a problem, being at the junction of the parishes of Nynehead, Wellington and West Buckland, as to who shared the cost of maintenance. In 1894 the new Wellington Rural District Council took over responsibility, rebuilding it in 1912 (not 1812 as carved on the parapet!).

A quarter of a mile downstream an aqueduct built in the mid-1830s carries the Grand Western Canal over the river. The bridge at Ash is another old crossing on the border between Nynehead and West Buckland but was rebuilt in the 1990s to cope with modern-day traffic. Finally, just before it leaves Nynehead the river is crossed by the bridge carrying the railway, built in 1842/3 but later modernised.

WITHIES, WILLOWS OR OSIERS

The production of willow for baskets, eel traps, cradles and other things needed by rural communities has long been important in central Somerset and osier beds remain characteristic of that area. The first commercial withy bed in Somerset is said to have been started in 1827 but withy growing was important in Nynehead well before this, as shown by the 'osier bed' recorded on the 1794 canal survey. From Lady Day 1802 for 11 years Robert Grant, a Taunton basket maker, leased from the Sanford estate about four acres of land 'commonly known as Willowbeere'. The lease required him to 'plant, set and preserve as many good thriving willow plants as shall be necessary for keeping the said piece or plot of ground full and in good repair' and at the end of the lease yield it up 'sufficiently planted and filled up'. There were almost seven acres of willow beds on Hornshay Farm in 1823, which the Tithe Map shows adjoining the south side of the canal to the east of the Tone aqueduct. By 1888 these had disappeared. In 1837 there were other small withy/osier beds on the Luckham stream.

Successful withy growing requires a good supply of water and suitable ground conditions. Today withies are planted in the spring at a density of 16,500 per acre, which would have given the Nynehead bed some 50,000 plants. The land would have been flooded in the winter before planting. At Nynehead water was taken to the willow beds by a leat from an intake on the north side of the Tone downstream of Hornshay Bridge. There was a weir with sluice-gates to control the flow. Remains of the brick intake structure can still be seen, as can the base of the weir at low water. The leat followed the edge of the flood plain roughly parallel to the river, entering the willow beds through a culvert under the canal. An outflow at the eastern end of the beds took surplus water to the river near Ash. The leat is not mentioned in the 1802 lease and it is possible that the estate was responsible for its

upkeep. The Tithe Map shows a 'willow bed cottage and garden' on the north side of the canal, but it was not included in the 1802 lease (presumably Robert Grant lived in Taunton) and by 1888 had disappeared.

Withy growing in the village is remembered by Doug Lentell in more recent times:

Reg Arberry and father cut withies on the Tonedale side of the Park Bridge, stripped the bark on site and transported them to his shop at the bottom of Cornhill where the baskets were woven. To protect him while working in the rain he sheltered in one of his basket shelters.

THE HORNSHAY FARM TURBINE HOUSE

At the northern end of Hornshay Weir stands the farm's disused turbine house, a small brick building with a water intake and outlet bypassing the weir. Hornshay Farm had expanded markedly in the late-nineteenth century, with the erection of several brick buildings. The tenant in the 1880s was Stephen Bailey who also acted as the Sanfords' agent on the estate, owner at the time being William Sanford, a man with scientific interests who introduced electricity to the Court. It is not surprising that the opportunity should have been taken to introduce the latest technology to the estate farms. At Hornshay the closeness to the Tone and the weir built in the 1810s at the end of the canalised river provided an ideal opportunity to generate power for use on the farm.

The turbine was first mentioned in a letter on 5 May 1882 from Robert Nailer of Glastonbury to

Machinery in the Hornshay turbine house.

Turbine-house bevel gears and
bases of the drive-shaft.

Right: *An extract from the Gilkes of
Kendal order book showing part of
the Sanfords' order for the turbine
machinery, 1882.*

**Hornshay Turbine House with
remains of the drive-shaft
to the farm buildings.**

The end of the drive-shaft from the turbine house – machinery in a building at Hornshay Farm.

William Sanford. Nailer was writing about the possible installation of electric light at the Court but added, 'I suppose your trout have not recovered from the chemicals, yet the fall remains and the water however soapy will turn a wheel.' (The chemicals and soapy water originated from Fox's works upstream at Wellington.)

A month later Mr Gilkes, a turbine maker of Kendal, came to see Mr Sanford and Stephen Bailey about the water-wheel. This was followed by an order on 31 July. The firm's order book sets out in detail what was required but not the type of turbine, which is thought to have been of the Thomson Vortex type. The machinery was to be delivered by 30 September.

Work on the weir and the turbine house itself did not go smoothly, partly because of floods. On 21 October 1882 Stephen Bailey wrote to Mr Sanford:

The flood of Monday and Tuesday has I am sorry to say done considerable damage to our works at the cascade. The water was higher than ever known and has broken through the bank and washed away a considerable quantity of soil, so that we cannot at present proceed with it... It has done considerable damage all the way down the valley.

Eleven months later work was still going on. Bailey reported to Mr Sanford on 13 September 1883 that:

We are fixing the piles at the cascade but we cannot tell what the result will be until the concrete is in, and we cannot get the heavy piling engine until tomorrow to finish driving them.

A few weeks later things were looking better, Bailey reporting on 2 October that:

I am glad to say we are now making good progress with the masonry at the Cascade and if the weather continues fine this week I shall hope to get all the walls up out of danger.

A supplementary order to Gilbert Gilkes followed on 8 November 1883 for the 185ft horizontal shaft to carry the power to the farm buildings, followed by one on 14 November which specified a new turbine spindle and guide blade shaft. The problem of floods required the horizontal shaft to be laid two feet higher than first arranged and means were provided to catch the silt at the turbine itself.

The turbine was in operation by early in 1884 and continued to serve the farm for almost 100 years. After the sale of the estate in 1940 the new owners installed a Francis turbine to generate electricity, again provided by Gilbert Gilkes of Kendal. Two men came from Kendal to do the work, staying with the Sparks family in Higher Nynehead. When Hornshay Farm was sold by the estate in 1967 the sale details stated that:

... adjoining the weir is a brick and slate roofed building used as a TURBINE ROOM with David Brown Turbine and Governor and Electric Construction Co. D.C. Generator No. 187663 compound wound 12 k.w. 240 volt and switch board.

The new owner, Mr Ian Darby, briefly continued to use the turbine to power the machinery. However, in 1968 a mains supply was brought to the farm and a new bulk tank was fitted which needed an AC rather than the DC supply provided by the turbine. The turbine did, however, continue to supply electricity for lighting the farm buildings and the farmhouse until 1981. Fluctuations in river levels and siltation continued to be a problem and it was sometimes affected by the diversion of water for industrial use at Fox's Tonedale works. The weir was altered again by the Wessex Water Authority in 1987 and there have been proposals to install fish ladders, although the money for these is unlikely to be forthcoming.

In 2003 the turbine house, its inlet and its outlet are completely silted up, the building is partly overgrown and the slate roof is deteriorating. The horizontal shaft with its supports was taken up over a number of years and used to repair farm buildings. The last remains were removed in 1987, although some machinery remains in one building at the farm.

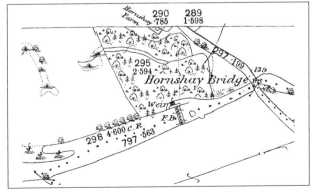

Hornshay Weir in 1887, as shown by the Ordnance Survey. It had been rebuilt four years previously. The turbine house is at the northern end of the weir.

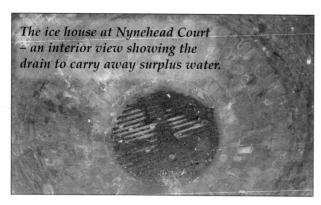

The ice house at Nynehead Court – an interior view showing the drain to carry away surplus water.

THE NYNEHEAD COURT ICE HOUSE

It is some time since the river froze but at the beginning of the nineteenth century things were different. This was a period of cold winters, the end of the 'Little Ice Age' which began two centuries before. Meteorological Office records show that between 1786 and 1827 the mean January temperature in central England was 2.1°C, compared with 3.71°C between 1956 and 1997. The seventeenth and eighteenth centuries saw the building of many ice houses on estates to store ice during the summer. At Nynehead ice was taken from the river and stored in the Court's ice house, one of the finest in Somerset. It is an egg-shaped brick structure with an arched entrance, the present one replacing an earlier entrance the remains of which can be seen. When the ice house was renovated in the 1990s 50 cubic yards of rubbish were removed. It was built in March 1803 when miller Thomas Bond was paid £18.10s.2d. for grinding and drawing the bricks and lime needed.

The blocked north entrance to the Nynehead Court ice house, from the inside.

The availability of ice depended on a long spell of below-freezing temperatures and water in a slow-moving river, or in a lake or pond. In February 1814 William Sanford paid £1.3s.6d. for three men to spend one day drawing ice. A year later, in January 1815, £1.18s.0d. was paid for three men and two boys to take ice out of the river and draw it to the ice house, with 2s. being spent on two seams of straw. The ice would have been taken from the canalised river or abandoned parts of the old river. In 1831 John Brown was paid 1s.6d. for a day's work on the ice house, so it was certainly in use over a number of years. It is likely that an ice house of this size would have taken much more than one day's work to fill if the ice was being cut locally and then taken to the building. This might support the idea that the ice was actually being imported from elsewhere. The ice house eventually became redundant when improved communications allowed ice to be imported from North America and northern Europe via an agent in Bristol.

RECREATION

The river has always been an important amenity for the village and the venue for a variety of activities. Fishing on the river was let by the estate in the nineteenth century, people travelling from many parts to use licences granted by the Sanfords. Poaching must have been a problem, however, as in 1820 William Sanford and others felt obliged to publish a notice in the local paper reminding the public that fishing in the Tone was private and that transgressors would be penalised. Today the fishing is let to local clubs. The creation of the canalised river created opportunities for boating and swimming. A boat-house was built on the northern bank and in the late-nineteenth century a regatta was held, despite the fact that the river was beginning to silt up. In postwar years the river was the venue for a different form of boating – the 'Tone Struggle', a race between home-made rafts.

POLLUTION

The Industrial Revolution brought pollution of rivers by waste from riverside factories. In the late-nineteenth century there was a protracted dispute between the Sanford family and Fox Bros about the pollution of the Tone from the latter's textile factory on the northern side of Wellington. The problem arose as early as 1856, while in March 1863 Edward Sanford received a letter commenting that 'It must be very annoying to have the quality of your fish deteriorated by that factory'. Further complaints from fishermen were received, such as that from Mr Charles Ballance of London in July 1868:

I cannot leave Taunton without a line to thank you for your prompt reply to my request for permission to fish on your estate at Nynehead Park. My eldest little boy... has much enjoyed the Dace fishing at the upper weir. I have been with him three times, but we have scarcely

Nynehead Court ice house in 2003, after restoration sponsored by Taunton Deane Borough Council.

The Tone Struggle at Hornshay Weir in the 1980s.

seen a trout – it seems such a pity that your beautiful water should continue to be polluted by the nuisance from the manufactory above. The Dace seem to thrive under it but the effect on the trout is disastrous. I can recollect years ago when the water was perfectly alive with fine fish for 4 or 5 miles.

By 1890 the dispute had become serious – lawyers were involved and the case ended in the High Court. There was a case of cattle poisoning and pollution continued to marr the enjoyment of the area, as witnessed by a poem from about that time, written by 'Wellingtonian', the last two verses of which read:

> But while my thoughts were musing,
> On pleasant things gone by;
> My feet had slowly borne me
> The flowing river nigh.
> But not a fish, or moorhen,
> Could anywhere be seen;
> For a dirty frothy substance
> Was floating on the stream.
>
> And a most offensive odour
> Seemed to have filled the air,
> And as 'twas so unpleasant
> I did not tarry there,

> But onward bent my footsteps
> And as the glorious sun
> Sunk 'neath the west horizon
> I landed safely home.

The problem was complicated by the growing problem of sewage from Wellington's rapidly increasing population, with increasing concerns about the dangers of enteric fever. In 1894 it was proposed to store the town's sewage in Fox's dye pits, which would only have exacerbated the problem downstream in Nynehead. The matter came before the County Council's Sanitary Committee during the following year, and a year after that William Sanford offered land at Tone for the construction of the sewage-treatment plant. This did not completely solve the problem in the short term, as witnessed in a letter from Mr George Stone stating his intention to give up Gundenham and Tonedale Farms:

> I find I cannot battle with the sewage of Wellington which has become deadly to my cattle and sheep and Messrs Fox Bros will do nothing to help me in the matter. If I go to law with our Urban Council I must do it single-handed so I prefer giving up farming instead. I have lost over 200£ worth of stock in consequence this year.
> The filter pits the Council placed in Steadham Lane have not been used since Lady Day last. I enclose a copy of some of the correspondence I have had and I think from that you will see how harshly I have been dealt with. Tonedale Farm and your park has become simply a receptacle for the sewage of Wellington and it is high time it was stopped.

A century later the Wellington Waste Water Treatment Works is run by Wessex Water Plc and pollution levels in the River Tone have decreased markedly.

Bringing up the ice from the river

19

Hornshay Weir and the turbine house from upstream, showing the structure before it was rebuilt in 1987.

The Tone Struggle raft race at Hornshay Weir in the 1980s.

Chapter Three

WILDLIFE

Although predominantly a farming parish, Nynehead has a variety of habitats within its boundary. Of these the River Tone is probably the most widely known feature, meandering through the southern part of the parish and fed by several streams, some of which flow with enough gusto to provide a habitat for water birds. The river floods on average two or three times each year and the extensive area of pasture land through which it flows becomes a huge inland lake for a day or so. Pasture, while not presenting the same high percentage as it has in times past, is still the most significant type of habitat at approximately 35–40 per cent of the parish, whilst arable farming, which is on the increase, accounts for the next highest proportion at around 30 per cent.

There are no significant ancient woodlands, the majority being either secondary, such as along the line of the canal, or what the Tithe Survey calls 'plantations', primarily for amenity or sport. These are now principally of mixed species, their ages do vary and some have evolved more naturally than others. Individual trees are very important scenically and for wildlife, as in the formal parkland at Nynehead Court which holds the oldest and largest specimens. In the Court grounds and adjacent to the churchyard is a magnificent yew tree which in itself is almost an entire habitat. There are also a few well-established specimen trees in the former parkland by the river as well as in the arboretum to the south of the church. Woodland accounts for only ten per cent or so of the parish.

The parish has several areas of land which are used as cover for game birds, some being sown with sunflowers, some with maize and some left to become meadow or fields of teazel and thistle. The significant increase in the number of goldfinches may be directly attributable to this fact.

In addition to the river there are other areas of water. Although there are no reservoirs or major

A young cuckoo being fed by the surrogate parent in a Nynehead garden.

lakes to attract large numbers of birds, a private lake has recently been created at Chipley which, even after only two years, is clearly beginning to attract wildlife. Most other areas of water are pond-sized and are the remains of borrow pits. Garden ponds are of course an important contribution to the survival of aquatic and amphibian species. The floods of the River Tone do not usually last long enough to attract any water birds at all, although it is not unusual to see a cormorant looking down from a pylon perch. In fact such flooding is a mixed blessing for wildlife. Water-living creatures such as otters can suffer injury in the violent and fast-flowing muddied waters, while the erosion of river banks destroys many burrows of smaller mammals. On the plus side, freshly deposited silt creates sandbanks which quickly become impressed with the footprints of waterside residents giving invaluable clues to just who is living there. In the parish of Nynehead water accounts for only two to three per cent of the area.

Residential land should not be discounted, given the huge increase of interest in garden birds begun in England about 25 years ago and now prevailing throughout Europe. Nynehead, being a fragmented village, has garden land scattered throughout the parish and this enables the many species of garden birds to have relatively short journeys in search of food should their regular trusted place be temporarily disappointing. Residential land amounts to probably ten per cent of the whole parish.

The fruit farm located on the southern slopes of East Nynehead is an untypical piece of farmland. It has been widely adopted by birds and animals because, despite the busy workers who are present for much of the year, there is good cover provided by the hedges and by the furrows between the strawberry plants. This farm takes up about eight per cent of the parish.

Finally, a small but distinct habitat is the church-yard where the building, the gravestones and the grass combine to provide a safe haven for birds, plants, insects, lichens – in fact all forms of wildlife.

BIRDS

Pasture land

Historically pasture attracted relatively few birds, owing principally to the disturbance from large numbers of livestock who churned up the surface of the land. Generally, this is still the case today and the crow family (Corvids) fare best here. Nearly all the British crows, including carrion crow, jackdaw and rook, feature on or near the pasture land in Nynehead. (In 1889 a rookery of 10,000 birds was recorded in Nynehead.) Crows are scavengers and are interested in ill or deceased creatures, in their droppings and in the flies that they attract. They do not mind the damp nature of the pasture land, which positively deters many other birds.

The same food source is attractive to the buzzard, as well as the worms, which are easy to find. Like all birds of prey and owls, buzzards are lazy creatures – picking up worms is far easier than searching for a rabbit at dusk and dawn. Other members of the crow family include the magpie and jay, the latter often being seen around the more wooded areas. The kestrel will frequently be seen hovering above the fields and hedgerow banks. In winter groups of linnet, fieldfare and redwing, along with occasional parties of seagulls from the Poole Tip roost (principally black-headed), swell the throng.

Arable land

A new crop, maize, dominates arable land in Nynehead and continues to baffle birds. Some roost in it, some hide in it and a few feed in it, yet all do so somewhat around the edges. Foxes and hares have been quicker to colonise the interior of the maize field. Wheat fields have historically attracted birds, especially ground nesters such as the skylark who can raise their young before the corn grows tall and is harvested. There is some wheat grown in the village but nowadays the skylark's lovely song is rarely heard.

A feature of both wheat fields and the new maize is the sight in late summer of swallows and house martins swooping fast and low over the heads of the crop as they build up their physical strength for the massive journey of migration that lies ahead. It is also possible at this time to see a hobby searching over the same fields for a sick swallow or preferably the dragonflies of late summer which it spectacularly catches and eats on the wing. After harvest, arable fields typically take on a totally different appearance and could almost be classed as another habitat. Many smaller birds move on to the fields picking

their way around for grain-size food and regularly giving uplift to the dull dark browns of winter.

At ploughing time the machine is still followed by gulls seeking worms in the freshly turned soil, but in Nynehead both heron and buzzards may be seen too. A total of 33 buzzards were once counted in a single such field. This habitat is popular with meadow pipit and yellowhammer, as well as game birds including pheasant, small numbers of red-legged partridge and very occasionally quail.

Woods and hedgerows

Hedgerows have been included here as the bird species which favour them tend to complement those of woodland, but they could be considered a habitat in their own right. Whilst there are now far fewer than historically there are still good numbers of hedges beside the lanes, some of which are the double type, preferred by birds for the cover they afford. They are managed somewhat brutally with huge mechanical cutters which level off the tops and often account for the nests of early birds such as blackbird and possibly song thrushes too, given the reduction in their numbers. The hedgerows are also the domain of Nynehead's most exciting bird, the sparrowhawk, which still astonishes local people as they follow it in their cars down the Hollow or along a lane before it flips up and over the side busily searching for spooked prey. Sometimes sparrowhawks have been seen perching on our village signs after such a chase and they look with a bright yellow eye as if to say, 'There, you can't catch me mate!'

Apart from the formal woods at Nynehead Court the most significant areas of woodland are around Chipley and at Long Copse and Blackham Copse along the canal. This mixed woodland, planted in the 1830s and subsequently replanted, holds all the predictable bird species, but owing to a number of factors – the public footpath running through it, its narrow width and the very close proximity of the railway line – it does not attract the rarer species of South West woodlands such as redstart, wood warbler or pied flycatcher. Nevertheless, two species of woodpecker (the green and great-spotted wood-pecker) occur and so does the nuthatch, which otherwise only inhabits the Court's garden and is the village school's emblem. The shy treecreeper might also be seen by the fortunate observer.

Water

Watery areas in the parish are varied, including the regular floods that are by and large of little use to birds. There is a decent piece of wet pasture unsuit-able for stock which attracts a couple of rarer birds in the winter. The large freshwater lake at Chipley is on private land so a study of this has been difficult. Species to be expected here would include great-

Otter footprints and spraints (droppings) can often be seen on fresh silt deposits at the edge of the river.

crested grebe, coot, moorhen and species of duck. The River Tone attracts quite exciting birds including the kingfisher and dipper, although these are not seen as a matter of course. Green sandpiper and snipe have both been recorded near the river. Riverside alder trees provide food for redpoll and siskin. The sandy river banks have provided nest sites for visiting sand martins, first seen swooping above the water in early summer, but sadly the loss of suitable banks from erosion means they are now rare. What a shame that they no longer nest in Nynehead Hollow.

Gardens

Birds and people often mix quite well. It is almost certain that the species list for London will be greater than that for Nynehead. Nevertheless, some species are becoming increasingly disenchanted with our modern habits, for example the modern 'barn conversion' is driving away swallows in huge numbers. Conversely, there are some success stories, with birds such as the great-spotted woodpecker now a daily visitor to many gardens where it has learned just how nice peanuts are. More people now feed the birds and their rewards, whilst generally costing them more than they may be prepared to admit, are great. Many of the species referred to earlier are now regular garden visitors in the village alongside more common garden-loving birds, and the checklist can be increased by including those which use the airspace overhead.

Historical bird records

Historically no completely researched list exists of the birds of Nynehead but *The Materials for the Town of Wellington, County Somerset* by A.L. Humphreys (published in 1889) does provide a fascinating glimpse or two of how things have changed.

Imagine Nynehead, or Somerset even, without the buzzard. Humphreys refers to them as 'rare' with the last individual being 'shot near Burlescombe' in 1887. Sadly for bird-watchers, the number of birds that Humphreys was able to write about is greater than that available today. Birds that have disappeared from the parish include turtle doves, corncrakes (or land rails as they were known), long-eared owls, grasshopper warblers, red-backed shrikes, nightjars and even black grouse. Reading Humphreys brings back memories of a Dorset woman who was relatively interested in the nature around her. When a particular bird walked on her grass she would call it a 'polly wash dish'. It was a pied wagtail, referred to by Humphreys as a 'dishwasher' and a bird still to be seen locally in good numbers. Not only the 'land rail' has a new name these days, but Humphreys writes of the golden-crested wren and the ray's wagtail, the mountain finch and cole tit. Over 100 years on these names have all but disappeared, along with some of the birds. Nevertheless, it is reassuring to see that most of Humphreys' birds are still around and that the cuckoo was as noisy then as it is every May!

LARGE MAMMALS

Habitats in the parish are sufficiently varied to provide the necessary support for a number of Britain's larger mammals. The species within this group include those which have a definite home base and those which lead a more 'nomadic' lifestyle.

Within the first group, the red fox and the badger are both present in the environs of the village. Indeed foxes are frequently seen in and around gardens, some on a regular basis. Badgers have been present in the parish for many centuries, in common with the species' distribution in Britain. Some of their 'setts' will have been used for many generations before today's resident animals. Around the village there are many examples of their regularly used pathways and also their toilet areas, thought to be used as part of their territory-marking activities. Like the fox, badgers frequently visit gardens which promotes mixed feelings amongst gardeners, since they will often leave a trail of evidence in lawns after digging in search of worms and grubs.

Roe deer can be seen in the parish. While they tend to favour bases in copses and woodland they will often cover considerable distances in their search for suitable grazing. They do breed locally so the sighting of a small family group is not uncommon. There are reports of red deer having been seen also, but these are probably individuals having fled to the area following disturbance by hunting on the Quantocks.

The River Tone is an important habitat for the rare and elusive otter and whilst a fleeting glimpse of one is possible, their presence is most likely to be proven by spotting telltale footprints in the sandy silt on the riverside, or perhaps finding their 'spraints' (droppings). Occasionally, the remains of a fish meal will be found, which of course is also an indication of a thriving fish population in the river. Two positive sightings of footprints and one of spraints were recorded at two separate locations within the parish during the winter of 2002/3. Other regular sightings of footprints elsewhere in our area indicate that there is considerable activity. One road death has also been recorded in recent years.

Otter numbers are increasing slowly along the River Tone, after an absence for a number of years. Their return was noted in around 1988, and since then the numbers of records have increased steadily. Sadly records of road casualties can number as many as 12–15 per year along the length of the River Tone, and several such deaths result from animals using the stretch through Nynehead parish. Otters do not set up permanent homes (holts) except for breeding purposes, so any records will probably be of individuals as they travel along the several miles of their river territory or as they cross roads and lanes on their journeys to other suitable streams in the area. Otter numbers

nationally are well known to reflect pollution levels and therefore it can be assumed that this situation has improved along the river locally.

Otters are often confused with the slightly smaller and more commonly seen mink, which also frequent the river. Interestingly, the numbers of mink recorded for the Tone have declined, along with the increase in otter numbers, but it is uncertain whether this fact is linked in any way.

SMALLER MAMMALS

Rabbits are numerous, as would be expected in a grassland habitat, and there are a number of records of the scarcer brown hare, including one which hopped casually into a front garden one summer's evening. Hedgehogs are regularly encountered around the village and these useful garden visitors help control unwanted garden pests, such as snails and slugs, and will return to gardens if encouraged to do so.

The habitats within the parish boundary undoubtedly provide suitable support for a number of members of smaller mammal groups, including stoats, weasels, voles, shrews and mice. Evidence of their presence can be based not only on chance sightings, but also from 'trophies' brought home by pet cats. Both field voles and bank voles are recorded, as are common shrew and the rarer pygmy shrew. The presence of shrews is often noted by hearing their persistent high-pitched squeaking as they scurry along under the undergrowth of hedgerows and garden boundaries in their relentless quest for small insects and grubs. Both the house mouse and the slightly larger wood mouse, also sometimes called the common or long-tailed field mouse, are present. The dormouse has been recorded on the borders of the parish, but as there are no large stands of hazel coppice and woodland, where it is normally expected to be found, it is probable that this delightful creature could be quietly living in the area in hedgerows, copse edges or even gardens.

The River Tone provides a habitat suitable for the rare water vole ('Ratty' of *Wind in the Willows* fame). Whilst not proven to be present within the parish, the scarce water shrew could well be present as it has been recorded at the river not too distant from Nynehead. As both of these secretive creatures increase their activities in parallel with the increase in waterside vegetation in the summer months, they become more difficult to observe. Casual sightings are therefore the most likely, although footprints in sandy silt, or burrow entrances in the river bank might be found.

Inevitably in a rural area, the brown rat is present. It would seem that they are most frequently seen when they enter gardens and outbuildings in search of food and shelter towards the end of harvest time. Unpopular they may be, but they must be included on the record list. Grey squirrels are numerous in the areas with larger trees and woodland and are regular garden visitors. Less popular for gardeners are moles which occasionally invade lawns. Good numbers exist in surrounding fields, especially those used chiefly for grazing and which enjoy little ploughing disturbance.

REPTILES, AMPHIBIANS AND FISH

Records of only three of Britain's reptiles have been made for Nynehead. The grass snake is regularly seen and is known to breed in the area, as are common lizards and slow-worms. Most sightings have been made in gardens but also all have been seen occasionally in other parts of the area.

With a good number of natural ponds surviving within the parish, together with garden ponds encouraging the breeding of amphibians, reasonable numbers of records have been made. The common frog and the common toad are the most frequently noted species. Newts are regularly seen in ponds and pools around the village, especially in gardens, where wildlife havens are created successfully for the support and breeding of many amphibians. The common or smooth newt is the most likely species, although the smaller and rarer palmate newt may be found. No records of the great-crested newt have been made at the time of writing.

The River Tone is now sufficiently clean and unpolluted to provide a suitable habitat for many freshwater fish, a fact supported by the thriving otter population referred to earlier. Fairly recent records of salmon travelling upriver during the summer months exist for parts of the Tone just east of the parish boundary. Chubb are to be found in the slower-moving and deeper waters of the river, as are brown trout. Shallow stony-bottomed waters will undoubtedly support the bullhead or miller's thumb.

The white-clawed crayfish was recorded in 1990–95 in the River Tone within the parish, but recent sightings do not appear to have been made for this now rare and protected creature. Normally associated with very alkaline waters (e.g. on chalk soils), this small crustacean is susceptible to pollution and also pressures from the larger introduced North American signal crayfish, which has also been recorded as being present in the River Tone.

INSECTS

Butterflies and moths

Whilst no exhaustive survey of the butterflies and moths in the area exists, many records of sightings in and around gardens have been made. Most of the commoner species of British butterflies including peacock, red admiral, small tortoiseshell, comma, painted lady, speckled wood, meadow brown, gatekeeper and small copper have been seen in Nynehead. Less popular is the large white, which frequents our gardens in search of egg-laying sites amongst our cabbages and nasturtiums. The related small white and green-veined white are also present.

Scarcer and more local species might be seen, such as holly blue (particularly in gardens in late spring feeding and egg laying around holly and ivy), the brimstone in early spring and later perhaps the migrant clouded yellow. In damper areas, especially where lady's smock (cuckoo flower) is abundant, many orange tip butterflies can be found.

Nynehead is 'sandwiched' between some well-known locations for some of Britain's rarer butterflies and, whilst there are some suitable potential breeding sites within the parish, no sightings have been made of brown hairstreak or silver-washed fritillary. Two factors in particular may contribute to this absence. Firstly, suitable habitats for these species may not be sufficiently large nor sustainable as compared to known neighbouring locations. Secondly, the presence of the M5 motorway a short distance south of the parish may have an effect. It is known that butterfly colonies are reduced in many similar situations in Britain where such roadways are situated.

Fewer records exist for the moth populations in Nynehead parish, probably because so many of these insects are notably small and dull! However, one very spectacular late-summer visitor seen in gardens is the hummingbird hawkmoth. This small moth visits Britain in warmer summers and can be seen hovering as it feeds from flowers. Quite often it is mistaken for a tiny hummingbird (hence its name).

Beetles

Like moths, beetles seem to capture the imagination much less than butterflies, birds and mammals, probably again due to the vast numbers of species in Britain and also because of 'bad press'. Interestingly, one species which has been recorded in a Nynehead garden is the lesser stag beetle. Requiring the presence of rotting wood for its breeding cycle, this is a shy and seldom-seen species which is quite widespread throughout the British Isles.

Dragonflies

This group includes both the larger dragonflies and the smaller damselflies that make up the 50 or so species in Britain. Garden ponds now provide excellent breeding grounds for dragonflies and most of the commoner species have been seen. Occasionally, the less-common golden-ringed dragonfly has visited gardens, which is a bit of a surprise as this species prefers heathland habitats.

Parts of the River Tone and its tributaries are sufficiently slow flowing to support damselfly species that favour such conditions. The slightly muddy water also helps. The beautiful demoiselle, the males sporting rich metallic-blue, almost-black wings, are to be seen fluttering gently around quieter waters in the area.

TREES AND FLOWERING PLANTS

Although Nynehead parish has a wide range of habitats the species present are to be expected for such an area and there seem to be no exceptional rarities or uncommon species to be found.

Trees

Notable trees include black poplar, a scarce species in Britain, but one which is more abundant in Somerset, beside rivers and ponds, although numbers are declining. There is a good stand at Ash but erosion due to the frequent winter floods along the River Tone has caused the demise of many mature specimens over the years and replacement by natural suckering does not seem to occur in very wet situations. Almond willow is represented by a handful of specimens close to the three-arch bridge below the Court. This willow is sometimes grown for basket making and interestingly there are records of withy beds here.

One fine veteran tree is a plane in the grounds of Chipley Park, said to have been planted in 1760. At the entrance to Nynehead Court is a large tulip tree which must now be of considerable age. This tree produces a good mass of blooms, only associated with well-established specimens. The grounds of the Court also have an arboretum and an avenue of large sweet chestnut. More good specimens of this tree grow in the nearby churchyard. Elm was once widespread in the parish, but losses to Dutch elm disease have dramatically altered the landscape. As this species can regenerate by suckering growth, it is likely that we shall see a return to the former views of the hedges and woodlands.

Flowering plants

Species that are less common include common stork's-bill, scarce in Somerset and certainly not in its expected habitat at Nynehead. The rarer related small-flowered cranesbill is recorded from one roadside as is grass pea. Such habitats can be surprising in their flora populations. In many such locations around the village, populations of violets brighten the banks in early spring. In springtime groups of 'nodding star of Bethlehem' can be found, together with winter aconite, both probably being garden escapees. Moschatel, sometimes called 'Town Hall Clock', also grows in similar habitats along with opposite-leaved golden saxifrage and the curious butchers' broom.

Orchids are always an exciting find. Early purple orchid and common spotted orchid are both recorded for the parish and, whilst not being amongst Britain's rarer orchid species, hopefully they will remain safe in their sheltered hedgerow locations for years to come.

The churchyard of All Saints' Church supports a rich diversity of plants. Meadow saxifrage is present, probably an introduction, but not previously recorded in the *Atlas Flora of Somerset* (1997) for this site. An opportunity certainly exists to survey this area botanically in the future and perhaps more localised species will come to light.

Riverside plant populations include the ubiquitous Himalayan balsam (also known as 'Policeman's Helmet'), which whilst providing a splash of colour in summer, is very invasive and spreads rapidly thanks to the regular flooding of the river. Adjacent parishes have records of trifid bur-marigold from the banks of the River Tone. This is a scarce plant usually associated with peaty areas. Seeds deposited in flood silts mean there is a good chance of finding it in the parish area.

Somerset is a rich location in Britain for mistletoe and Nynehead has some excellent populations, notably in the lime-tree avenue of Chipley Park. Contrary to popular belief, parasitic mistletoe grows on a range of host trees, not just apple. Therefore, despite the loss of the orchards in the parish, this plant can be found growing on lime, some poplar species, hawthorn, field maple and some willows. A surprising number of ornamental garden trees will also host mistletoe – for example, laburnum, cotoneaster, rowan and cherry.

Grasses

It can be a bit difficult to get excited about grasses, but there are some records of scarce and rare species in the parish. Hybrid sweet grass is not recorded in the *Atlas Flora*, but a small population grows in a tiny pond with floating sweet grass and plicate sweet grass, so there is something to offer for grass enthusiasts.

FLOWERLESS PLANTS AND FUNGI

The Hollow has an interesting population of flowerless plants, the habitat being both damp and shady. Ferns grow in abundance, especially hart's tongue, while liverworts are represented by pellia and marchantia growing alongside the many mosses on the steep rocky walls. It is obviously very difficult and dangerous to carry out a detailed survey of this area, but no doubt some interesting surprises await an intrepid botanist. Real enthusiasts will also be pleased to know of the presence of a good population of the tiny least duckweed in a small pond. This species is not uncommon on the Somerset Levels, but requires some critical examination with a magnifier to be sure of its identity.

Fungi represent another much-under-recorded group of flowerless plants. There will be a large and varied population of the commoner species throughout the parish, because of the diversity of habitats. One good colony of shaggy ink cap or lawyer's wig has appeared on a garden lawn in the autumn for some years. Once again there is an opportunity here for further study.

Chapter Four

ORIGINS & EARLY HISTORY

Although the landscape of the Vale of Taunton Deane is largely the product of changes since the last Ice Age – that is of say the last 10–15,000 years – working on the underlying geology, we know that there was a human presence in the area as long ago as 200,000 years. The coming of the ice changed the local environment massively. Although at its greatest extent the ice sheet reached probably only as far as the Somerset coast, South West England would have been covered with deep permafrost, akin to much of northern Siberia today with its tundra vegetation.

The retreat of the ice and the increase in temperature from 15,000 years ago had two main results. Firstly, the thawing of the permafrost relatively quickly released vast quantities of water which scoured out river valleys and brought down eroded material. The deep valleys in the headwaters of the Tone could, in part, be the result of this process. Secondly, the tundra vegetation gave way to birch and eventually led to deciduous forest, although the improvement of the climate was not a smooth process and long periods of wet and warm weather alternated with drier and colder conditions.

The retreat of the ice, the better climate and more fruitful landscape brought the reappearance of people in the Tone valley. At first they were, as before, migrant hunters, but in due course they became settled and in the Neolithic period began clearing the forest in order to cultivate the land. Little is known about the impact of these people on the parish or whether indeed they did settle here. The total population of the area would have been very small. Nevertheless, there were important pre-Saxon finds in the parish in the nineteenth century. A 'British urn' was found in the Tone valley below Nynehead and bronze axes at the Burrows overlooking Lower Nynehead. Here there are slight indications of earthworks but whether they

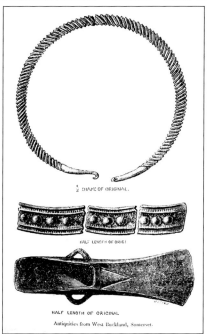

Prehistoric finds from Nynehead. W.A. Sanford of Nynehead Court was an antiquarian and palaeontologist and a leading member of the Somerset Archaeological and Natural History Society in the late-nineteenth century.

are man-made is arguable, although the name 'Burrows' does suggest that there might have been a tumulus on the summit. The axes were exhibited at the Wellington Museum. A Bronze-Age hoard – celts, torque and amulet – was found near Ash Farm.

The Roman impact on Somerset was chiefly in the east and south of the county around the Fosse Way, a settled landscape contrasting with the 'militarised' zone in the uplands to the west of the county. The Taunton area would have been settled, if not by Romans at least by Britains leading their lifestyle. A Roman presence near Nynehead is indicated by coins found near Wellington and pottery of the second and third centuries, discovered at Cade's Farm on the eastern edge of the town. Within Nynehead itself Roman coins were found in the nineteenth century in the river valley and a fragment of a third- or fourth-century black-burnished ware jar was found in a garden in East Nynehead in 1988.

Between the end of the Roman occupation of Britain in the early-fifth century and the coming of the Saxons there is a virtual silence, but it must be assumed that the land continued to be farmed even if towns such as Bath were abandoned. The Saxons arrived in Somerset in the mid-seventh century, in 658, the British being forced westwards to the line of the River Parrett. By about 682 the Saxon king is recorded as making a grant of land at Creech St Michael to the abbot of Glastonbury and by 722 there is the first mention of Taunton. The area would already have been well developed and settled and it is debatable whether the British inhabitants were driven westward into the hills or stayed to integrate with the newcomers. However, the Saxons made a great impact on the area through the naming of places, although pre-Saxon river names such as 'Tone' continued to be used.

Studham Lane. This sunken track was possibly once the main route from Wellington to Nynehead.

Nynehead is mentioned in the the record of a grant of land here in 890 to Wulfhere Cidding, at a yearly rental of 20s. on condition that the tenant should be a 'follower of the Lord of the Church'. In 904 the Bishop of Winchester was granted possession of the manor of Taunton with its widespread territories, including Nynehead. At this stage Nynehead and other places with Anglo-Saxon names were probably not clearly defined villages but were attached to estates.

The period of the Saxon occupation up to the Norman Conquest was by no means peaceful as we know from the stories of King Alfred and his time in the Somerset marshes. In AD1000 Aethelred II (the 'badly-advised' rather than the 'Unready') was facing threats of invasion. In 997 the Danes had sacked Watchet for the second time in ten years and in 1013 Swein Forkbeard swept up from the South Devon coast on his way to the heartland of Wessex. The effect on the daily life of the Nynehead resident is difficult to say but we can make some guesses about what the village was like.

By AD1000 the Vale of Taunton was already a rich mixed-farming area dominated by the estate of the Bishop of Winchester. Nynehead was one of almost 30 manors in the estate's outer areas, operating independently in most respects but acknowledging the bishop as overlord. Most people would have worked on the land and life for them would have been hard with a poor diet, relieved only by the yearly round of seasonal celebrations. While at the highest level the Anglo-Saxons had a rich culture, few if any ordinary people would have been literate and any news of events outside the village would have been obtained by word of mouth.

We cannot tell how many people lived here, although there would have been far fewer than today. Houses would have been small and thatched, in small groups and isolated farms, perhaps in the hamlets that still exist – Lower, Higher and East Nynehead and Chipley, together with the lost settlement of Pixton. Next to the predecessor of the present-day Nynehead Court there could have been a thatched and wood or stone church with a priest who might have been resident or one of a group of 'missionary' priests from Taunton. He would have been one of the important and (possibly) literate members of the community along with the steward who represented the bishop's estate.

From the high point of the Burrows above Lower Nynehead one would have seen a farmed landscape of small fields, hedges and woodland as today. It would have been a less-tidy scene, created and maintained by hard physical work and hand tools. Roads and tracks would not have been surfaced and there would not have been today's distinction between roads and footpaths. The River Tone was, as today, a major feature of the parish although not necessarily on its present line. The valley would have been wetter with willows, alders and other riverside vegetation and was an important source of water, food (fish and wildfowl), reed for thatching and possibly water-power for a mill. Nearby villages were very similar with generally small and scattered groups of houses. The nearest 'town' was Taunton, already a marketing centre with a mint and some of the freedoms of a borough. Wellington was still only a village, not being recorded as a town for another two centuries.

AFTER THE NORMAN CONQUEST

The Norman invaders had a dramatic impact on life in England and in particular on the ownership and organisation of land and on the church. It is on land ownership that most hard information is available but even so the situation in Nynehead was not simple. Under the Normans land was ultimately owned by the Crown but held by tenants who owed the King defined duties and who could in turn sub-let their land. After 1066 most of Nynehead continued to be part of the Bishop of Winchester's Taunton estate but the situation was complicated with different and separate areas of ownership.

By 1166 the area of Lower Nynehead was held by Hugh Fluri while in 1208 Thomas Fluri was named as one of the bishop's tenants. It was known as

The Burrows, a local landmark overlooking Lower Nynehead and Hornshay Farm.

Nynehead Florey in 1242 when Ranulph de Fluri held the land. This is the last record of the Fluri ownership, the estate then being divided between two heiresses who owned land both in Nynehead and in Withiel Florey on the Brendon Hills. These estates were reunited under the Wykes in the fourteenth century. John de Wyke was lord of the manor in 1382 and the estate passed through his descendants, ending with Richard Wyke, who died in 1590 and is buried in Nynehead church. The manor then passed to the Sanfords.

The Bishop of Winchester's earliest known tenant at East Nynehead or Nynehead Monks was Robert de Beauchamp. He granted the land to Montacute Priory who held it until the Dissolution of the Monasteries in the sixteenth century. By 1275–6 it was known as Monks Nynehead. In 1544 it was sold by the Crown to William Ayer of Warminster and Richard Gonnyng of Mells, but a year later they sold it on to Agnes Wyke whose family held it until it was divided early in the seventeenth century.

The manor of Chipley at the western end of the parish was also held by Montacute under the Winchester estate. In 1208/9 records refer to Thomas of Chipley and Albreda, widow of Chipley, and in 1248–9 Walter of Chipley is mentioned. In 1327 only four names are listed in the Lay Subsidy Rolls suggesting that then, as now, it was a small settlement. In 1408–9 the land passed from Thomas and Elisabeth Chipley through their daughter to the Warre family of Hestercombe and then, again through marriage, to the Lottishams, from whom it passed to the Clarkes.

Taunton Priory had important landholdings in Nynehead. After the Conquest the rectory at Nynehead was initially held by Montacute Priory but was passed to Taunton Priory when it was founded circa 1120–25. In 1214 the Priory was granted by the de Fluris the right to appoint vicars to the benefice of Nynehead and continued as patron of the benefice until the Dissolution of the Monasteries. The Priory's income came from land granted to it. In addition to the Nynehead rectory estate the Priory was given land at 'Pykeston' (now Pixton) and 'Linegeresland' or 'Lyngyegereslaunde at Nygahide'. Pixton in the northern part of the parish was recognised as a separate settlement in the Middle Ages. Linegeresland on the road to Langford Budville became known as Liquorisland until its recent change of name to Blackberry Farm.

The three centuries up to the mid-fourteenth century showed an increase in population, the spread of settlement and a growing economy. In 1215 the 'town' of Wellington was established on land owned by the Bishop of Sherbourne. Milverton, two miles away, had been made a borough by 1265, both towns providing markets within easy reach of Nynehead which had meadows, pasture, arable land and woods as well as at least one mill. It is not known whether Nynehead had an 'open field' divided into strips, although the Tithe Map of 1837 shows an area called 'Western Common' at the eastern end of the parish, apparently shared with Bradford-on-Tone.

The Lay Subsidy Rolls of 1327 give the first list of names of Nynehead residents. These lists were prepared for the purpose of raising taxes for foreign wars, recording inhabitants and occupiers whose goods (i.e. movable assets, not land) were worth more than 10s. A total of 35 people are listed, three of them women – 14 in 'Neghenhude Flory', 12 in 'Nygenhude Monachorum', five in 'Pixtone' and four in 'Chippelegh'. Individual surnames include some probably derived from places in the parish or nearby – 'Bamptone', 'Chippelagh', 'Uppecote', 'Lynegereslond', or from local features – 'Brigge' (bridge), 'More' (moor).

Nynehead cannot have avoided the devastation caused by the Black Death in the middle of the fourteenth century when about one-third of the population of England was lost. Specific evidence of its effects on Nynehead is not to hand but it has been suggested that the rapid change-over of vicars in 1350 was caused by the plague. William Wysman left after three years in the post to be succeeded by John Cryspyn on 22 June 1350. He did not last long, resigning to be replaced four months later by William Esch on 18 October. Wysman and Cryspyn actually exchanged livings, Wysman taking up the latter's post at 'Rovyngton' (Runnington?). There is no evidence of death by plague here but there could have been some knock-on effects from elsewhere. The severe reduction in population reduced the pressure on land and in some areas the abandonment of houses and even whole settlements. There are signs of possible former settlements to the north of Nynehead Court and at Upcott that might reflect this trend, although there is no firm evidence to support the theory.

The day-to-day concentration on raising crops and livestock did not exclude the need to contribute to the national demands for money to support the aspirations of the King and other authorities. A prosperous agriculture was essential for this duty to be fulfilled. From 1288 for six years all ecclesiastical benefices had to contribute to the cost of a crusade, while Muster Rolls in the sixteenth century identified the men and arms available in each village. In 1321–22 the rectors, vicars and other ecclesiastical persons in the Deanery of Taunton gave 'of their own free will' one penny in the pound of their incomes, according to the taxation of their benefices, towards the erection of a new bell tower at Wells cathedral.

The 200 years after the Black Death showed signs of increasing prosperity in Nynehead. Nynehead Court was a stone house by the end of the fourteenth century, while in 1410 John Wyke left £10 in his will for the building of an aisle at the church. Religion was central to life in the village and Nynehead was affected by the religious turmoil of the sixteenth century. In addition to the changes of ownership following the Dissolution of the Monasteries, including Taunton Priory, the spiritual lives of ordinary people were changed. Two wills from the middle of the century might reflect this. Agnes Pirry, widow of Nynehead, died in 1536. As well as leaving sheep to most of the beneficiaries she left 3s.4d. to each of five local churches, 20d. each to Runnington and to 'the mother church of Wells'. To Nynehead church – her parish church – she left 'my crosse of silver and 6 yewes to have my anniversary

by the year by the wardens there for ever', and 8d. 'to the light of all souls'.

Sixteen years later Agnes Wyke died. By then the Protestant Edward VI and the Catholic Mary I had come and gone and the throne of England was back in the hands of another Protestant, Elizabeth I. Apart from requiring her body to be buried in the church of Nynehead all the provisions in Agnes' will are purely practical – oxen to her sons, donations of money to offspring and wives, a feather-bed, cows and sheep. The church did not benefit in any way.

At the end of the sixteenth century we have two pictures of Nynehead which suggest that life was not always easy, despite the rosy view sometimes given of the time of the first Elizabeth.

In September 1594 the parishioners of West Buckland and Wellington were indicted at the General Session of the Peace in Bridgwater for a 'founderous market way' from Nynehead Florey to Wellington. As West Buckland people were involved this must have been the road across the flood plain from Hornshay Bridge which fell at the meeting-point of the three parishes. This was clearly a common problem as six out of the 105 indictments made at the sessions included roads and waterways out of repair, blocked or diverted. Also in 1594, Bishop Still made his visitation to enforce Church law and to correct faults brought to his attention by the churchwardens of the parish. The picture that emerges is not good. The church had been in decay for four years and the churchyard was in a poor state. In addition the vicar was alleged to have taken part of the churchyard for his own 'proper' but unspecified use. He also had not read the Queen's Injunctions for a year, nor gone on perambulations of the parish, his defence in the latter being that the parishioners were 'negligent thereon'. It seems that there were disputes between the vicar Anthony Middleton and the wardens.

At the end of the sixteenth century the Sanford family arrived at Nynehead Court and a new and exciting chapter in the history of the village began that was to last for the next 300 years.

Nynehead Place Names

Nynehead in Somerset appears to be the only settlement in the world with this name. There is a Nynehead Street and other local names in Deptford in south-east London, and a Sanford River in Western Australia, all stemming from the activities of the Sanford family in the nineteenth century.

The name 'Nynehead' is of Anglo-Saxon origin 'Whose very name shewes what quantity of grownd is comprized', as Thomas Gerard noted in 1633 in his *Particular Description of the County of Somerset*. It is generally accepted to mean 'nine hides', a hide being an area of land, about 120 acres, adequate for the support of one free family, or as much land as could be tilled with one plough in one year. Other unlikely derivations have been suggested, such as the head of nine streams or parishes, or somehow from the Hollow. Nynehead's name has reached its present form relatively recently. The earliest version – Nigon Hidon – in AD897 was followed over the next 1,000 years by at least 25 different spellings (e.g. Nichehede (1086), Neghenhude (1327), Nyenhide (1410)), until in the nineteenth century 'Ninehead' was eventually superseded after a short period of overlapping use by 'Nynehead'.

The settlement that developed around the church and the Court is now known simply as 'Nynehead' but was previously Nynehead Florey after the de Fluri family who came here after the Conquest. It has been suggested that the name 'Fluri' or 'Fleuri' comes from the French village of Fleury-sur-Loire, but this is debatable. There are at least 17 places incorporating the name in France and a village in Normandy is a more likely source (e.g. Fleury la Forêt). Higher Nynehead was known until the early-nineteenth century as Upcott ('higher house'), after the farm on the road to Milverton, and then as 'Middle' Nynehead, until reaching its present name. Chipley is an Anglo-Saxon name – Cyppan Leage in AD854 and Chippeleg in 1254. There appears to be no dispute about the second part of the name – leah (field) – but at least three meanings have been suggested for the first – a personal name, onion (hence 'onion field') and cattle.

The hill on the road to Oake is locally known as the Knap(p), probably derived from the Anglo-Saxon 'cnaepp' or 'top, mountain top'. It is certainly in a prominent position with extensive views across the valley to the north. Although there is no evidence of prehistoric use it has not surprisingly been used in modern times for celebrations – a bonfire for one of Victoria's jubilees – and more secretively as the location for a Cold War observer post, now disused.

The Tithe Map shows 430 parcels of land in the parish with a such a variety of names that a detailed study of farm and field names would be worthwhile – many that are named 'mead' or 'meadow', those with areas ('Eight Acres') and the intriguing Great Downs and Western Common.

FIXING THE PARISH BOUNDARY

While Nynehead is identified as a place as early as the ninth century, defining the area to be known as such – the parish – took a lot longer. Generally speaking the historic parishes in England came into being during the Middle Ages as ecclesiastical parishes, the areas in which the church's spiritual and pastoral care of local people was delivered. These were essentially complete by the fifteenth century and were subsequently adopted for secular and judicial purposes. However, the precise delineation of the boundaries in map form often did not happen until much later, in Nynehead not until the Tithe Survey in 1837. The collection of national data, such as population on a consistent basis, required accurate and rational definition of these boundaries and several Acts of Parliament in the nineteenth century sought to tidy up the boundaries.

The parish boundary in 1837 follows to a considerable degree the boundary of the manor of Taunton as shown in the Great Charter of AD854. The boundary of the manor followed the River Tone from Bradford, westwards to the stream that joins the river to the west of the Court, then headed north towards Chipley. From there it followed the stream eastwards which today forms the northern boundary of the parish of Nynehead before turning north to Oake. The position of the manor boundary around Chipley is not clear. The eastern boundary of the parish, where it abuts Bradford-on-Tone, cannot be related to the charter boundaries. It is here that one of the landscape puzzles exists with the presence in Nynehead of 'Western Common', fields adjoining land in Bradford named 'Headlands'. This, together with the pattern of hedges, suggests that the boundary here might have been fluid, with common land shared in the Middle Ages between the two parishes.

The parish in 1837 covered an area of about 1,400 acres with some significant differences from the present: it did not extend south of the river; a detached part of Hillfarrance was completely surrounded by Nynehead around Perry Farm; another detached part of Hillfarrance lay to the south of Chipley; and a small area of Nynehead (Whiteheathfield) was surrounded by Hillfarrance. The area to the south of the Tone was divided between Wellington and West Buckland with the three parishes meeting at Hornshay Bridge on the Tone.

In the nineteenth century legislation was passed to remove the problems caused by the fragmentation of parishes. From March 1883 detached parts of parishes wholly surrounded by another parish were to be amalgamated with that parish in time for the establishment of parish councils under the Local Government Act of 1894. Thus, in 1883 the two detached parts of Hillfarrance were transferred to Nynehead and the detached part of Nynehead known as Whiteheathfield was given to Oake.

The parish boundary changes made in the late-nineteenth century were not the end of the matter. In a further extension of the parish in 1933 land south of the River Tone was transferred from Wellington and West Buckland to Nynehead, while in another review in 1986 the present boundaries were achieved. Nynehead was extended south to include houses and commercial property at Poole, one argument being that this would give the parish access to income from business rates, although subsequent changes in the rating system have since removed this benefit.

Above: *An indenture of 1693 signed by John Sanford of Nynehead Court and Edward Clarke of Chipley.*

Left: *An enlargement of the Sanford and Clarke signatures on the indenture.*

The monument on the Blackdown Hills above Wellington (a picture taken c.1908). The monument was erected at a suggestion by William Sanford made in 1815, after the Duke of Wellington's victory at Waterloo.

Chapter Five

THE SANFORDS OF NYNEHEAD

'Nynehead without the Sanfords during the last three centuries would indeed be the play without Hamlet.' These words in Charles Tite's obituary to William Ayshford Sanford (1818–1902) sum up succinctly the importance of the Sanford family to Nynehead.

It is believed the Sanfords arrived in Nynehead in 1599. They had long been landowners along the Somerset/Devon borders and are traceable back to John Sanford seated at Brook Sanford (now Edbrook) near Winsford in the reign of Richard II, at which time they also owned property in Milverton. They were destined to play a prominent part in the district over the following centuries. The Sanfords were to provide Somerset with five High Sheriffs and two Members of Parliament. They were part of an extended network of landed gentry linked by marriage to many West Country families.

We have much detailed information about Nynehead from the Sanford family papers held in the Somerset County Record Office. They provide a wealth of data for local historians, containing legal documents, letters, account books, parliamentary papers, diaries, inventories, wills and other material, even the occasional oddity such as a packet of 2,000-year-old wheat seeds from Egypt. The catalogue for the collection has over 4,600 entries, many in bundles, and includes documents dating back as far as the twelfth century.

Martin Sanford, the first of his family in Nynehead, became High Sheriff in 1641, the year the Civil War broke out. The Sanfords, like Popham in Wellington, sided with Parliament. Martin called together a Parliamentary Grand Jury which petitioned the King to recall the Commission of Array. Ordered to search for arms, he reported to Parliament the finding of quantities of armour in local houses, including the discovery of 40 men's armour pikes and muskets in the house of Master Sheers, his neighbour in Nynehead. He received Parliament's commendation for these actions.

Events were developing in the county and Wells was chosen as the Cavalier rendezvous. The leading Parliamentarians met at Shepton Mallet where an angry confrontation with the Royalists took place. Henry Sanford, acting for his elderly father, formed a 'posse comitatus' over 1,000 strong.

Within a few days the number of supporters built up to over 12,000 and the Royalists, under the Marquis of Hertford, withdrew to Sherborne Castle in Dorset. Henry, who put unity of the county above partisan considerations, was pardoned by the King in 1644.

Henry's marriage to Mary Ayshford of a long-established Devon family brought with it their large estate around Burlescombe, and linked the Ayshford name to future generations of Sanfords. Henry's son Martin died without living children and his brother John inherited. John at the time was a cloth merchant in London trading with the Dutch and Germans. In 1675 he was responsible for major rebuilding at Nynehead Court. In 1688 he stood for Parliament in Taunton as a Tory, taking the Wellington 'cudgel men' to support him at the polls. He and Sir William Portman were returned.

These were exciting times in politics as this was the year that William of Orange landed at Torbay and James II fled to France. Two years later, after John Sanford was beaten by the Whig Edward Clarke of Chipley, he moved to represent Minehead in Parliament. We now had two Members of Parliament, one Tory and one Whig, living in the same small parish. However, whatever their differences, two of John's sons were to marry two of the Clarke girls.

The eighteenth century appears to have passed comparatively uneventfully. William, the grandson of the MP, was High Sheriff in 1743. His death in 1770 was followed nine years later by that of his son John, leaving the latter's seven-year-old son William as head of the family. It seems the Court must have been let at this time and William may have been brought up in London by his mother. He is known to have visited Hanover for four months in the winter of 1798/99 when he became friendly with Prince Adolphus Frederick, Duke of Cambridge, youngest son of George III. They corresponded for over 30 years and Adolphus stayed with William at Nynehead in 1809 when the Court became the scene of lavish entertainment. The Prince agreed to become the godfather to William's first grandchild, although he was unable to attend the christening.

William was well aware of the distress caused by the agricultural depression after the Napoleonic Wars and actively campaigned for social and economic

Above: *Old Boys' School, Perth, Western Australia, designed by W.A. Sanford in the 1850s while he was there as Colonial Secretary.*

Right: *Edward Ayshford Sanford (1794–1871) in a portrait commissioned by his admirers in Wellington.*

Left: *William Ayshford Sanford (1818–1902), from a special feature in the* Wellington Weekly News *on his death.*

*A song written to celebrate the election of
Edward Sanford to Parliament in 1830.*

improvements. He provided work for local men by remodelling the parkland at Nynehead Court. In 1815 he chaired a meeting at the White Hart Hotel in Wellington to carry out his plan to raise a monument to commemorate the Duke of Wellington's great victory at Waterloo. It took many years to complete, but those passing through the Taunton Vale today can see it standing high on the Blackdown Hills.

At about this time, William acquired a holiday home in Lynton on the North Devon coast. His house has now become the Cottage Hotel. There, in 1817, he was responsible for the construction of the North Walk high above the Bristol Channel linking Lynton to the Valley of Rocks. In about 1820 he retired to Lynton, where he lived until his death in 1833, leaving his son Edward to manage the estates.

William's brother John was the rector of Nynehead from 1810 to 1834, but his duties were undertaken by a curate because, as he had married a divorcee, he decided to live in Florence. There he built up a notable art collection. This descended to his daughter Eliza, who married the Second Lord Methuen, and now forms part of the magnificent collection at Corsham Court in Wiltshire. John was also chaplain to the Duke of Cambridge.

Next we come to Edward Ayshford Sanford, educated at Winchester and Trinity College, Cambridge; his coming of age was marked by a big party in the grounds of Nynehead Court. His first marriage to Henrietta, a daughter of Sir William Langham Bt, was to bring a farm in Deptford, south-east London, into the family. In time this was developed with housing and one can still find Sanford, Nynehead, Chipley and other estate names on the street signs. In 1830, the last of the Clarkes having left Chipley, the property came to Edward, but within a few years, as he had two large houses so close together, he pulled down the mansion built by Edward Clarke.

Also in 1830 Edward was elected to Parliament. As a Whig he supported the Great Reform Act of 1832. A description exists of the party he gave for his supporters at Chipley, at which immense amounts of food and drink were consumed and the evening finished with a spectacular fireworks display. Henrietta died in 1837 and in 1841 he married Lady Caroline Stanhope, daughter of the Third Earl of Harrington. She brought two Dukes into the family circle, one sister having married the Duke of Bedford and another the Duke of Leinster. Edward had an impressive London house in Cavendish Square at this time.

Edward stood down from Parliament in 1841, but continued his many interests. He was a Fellow of the Royal Society, a founder member of the Somerset Archaeological and Natural History Society, and Chairman of the local Quarter Sessions. He was High Sheriff in 1848 and became a Deputy Lieutenant for Somerset. It was during his lifetime that first the Grand Western Canal and then the Bristol and Exeter Railway came through the estates of Nynehead and Burlescombe, and the Tithe Survey was conducted by his agent Charles Bailey.

Edward was followed by his son William who, as a young man, served in the Colonial Service. He was Colonial Secretary in Western Australia from 1852–55. At the time of his appointment the Colony had only been in existence 24 years and, with a population of fewer than 10,000 in an area the size of Western Europe, it struggled to survive. While at Cambridge Edward had joined the Camden Society, which promoted interest in medieval architecture. He developed this interest by planning schools and other buildings in the Colony. The Perth Boys' School, which he designed, is now owned by the Western Australian National Trust. A small Gothic building of church-like appearance, it now stands in the centre of the city surrounded by towering office blocks. William also supervised an expedition to explore the northern and eastern interior of the Colony. It was lead by Robert Austin, the assistant surveyor, who named a watercourse he discovered the Sanford River.

At about the same time one of William's brothers, Henry, had arrived in Western Australia. He

Col E.C.A. Sanford (1859–1923)

Hornshay Street, Deptford, London SE15, built in the 1880s on land owned by the Sanford family.

leased 48,000 acres on the coast at Port Gregory and built a substantial house that still stands at the time of writing. He named his property Lynton. In addition to farming, Henry was involved in lead mining and whaling. He was Governor of the Convict Depot that was established in Port Gregory in his time and was also a magistrate and sub-collector of customs. He became a local hero, rescuing the crew of a ship wrecked on the reef in a storm. On a trip back to England he married Emily Somerset, granddaughter of the Duke of Beaufort, but pioneering life in the Australian bush was not to her taste and they both returned to England.

William was also back in England and pursued his interests in natural history and archaeology. He became Secretary and finally President of the Somerset Archaeology and Natural History Society. He also became President of the County Agricultural Association. He was a Fellow of the Geological Society and the Zoological Society in London and wrote learned papers on geology and fossils. In 1859 William was in the chair at a meeting when the local Volunteer Rifle Company was raised for fear of a French invasion. A total of 32 members joined and he was appointed Captain. The Company survived until 1908. He also continued his interest in architecture and was responsible for alterations to the village church and probably for cottages and other buildings on the Nynehead estate. He introduced electricity to Nynehead Court and constructed a water-wheel on the River Tone to supply energy for Hornshay Farm.

William leased Martinhoe Manor at Woody Bay near Lynton where they kept a yacht and spent many family holidays. He took over the estate on the death of his father in 1871. In John Bateman's book, *Great Landowners of Great Britain and Ireland* compiled in 1883, the Sanford landholding was given as 5,057 acres in Somerset and Devon, producing an annual income of £8,170.

Colonel Edward Charles Ayshford Sanford was next in line. He served in the Army, finally commanding the Third Battalion of the Duke of Edinburgh Wiltshire Regiment, and was later made Honorary Colonel of the Battalion. He served in the Boer War and was with Methuens Horse from 1884–85, after which he was posted to St Helena as Governor of the Boer prisoner-of-war camp. He was appointed CMG for his service. He returned to run the estate and served the community as JP and High Sheriff in 1908. This was the year that Edward VII gave the Lord Lieutenant precedence over the High Sheriff. By the early-twentieth century Nynehead was let and Chipley was the principal Sanford residence. A very attractive rambling building with a red-brick Queen Anne façade, it probably incorporates the original house built by the Chipleighs in Plantagenet days. There was also a large house in Ennismore Gardens in Knightsbridge.

The Colonel was succeeded by William Charles Ayshford Sanford, known as Aysh, in 1923. The estate was run by trustees until he was 25. In the meantime he had married Rosemary Lindsay, a granddaughter of the 26th Earl of Crawford and Balcarres. In 1939, following the agricultural depression of the 1930s, Aysh sold the Burlescombe estate, keeping the Ayshford Chapel. Nynehead Court, with a large portion of the Nynehead estate, followed in 1940. The remaining farms and the Deptford houses were gradually disposed of over the next 30 years. Aysh served in the Second World War in the Royal Horse Guards and his brothers Martin and Roger in the Coldstream Guards and the Black Watch, respectively.

Edward William Ayshford Sanford, known as William, was born in 1929. He inherited Chipley in 1974 when his father was killed in a car crash. With the help of his wife, Judy, he restored the house to a habitable state and on retiring from the Central Office of Information, where he worked for the Foreign and Commonwealth Office, he moved down from London to reside in Somerset. William played his part in county life, serving as High Sheriff in 1992. The office of High Sheriff is the oldest, continuous crown appointment in the land and in his year of office it celebrated its millennium with many special events, including a garden party at Chipley.

In 1978 Edward Samuel Ayshford Sanford was born, and in the same year Chipley was to have a moment of national exposure. The house was used as the principal location by the BBC for the TV play 'Matilda's England' written by William Trevor, with Celia Johnson in the lead. A number of local people including William and Judy were used as extras.

The Sanfords have now been associated with Nynehead for over 400 years.

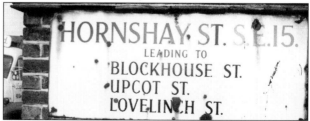

Nynehead names on a street sign in Deptford, London SE15. The Sanfords owned about 80 acres of land here in the nineteenth century.

THE SANFORDS OF NYNEHEAD

The main line of descent with the most important to the history of Nynehead in bold,
other offspring mentioned in [brackets]

John Sanford of Brook Sanford (late-thirteenth century)

Hugh Sanford of Brook Sanford m. Matilda Bassett (early-fourteenth century)

William Sanford of Brook Sanford m. Agnes Rodway (late-fourteenth century)

Philip Sanford (eldest son – died without issue)

John Sanford of Halberton and Sidmouth
m. Elizabeth Bonville (early-fifteenth century)

John Sanford of Halberton m. Margaret Harlewyn (mid-fifteenth century)

Christopher Sanford of Halberton m. Anne Balshe (late-fifteenth century)

Martin Sanford of Halberton m. Jane Champnies (early-sixteenth century)

Martin Sanford of Nynehead (d.1643) m. Susanna Sydenham

Henry Sanford (1612–44) m. Mary Ayshford

Martin Sanford
(eldest son – all children died young)

John Sanford (1638–1711) m. Elizabeth Knightly

William Sanford (d.1718) m. Anne Clarke

William Sanford (1717–70) m. Anne Chichester

John Sanford (d.1779) m. Hon. Jane Anstruther

William Ayshford Sanford (1772–1833) m. Mary Marshal
[his brother – Revd John Sanford (1777–1855)]

Edward Ayshford Sanford (1794–1871) m. (1) Henrietta Langham, (2) Lady Caroline Stanhope

William Ayshford Sanford (1818–1902) m. (1) Sarah Seymour, (2) Sarah Hervey
[his brother – Henry Sanford (1822–1905)]

Col Edward C. Ayshford Sanford of Chipley (1859–1923) m. Elizabeth Griffith

William C. Ayshford Sanford (1905–74) m. Rosemary Lindsay

Edward William Ayshford Sanford (b.1929) m. Judy Vickery

Edward Samuel Ayshford Sanford (b.1978)

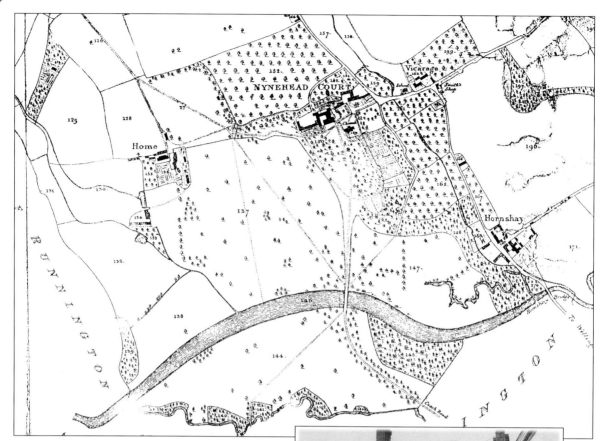

Above: *Nynehead Court as shown on the 1837 Tithe Map.*

Right: *The east front of Nynehead Court in the late-nineteenth century with a family group. The former orangery is to the right of the picture.*

Nynehead Court and church in 1792. The picture includes the church house (left), the orangery and cottages (right), all since demolished.

Chapter Six

NYNEHEAD COURT

'A remarkably early example of the classical
style in Somerset' (Pevsner)

The manor-house of Nynehead Court stands next to the Parish Church and is approached by a short drive from the village shared by the church into a forecourt dominated by a fine tulip tree. The Court is an attractive two-storey mansion with projecting wings, a steeply pitched hipped and slated roof with dormer windows, and a stone entrance porch with a venetian-style window over. The front of the house is rendered cream/yellow with white surrounds to the openings and white quoins, but behind the façade lies a complex of buildings of different materials – stone and brick – indicating a development over a long period. To the rear of the house is a small attractive courtyard from which the former rear porch in stone matching the entrance porch can be seen. Brick is the dominating material in this façade, as it is in the two-storey range on the west side of the courtyard.

Associated with the house are buildings which served a range of functions – the remains of an orangery to the right of the entrance, farm buildings and stables in brick and stone, a brick building now used by the gardeners but which once housed the generator for the main house, and the ice house. Behind the Court is a long low range in brick enclosing an open space (once a farmyard?), in which a large mulberry tree is the main feature.

The present drive from the village has only been the main approach for the last 150 years or so. Before, 200 years ago, the Court was reached from Wellington by a track through Stedhams Covert and across the Tone below the Court. By 1820 a new coach road had been built from the road near the present Wharf Cottage, but when the Grand Western Canal was built this was superseded, in 1833, by a tree-lined avenue from the Wellington to Nynehead road. This approach was used until the late-nineteenth century when the present entrance came to be favoured, although even then it was still used when the Hornshay road was flooded.

There is little if any direct evidence about how the Court came into existence. By 1086 the manor was recorded as part of the Bishop of Winchester's Taunton estate and it is probable that there was a house here at that time, if not before. Its position next to the church also suggests an early date and its site below the ridge shielding it from the south-westerly winds reflects a concern with practicalities rather than providing a prestigious position with good views across the Tone valley. This early house would have been a simple, thatched, single-storey timber building on stone foundations orientated north to south. There would have been one large room with a central hearth, a louvre in the roof to let out the smoke and an earth floor laid with rushes. All members of the household lived, ate and slept in the hall but the kitchen was probably detached from the hall in order to lessen fire risks.

By the end of the fourteenth century there was a stone house here and there is evidence that a gallery or solar was added at this time. The western porch was the main entrance with a door that has been dated to 1380. This door, with its original knocker, has since been moved to the front of the present house. There is a half-built-up window visible on the outside of the porch which suggests that it lit a spiral staircase to the gallery or solar. In the old porch there is a curious little niche in the north wall (which evidently was not then blocked) with an ogee-headed opening to allow the light from a lantern to shine out. The eastern porch is thought to be later, but earlier than 1675, as shown by the blocked window of the wall running into the north wall of the south-east wing. Another relic of the old house is the curve of a roof beam over the gallery or solar which is still visible on the landing of the first floor behind the lift. The original roof level was also visible when the rendering was removed during restoration in 1991.

The greater peace and security of the country in the sixteenth century encouraged building. Forde Abbey, Montacute and many more in the district were going up or being rebuilt during this period. At Nynehead the great fireplace in the dining-room and the range of buildings which forms the western side of the rear courtyard are evidence of this improvement. These brick cottages probably housed servants and farm workers. The room on the north end of these cottages used to be the old dairy and until the early 1990s still had the slate tables around the room. It is thought that the southern end of this range, then standing apart from the main house, might have been a dower house, a 'hall' complete in itself. Its shape,

A view of the interior of Nynehead Court during the late-nineteenth century.

strong and simple, with its mullion window, gabled roof and great fireplace, give the impression of independent importance.

At the end of the sixteenth century the Court passed from the Wykes to the Sanford family who owned the house for the next 350 years, making major alterations. The first owner of the family was Martin Sanford (1575–1643) who had eight children and many grandchildren, all of whom had to be accommodated. He built a chamber over the present dining-room with a lovely plaster wreath in the ceiling. The room also had an ornate fireplace bearing the arms of the Sanford family and the date 1633. The fireplace belonged to the large chimney from the dining-room and was part of an external wall. The wide staircase with its 'dog-leg' angles and shallow steps replaced the narrow winding spiral staircase leading to the gallery. Windows were still small like the mullion lighting the lavatory on the first floor, which must have been part of the gallery or solar reached by the spiral staircase.

The house as we see it today is largely a result of the work of John Sanford (1638–1711), who was a cloth merchant. In addition to rebuilding the existing house in the classical style, John added the main block looking roughly east, the block to the west with the drawing-room (a 'double cube room') and the block projecting forward to the left of the main entrance. The initials of John and his wife Elizabeth Knightley with the date 1675 are deeply inscribed into the stone over the doorway connecting his new building with the original hall. It is thought that to achieve the rebuilding in a suitably prestigious manner John might have employed a London surveyor named William Taylor, who a few years later designed Edward Clarke's grand new house at Chipley.

An inventory ascribed to the year of John's death in 1711 shows that it was by then an impressive mansion.

It is difficult to identify all the rooms listed but the 'hall' is interesting because clearly it was still one large room, not yet divided into hall and dining-room. The fire on the floor, with the smoke going through the roof, had been replaced by the large fireplace with an external chimney in the east wall of the present dining-room. There were three 'parlours' – 'little', 'middle' and 'best' – and on the first floor six 'chambers' or bedrooms. On the top floor were the 'mayd's' room and an adjoining chamber and other spaces in which items were stored. There was a 'Great Stair' and two 'camp chambers' that are thought to have housed four-poster beds. The building identified as a possible dower house is not mentioned, suggesting it was not occupied by John Sanford.

The inventory does not refer to any of the rooms in the north range, which is not shown on the first known picture of the Court. This is a pen, ink and wash drawing entitled 'The S.E. View of Nynehead Court, the seat of W.A. Sanford Esq.' In a corner in minute script is inscribed, in different handwriting, 'As it was in 1792'. The drawing might have been done from memory as there are some curious anachronisms. The relative sizes and sites of the house and church are incorrect, while the drawing-room block, with its fireplace, attributed by Pevsner to c.1760, is omitted. The east–west wing is missing from the drawing and a one-storey building of inferior type stands on the projecting site of the present kitchen. The site of the orangery is occupied by a three-storey building of cottage type which blocks the present eastern archway. Adjoining this to the east is another building with a door (or windows), probably cottages. In front of the main block are shown rectangular lawns with a low wall, much as at present, but no drive. It is not clear if there was a main door to the house on this side, suggesting that the entrance from the inner court was still in use. Another circular lawn edges this but the tulip tree is not there. Beyond this again is another low wall with a double hand-gate leading apparently to a drive. In front of the church is a building of some size which might have been the church house, again no longer there.

Nynehead Court from the ice house, showing how the house has developed. The late-nineteenth-century brick building in the foreground once housed the generator and is now used by the gardeners.

The 1792 drawing coincides with a written description of the Court from a survey of the estate made in 1788 for William Sanford. The list of properties is headed:

The Capital Mansion house of Ninehead, Courts Courtlage, pleasure ground, gardens, the Home Court Field now divided into 3 pieces, the Plott late a garden and part of Conygear Orchard now occupied by Mrs Elizabeth Acland – in all 27 acres.

Edmund Rack's description of Nynehead in the 1780s states that the Court 'belonged' to the Aclands. Presumably Mrs Acland occupied the house while the young William was living in London with his widowed mother.

During the nineteenth century the house reached its present form externally, although internal alterations continued to adapt the accommodation to the needs of successive occupiers. The main changes included the construction of the north side of the Court running east–west, probably in the early part of the century. The junction with John Sanford's 1675 building is clumsily contrived, especially on the upper floors. The wing projects east at a curious wider-than-right angle and the size and height of the ground-floor room, now the kitchen, give the impression that it was intended to be of importance, as do the three tall north windows, embellished outside with stone panelling. It is thought that the odd angle is due to it being built on the much earlier building detached from the main house, possibly the original kitchen *(see 1792 drawing, p38)*. The north range is not shown on the Tithe Map in 1837 but does appear on the Ordnance Survey map of 1888.

By the early-nineteenth century the main entrance had been moved to the existing position on the east side of the house. The coach road from the north passed the west end of the church to a turning area in front of the Court. Modern facilities were provided, including electricity, in 1882. This was originally generated by a water-wheel near the house, although precisely where this was done is not known. Perhaps works near Home Farm (now Court Gardens Farm) are related to this. Later the generator for the house was installed in the brick building now used as the gardeners' workshop.

THE COURT AFTER THE SANFORDS

After William Sanford died in 1902 the Court was let and his son, Col E.C.A. Sanford, took up residence at Chipley. In 1906 the Court and 70 acres of land were tenanted by Mr J.S. Lysaght, until 1919 when it was taken over by Major Stobart. After he died in 1935 the Court stood empty until 1939 when Dr T. Waterhouse, a London mental specialist, established a 'Clinic of Psychotherapy' there. His prospectus stated that the clinic provided all that was necessary for carrying out modern treatments for neuroses including psychological analysis, treatment by suggestion, physiotherapy, convulsive shock treatment and continued narcosis. Occupational therapy was provided in workshops, specially arranged for all kinds of handicrafts such as carpentry, basket work and wool crafts. Tennis, bowls, gardening, excursions and other distractions suitable for each particular case were also provided. There was even a farm run in conjunction with the clinic where patients could learn farming.

In 1940 the Nynehead Court estate was sold to Colonel Kleinwort. In 1948 Mrs Jenson Potts bought the house, transferring it in 1960 to a limited company. Registered as a charity, it was run as a retirement home with nursing facilities. The Friends of the Elderly, a London-based charity, took it over in 1991 and spent a considerable amount of money on the house and gardens, selling it eight years later to the present owner, Mr Adam Marneros, under whose care it continues to be a retirement home for the elderly.

LIVING IN THE HOUSE

The story of the Court's development inevitably concentrates on the owners but life in a country house involved many more people, performing different, specialised roles. Life in such a house is about more than just bricks and mortar. The Sanford papers contain a wealth of information about what went on at the Court over 300 years – more than enough to warrant a book in itself. From these records we can learn what was in the house, what people did from day to day, who the servants were and where they came from.

The 1711 inventory shows that the hall, the main room in the house, contained:

... a long table, 2 forms, 2 ovall tables, one sideboard, four Turky chairs, one dozen leather chairs, one pair of Iron Doggs, one fine pair tongs, one pair of bellows, two window curtains, one screen.

In the pantry chamber were

One feather bed performed, 3 stools, 1 chair, a little table, one picture, one chest of drawers [the only one mentioned], *Doggs and tongs, 1 window curtain, 3 hangings, one close stool.*

The 'Mayd's room' up the 'little stairs', had two warming pans, one chest, one press and one candle box. The maids probably slept on straw or wool mattresses on the floor. In the inner top chamber there was a 'speaking trumpett'.

The most valuable items were the silver goods and next to that the bed in the nuptial chamber, left by John to his wife with much else, and an annuity of £250. His wearing apparel, watch and rings are also

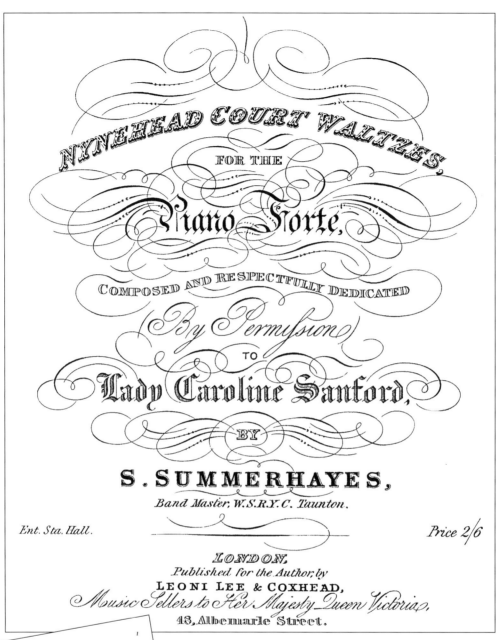

Left and above: 'Nynehead Court Waltzes' opening music and title page, c.1844. (Both reproduced courtesy of Oliver Davies)

Enjoying the Court gardens before a recital.

valued at £20. There is the surprising item of wool, worth £40, in the outer camp chamber, presumably thought valuable enough to be brought into the house for storage.

The accounts of John's heir William for 1740–59 show some of the items on which money was spent:

Livery lace – £2 6s 8d
One years wages for Betty Holly – £3 [her job is not specified but presumably she lived in]
A snuff box – £1 16s.
A horse – £7 10s.
A cow – £5 17s 6d
For painting the little parlour – £3 3s.
Soap and candles – £12 19s 6d. [evidently these were no longer home-made].
A half year's salary for the chimney-sweep – 10s.
A quarterly item 'took out for pocket money'.
For meat from Thos. Arscott from March 1748 to Feb. 1751 – £19 15s 4d.
50lbs of honey – 16s 8d.

Travel was important. In March 1751 ten weeks were spent in Bath, incurring expenses for the journey, an extra horse, a doctor's bill, an apothecary, lodgings, housekeeping and wine. A French horn was bought for £3.3s.0d. and a set of livery buttons cost £1.14s.6d.

Surviving from this era is the bell, used to summon men to work and meals. Of high-quality metal and decorated with engravings it bears the inscription '1747. W.A. Sanford Esq.' and now hangs between two tall brick chimney-stacks over the tower room and kitchen. It was presumably moved there when the east–west wing was built.

The Court was the venue for many festive occasions, such as the visit of the Duke of Cambridge in 1809 and the coming-of-age celebrations for Edward Sanford in 1815, for all of which the servants would have worked hard as well as providing the music. There were inevitably more sombre occasions. In 1779 another John Sanford died, evidently abroad. A bill accounted to the Executors for bringing the body from Plymouth Dock to Nynehead (a six-day journey) states:

A lead coffin... covered with black cloth and 12 men paid for carrying it to the 'Herse' with a set of handbells, more black cloth Shellboard, fustian, buttons, silk twist, pockets, garters, hat, ribbed stockings, buckles, and belts, 24 yards rich black silk, 3 drivers, 2 mutes, gloves, ribbons, herse and horses for 6 days, 24 cloaks, coach and 4 horses for 6 days.

A mason was paid 18s.6d. for making the grave.

In the following century the Court was noted for its music-making. This was especially true of the ladies of the house for whom the piano and harp were favourite instruments, in keeping with the fashions of the time, but their support of music was not limited to members of the family. The staff at the Court formed a band or orchestra for celebrations and in 1810 William Sanford paid for piano lessons for 14-year-old Charles Bailey, who later became known as an organ enthusiast. The organ that Charles installed at his house at Lee Abbey in the 1850s came from Nynehead Court.

In the 1840s Samuel Summerhayes of Taunton composed a set of 'Nynehead Waltzes' for piano, dedicated to Lady Caroline Sanford. On 25 July 1995 they were heard in the drawing-room of the Court for the first time since the Sanfords left, in a recital by Rowena Bass (harp) and Oliver Davies (piano).

Later in the century the family was still very musically active. On 13 November 1873 Rosalind Sanford wrote to her father from Nynehead Court saying, 'Since Norman Neruda is going to play at Taunton next Friday may we please go as I have never heard her and I think it will help me with my violin'. In 1884 Miss B. Sanford was receiving harp lessons from Miss Edith Brand of West Kensington who was paid £6.16s.6d. for 13 lessons and 13s. for the music. The presence in Wellington of the noted violin-string maker John Toms was of great value to the Court. At midsummer 1875 he was paid for providing harp and violin strings, music and music lessons and for tuning the organ. In 1886 the Court had two pianofortes, one harp and a violin which Toms 'serviced'. The Court also had a comprehensive library and a collection of paintings reflecting the interests of the owners.

The family travelled a great deal and, despite the availability of train services, depended greatly on horses. The stable accounts, especially from around 1880, show frequent payments for post horses and post boys, items of £2.2s.0d. and £3.16s. The Sanfords owned a house at Woody Bay in North Devon so when a four-in-hand went there from Nynehead, 'gates' on the road, presumably turnpikes, had to be opened at a cost of 4s. The horses were fed at Porlock for 5s. and a man with Mr Crook's horses helped to get the carriage up Lynmouth Hill for 2s. Post horses and post boys took 'the young ladies to Taunton ball', while fetching Miss Sanford from Wellington station cost £1. She must have had a maid and an enormous amount of luggage for the cost to be so high.

Music recital by the trio 'Serenade' in the drawing-room at Nynehead Court, 1997.

A full staff was essential to the efficient running of the house. There were indoor staff, such as the butler, the housekeeper and maids, as well as men and boys to look after the horses and carriages and a posse of gardeners to maintain the extensive grounds.

THE GARDENS OF NYNEHEAD COURT

The basic history of Nynehead Court is fairly well known but the gardens are much more of a mystery and prior to the nineteenth century we can see very little from the records available. The actual form of the 'pleasure ground and gardens' noted in the 1788 survey is virtually impossible to surmise from the evidence that we can see today. Few features survive from this period, although some of the mature trees such as the sweet or Spanish chestnuts, *Castanea sativa*, probably date from this time. Their position within the gardens is somewhat problematical, as they do not seem to form any distinct avenue or feature and could, therefore, have simply been intended to produce chestnuts. According to the current staff they still produce a good crop of nuts each year. It may also be that they represent only a remnant of a larger planting which has been thinned over the years.

From today's perspective trees within a garden are usually viewed purely for their ornamental value, but at that time plantings could certainly have had a more utilitarian perspective. Two distinct forms of chestnut are to be seen clearly forming separate groups and were therefore obviously planted as such. Named varieties are known from the Continent, as would be found with any other fruit trees, but as the trees show no signs of being grafted this seems unlikely in this case. Chestnuts are known as a very variable species and it could well be that they were merely from a distinct source when planted. The timber is said to resemble oak but has the unfortunate habit of being liable to 'shake', that is split at the annual rings, making it much less valuable in practice. This could be why the trees have never been felled when so many other trees within the estate have been removed for timber.

One of the other specimens within the gardens, the mulberry tree, *Morus nigra*, in the yard behind the house, could also date from the late-eighteenth century. The estate accounts from around 1760 indicate that a number were purchased at that time. The difficulty is that we cannot be sure where the trees were actually planted because the Sanfords had quite extensive interests besides Nynehead Court itself. The present multi-stemmed specimen is clearly not the original but could well be a surviving 'sucker' or side branch, as mulberries will usually take root if they touch the ground. This, of course, helps to explain why many mulberry trees appear to be so long-lived.

The tulip tree, *Liriodendron tulipifera*, which stands at today's main entrance is a handsome specimen of its kind. The tree comes originally from North

The fine tulip tree at the front of Nynehead Court.

America, where it is regarded as a weed species in some areas. It was introduced to this country soon after the Americas were opened up and was certainly in cultivation in this country by the middle to late-seventeenth century. The Court's specimen stands at about 65–70ft high and has a girth of about 10ft 6inches. A photograph from 1892 is said to show it as well established and from tree records available from across the country an estimate can be made of its age. Specimens with a known planting date from around 1830–45 have much larger girths than this tree, usually in excess of 15ft, so we can perhaps surmise that it would have been planted around the middle of the nineteenth century, rather than earlier.

A similar story emerges from the maidenhair tree, *Ginkgo biloba*, so called because the leaves resemble the much-grown maidenhair fern, *Adiantum*. The specimen in the grounds has a similar girth to the tulip tree of 10ft 8inches and a height of approximately 65ft. Maidenhair trees were introduced from China, via the Continent, in about 1750 and again records exist which can help to date this specimen. Those planted from about 1750 onwards have recorded girths of over 12ft, somewhat larger than ours. Those planted in the mid-nineteenth century show girths of a little under 10ft, placing our specimen at around the first quarter of the century, or about 125 years old. The tree is a male, as are virtually all of those in cultivation in this country, and so will unfortunately never produce seed.

The lucombe oak, *Quercus x hispanica* 'Lucombeana', which stands a few feet away from the *Ginkgo*, is again a fine tree although in this case it is clearly in decline. The tree is a hybrid between the turkey oak, *Quercus cerris*, and the cork oak, *Quercus suber*, and was raised by Lucombe, the nurseryman from near Exeter, in about 1763. He propagated the tree vegetatively by grafting it onto turkey oak stock. However, this same hybrid does occur widely on the Continent in southern France and Italy, so it is not certain that the tree sold as lucombe oak actually originated from there. As with many garden hybrids the crossing of these two trees probably occurred many times. The tree at Nynehead has undergone major conservation work in recent years and is about the same height as the *Ginkgo*. Unfortunately, because of the structure of the tree, its girth cannot be used for comparative purposes. Nevertheless, it is unlikely to be less than 200 years old.

Once we reach the nineteenth century the present shape of the gardens starts to become apparent. Of the surviving features the ice house is one of the most clearly recorded. It was built in 1803 and is said to be typical of its time. The bricks were made locally and specifically for the job. However, the records give us very little idea of any details of the estate work at that time. Much of the work would of course have been directed towards providing food and materials simply to run the Court, but an account book of 1830 does provide a glimpse into this world. James Pyne and Richard Ward were paid 9s. each for a week's work in that year. In Christmas week everyone's wages were reduced by one day, presumably because they were not paid for the Christmas holiday that they took. The most persistent job appears to be that of the mole catcher. Throughout the year the sum of 1s. was paid out to various people for 'mole catching', the possible explanation being that for the horse-drawn vehicles and equipment of the time a mole hole was felt to be a considerable hazard.

The knot-garden is a key feature around which there seems to be much mystery and misinformation. According to legend the Sanford family visited Versailles and in about 1700 brought back the design and cuttings of 'French box' that now form the knot-garden. In truth this all seems highly unlikely. To begin with, what we see at the Court is not in fact a true knot-garden at all but a parterre. True knot-gardens would have featured, as well as box, *Buxus sempervirens* 'Suffruticosa', plants such as cotton lavender, *Santolina*, or hyssop, *Hysopus*, and the design would have literally formed complex patterns or 'knots'. In fact the earliest examples recorded despised the use of box, describing it as being 'evil smelling' and 'corrupting the air'. In addition the spaces between the patterns would usually have been filled with coloured gravel rather than flowers. What we see at the Court clearly does not fall into this pattern at all and should properly be called a cutwork parterre. The spaces between the hedges were intended to be filled with flowers.

We then come to the story that the plants and design could have been brought back by the Sanfords from Versailles. Box does indeed root easily and it would be possible to take a few cuttings and get them to root. If we examine the parterre carefully, however, we can see that it would have required many hundreds, if not thousands, of plants when it was originally laid out. Bringing back 'a few cuttings' would have only been a start and they would then have had to be bulked up until there were sufficient plants for the job. Examining the parterre we can estimate that it would have required in excess of 5,000 plants to do the job or many years of propagation. This all seems extremely unlikely when there were many excellent nurserymen around, such as Veitch of Exeter, with whom we know the family did business.

In addition to this, if planted at the time of William and Mary (1689–1702), the plants would now be just over 300 years old and a simple examination of the parterre reveals plants with nothing like that age. If we examine the photographic evidence a picture from about 1868 reveals a parterre with relatively small hedges that could scarcely be more than a few years old, placing the planting date at around 1850. As with so many parts of the Court the facts are not clearly available in the records that we have. Nevertheless, it would seem likely that the parterre is in fact a Victorian addition, planted around the mid-nineteenth century. The pattern, rumoured to have been 'lifted from Versailles' and suggested to be the 'work of a genius', was in fact probably taken from various books of designs widely available to the Victorians.

By 1840 greenhouse design had become fairly advanced and the introduction of half-hardy plants from abroad meant that bedding out plants became popular. A close examination of the 1868 photograph also shows the central feature of the parterre as a flower or ivy-covered tower of some sort, not the suggested fountain. There are water-pipes and a stop tap in place but this could well have been for an irrigation scheme, especially if we remember that the parterre would have been filled with bedding plants such as geraniums.

A covering of snow reveals the sculptural form of the hedges in the parterre.

The gardens of Nynehead Court before 1869 (i.e. before the north transept of the church was extended by the addition of the Sanford chapel).

Right: *An extract from the above picture. Note the style of clothes and the gun held by the boy*

The gardens of the Court in the early-twentieth century. Compare the appearance of the parterre with the pre-1869 picture above.

Right: *Graffiti on a stable wall. 'Helped load four loads of dung with Lenthall, May 2 1927, rather -?-'. Another worker has added, 'and then you woke up'!*

Below: *The parterre and the view towards the Blackdowns, May 2003.*

Left: *More graffiti reads, 'Putting down Weed Killer, 11th July 1932. L Sharland'. Some wag has added 'I hope it killed you!'*

One of the most evocative features of the garden must surely be the orangery, of which so little is now evident. Up to the late 1940s it is said that some iron-work remained but today we are only left with the site and the rear wall from which it was heated. Again we have to rely on conjecture, as there are no accounts of when the building was originally constructed. Construction of the orangery supposedly took place at about the same time as that of the knot-garden or parterre, inspired by the Sanfords' relation-ship at the time with the Royal household. A more likely source of inspiration would have been the Great Exhibition of 1851 and Sir Joseph Paxton's Crystal Palace glasshouse. The records do, however, contain a small clue perhaps of a design for a 'proposed new vinery' for W.A. Sanford stamped by Bishop Bros. Engineering, a local firm in Wellington. There is no date to this design and unfortunately no fragments of the ironwork remain to be compared with the drawing. An orangery of this type would have been used to grow a wide range of plants such as oranges and other citrus fruits but would also have housed ornamentals such as camellias, which were thought at the time to be tender. With the First World War, however, as the men were away fighting, many gardens and buildings such as the orangery fell into disrepair. This of course meant that collections of citrus fruits tended to die out, but it was found that the supposedly tender camellias had survived perfectly well. At Nynehead Court, however, it is believed that there was a separate section designed specifically for camellias.

The other greenhouse, which remains, is clearly Victorian in its design and construction although it has been drastically repaired and altered over the years. The original roof glass, for example, would have curved slightly towards the middle of the pane to allow water to run off the roof more easily. A good example of this can be seen at the newly restored Heligan gardens in Cornwall. The greenhouse would originally have been heated by a coal- or coke-fired boiler using four-inch cast-iron pipes to carry the heat to the building. In the mid-1970s the pipes were removed to provide more space and a modern oil-fired boiler installed. A similar heating system can still be seen in place at the Royal Botanic Gardens at Kew.

Until fairly recently the roof of the greenhouse was repaired on a regular basis. The head gardener, who carried out some of this work in his early days, told us that the lead flashing at the top of the greenhouse roof is full of graffiti from people who have worked on the roof over the years. Although graffiti is often unre-liable as a definitive source of information, this could eventually provide some useful clues about the origins of this building. Undoubtedly the greenhouse was used to produce a wide range of bedding and ornamental plants for the house and garden, many of which would have been familiar to us today. The rear wall was probably used to grow vines. Whatever the

methods, the gardens produced a great amount of fruit and vegetables for the household. The old walled garden at Court Gardens Farm had a great number and variety of fruit trees grown in it, and its remains can still be seen, including in places the lead wires used to hold the plants in place. For those who would like to see what this walled garden must have looked like, Barrington Court is probably the best-preserved example in this area.

The pinetum sited on the south-east corner of the gardens is again of Victorian origin, as can be seen from the trees which remain. At that time new trees were coming into the country and as with all country houses it would have been desirable to have the latest features. Fashion in the garden was regarded as being of major importance and would have frequently dictated the overall design and layout throughout its history. No records appear to exist of the original plantings but between the two world wars many trees were cleared away to allow for the planting of apple trees. In recent years history has repeated itself and some of these have been cleared away to allow for the replanting of 'pines'. Although referred to as 'pinetums' they would in fact have contained a wide variety of coniferous trees besides the true pines themselves.

We can still see a cedar of Lebanon, *Cedrus libani*, originally from North Africa and introduced to Britain in around 1650; a Corsican pine, *Pinus nigra* var. *maritima*, from the Mediterranean and introduced around 1759; and a Douglas fir, *Pseudotsuga menziesii*, from North America. The latter is of some value as the tree, although discovered in 1793 by Menzies, was only introduced to this country by Douglas in 1827. There is also a tree known locally as 'Wellingtonia', *Sequoiadendron giganteum*, originally from California, which was not introduced to this country until 1853. Even after their introduction it would have taken a number of years for these trees to become commer-cially available, firmly positioning the development of our pinetum in the middle of the nineteenth century. This cosmopolitan mix clearly shows us the way in which plants were being brought into this country from all over the world at this time.

A further feature of the gardens are the 'bee boles' situated on the wall which connects the house to the church. At the time of writing these features are best seen from the churchyard as they have been bricked in on the garden side. They are said to have been originally intended to provide wax for the church candles, although clearly the honey would have been of value as well. The problem with this as a purpose is twofold: firstly, if they were bee boles they would have been open at the back and the hives would have been inside the structure. It has been suggested that they are more likely to have been buttresses for the wall. Secondly, today the garden side of the wall is covered by a yew walk, which can also be seen in the 1868 photograph. Even at this time the yew appears to be well established so it can be assumed that the

The 'bee boles' in the wall adjoining the churchyard.

bee boles had been out of use for some time even then. At that time the yew hedge had a series of holes or 'windows' cut in it which were probably intended to allow some light into what would have been a very dark tunnel. The whole feature was restored in the 1980s, as the yew had been growing out of control for some time.

Overall we can see that the present garden is largely of Victorian construction with perhaps a few trees remaining from the late-eighteenth century. This illustrates very clearly the unsentimental attitude the Victorians had to previous garden features, which were swept away as they modernised, and their enthusiastic introduction of new plant varieties. Today of course we are far more concerned about our past and there will be further work at the Court to preserve and uncover the garden's history. The pinetum is expected to be restored further and work is underway on the boiler house which heated the orangery. It would appear that it was heated by an underfloor system of some sort, which deserves further investigation itself. While conservation is important it is also vital that the gardens continue to develop. To this end it is good to see that a scarlet oak tree, *Quercus coccinea*, was planted in 1977 to commemorate the Queen's silver jubilee.

THE LOST PARKLAND OF NYNEHEAD COURT

Passing down through a beautifully wooded valley, it reaches Nynehead, where Art, stepping in to its assistance, has converted this modest brook into a fine and handsome river.
(Edward Jeboult: 'The Valley of the Tone', 1873)

Below the Court is a feature which puzzles many who take the popular walk from Lower Nynehead across the River Tone to the old canal and to Wellington – an elegant classical stone bridge with water flowing through only one of its three arches. A clue to its origin is given by the plaque under its central arch – 'W.A. SANFORD 1817'.

By 1800 the Sanfords had been established in Nynehead for 200 years and the Court had developed into a substantial country house with gardens and pleasure grounds. A visitor then standing in the gardens of the Court looking south towards the Blackdown Hills would have seen a parkland dotted with trees, below which was the River Tone lined with willows and alders, winding through meadows. As it approached Nynehead from Wellington the river divided. One branch, possibly the main river but later known as the Back River, flowed along the southern edge of the flood plain. The other followed the northern side of the valley before reuniting with its partner just above Hornshay Bridge. Below Nynehead Court the road to Wellington crossed the river and the flood plain before climbing out of the valley on the other side. Here the road rose through what is now a stand of mature trees known as Stedhams Covert. Under the trees is a rectangular pattern of sunken tracks which was shown on the first Ordnance Survey map in about 1800, but of which the origin is as yet unknown. The paths are probably medieval if not older but whether the site was used for anything other than growing trees before the nineteenth century has not yet been established.

The 40 years from 1800 saw a dramatic transformation of the scene by the owner of the Court, William Ayshford Sanford, and his son Edward. In November 1816 the *Taunton Courier* brought to its readers' attention the changes that William Sanford had made in the past six years:

Among the benevolent exertions in favour of the poor, which do honour to society at the present crisis, we feel happy in adverting to the laudable conduct of W.A. Sanford of Ninehead Court, near Wellington. This gentleman with the sole view of giving employment to the unfortunate people of his neighbourhood, who were out of work, has engaged upwards of Three Hundred of them in digging a canal through his grounds of very considerable extent, the completion of which will necessarily require the continued labour of many months. At a time like this, when the rent roll of country gentlemen is shrunk to one half of its usual amount through the depreciated value of land, and the insolvency of tenants, it is peculiarly agreeable to find that the warm impulses of generous feelings are not chilled into inanition by such unpropitious circumstances. The sentiment of gratitude expressed by the labouring classes of people in the neighbourhood of Wellington, towards Mr. Sanford, for his humane

Thomas Lee's bridge over the Tone as it would have looked with water under all three arches, showing the amount of earth needed to bring the coach road up to the level of the bridge.

The canalised Great River as it would have looked from the three-arch bridge towards Hornshay.

Another view of Thomas Lee's bridge with water under all three arches.

The three-arch bridge over the Tone.
How were the huge coping-stones brought to the site?

conduct in general, and particularly in this instance, would be very imperfectly represented by any terms that our best efforts could supply on the occasion.

This 'laudable conduct' was the transformation of a 'modest brook' into a 'fine and handsome river' in an attractive parkland in which the northern branch of the river was widened to form 'the Great River' – a lake 1,000 yards long and up to 40 yards wide, with a weir at each end. The centrepiece of the scheme was a new elegant three-arch stone bridge designed by the architect Thomas Lee. Above this bridge the existing river was widened, while downstream a new watercourse some 500 yards long was created, cutting off the old channel and removing the Nynehead Mills. The southern branch of the river – the 'Back River' – was diverted into a new channel flowing eastwards under the Hornshay–Poole road to rejoin the Tone 600 yards below Hornshay Bridge.

In 1813 the Hornshay–Poole road was straightened and by 1820 a new coach road to the Court had been constructed from a lodge opposite where Wharf Cottage stands at the time of writing. Also in 1813 John Hewett, the tenant of Hornshay Farm, installed a new drainage system in the fields to the south of the new weir at Hornshay. A total of 100 wagons of stone were bought for the 'underdraining', standard practice before tile drains were available 40 years later. It consisted of 'digging the drains deep, filling part of them with clean picked stones, and covering with earth to the depth of six or eight inches.'

In 1816 over four acres of shrubs were planted by the river to form Laurel Covert and in February of that year five men spent 27 man-days planting shrubs. In addition there were seven acres of 'plantations' along the Back River, a belt of trees about 25 yards wide from the Court gardens to the river above Hornshay Bridge and many individual parkland trees.

A boat-house was built on the northern side of the Great River above the three-arch bridge. It had to be repaired in 1815, suggesting that it had been there for some time (or was badly built). No plan of the scheme has been found but the evidence suggests that the work was undertaken between 1810 and 1817. In 1811 surveying equipment (a station staff, a protractor and a theodolite) was purchased from Berger's of London and six hogsheads of cider (c.2,500 pints) were bought from the farm for 'the garden men and the men at the river'. Cider was the main drink of men working on the land and, at an average of four pints per man per day, this quantity would support 625 man-days' work.

The work was still in progress in November 1816, but was probably completed during 1817. Perhaps it was intended to have the new park completed by Edward Sanford's wedding on 4 November 1817. Even so, on Christmas Eve in 1816 a celebration was held at the Court for the men working on the river, as recorded in the *Taunton Courier*:

Thomas Lee's three-arch bridge in 2003.

THE DEVELOPMENT OF THE NYNEHEAD COURT PARKLAND IN THE NINETEENTH CENTURY

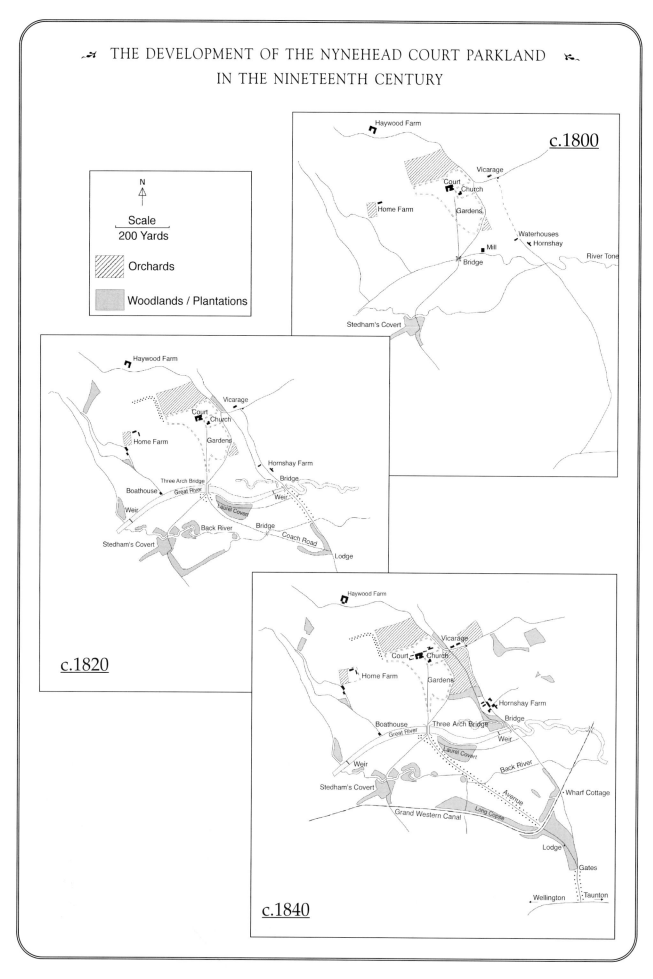

2

3

Ode

Inscribed to

*WILLIAM AYSHFORD
SANFORD, ESQ.*

Awake! companion of my leisure,
Rude and tuneless as thou art,
Awake, oh Lyre! to notes of pleasure,
Tracing, in thy varied measure,
The feelings of thy master's heart;–
And, oh! For that diviner spirit,
Whose sacred skill of highest merit,
In corresponsive strains could tell;
What vigour then would mark the song
What melody devout and long,
Would animate my shell!

Long had War's appalling thunder,
O'er th' affrighted nations rung;
Havoc fierce and ravening plunder,
Tearing nature's bands asunder,
Had far and wide their horrors flung;
What myriads, bold in conscious numbers,
Repose in death's eternal slumbers,
Who bled a tyrant's power to save;
What hosts that strove to quell his power,
Gained in the maddening battle-hour,
A victory and a grave!

Who can tell what desolation,
Riots in the march of war?
Where is all the gay creation,
Breathing joy and exultation?–
Vanished before his withering car!
The haughtiest nations learn to languish,
And fixed Despair, and writhing Anguish,
Famine, and Plague's consuming breath,
Mark where his meteor torch hath past,
And Ruin deep, and Fear aghast,
And Agony and Death.

Child of danger, Virtue's Minion,
Dove-eyed Peace at length appears,
Waving wide her balmy pinion,
She resumes her soft dominion,
And every hill and valley cheers.
Is there delight when day returning,
Pours from his high lamp, ever burning,
The living flood of light divine?
O Day! to realms benighted long;
O Peace! round thee a brighter throng,
Of varied glories shine.

Still with shadows vain surrounded,
Human kind their way pursue;
Grasping hopes on phantoms founded,
By unreal fears astounded,
Each transient as the morning dew.
With Vict'ry's banners round her flying,
Pale sand o'erspent see BRITAIN lying,
Victim of glory bought too dear;
And ere her wonted strength she shew,
Full oft must circling time renew,
The chorus of the year.

Want, o'er dreams of bliss prevailing,
Lifts his scourge and scowls around;
Hark, as to his rude assailing,
Echoes deep the voice of wailing,
And shrieks that tell th' unhealing wound.
With fixed gaze and bosom bleeding,
The haggard sire marks life receding,
Flit in his famished Infant's eye;
Hears the last cry arise in vain,
'Till kindly o'er his fever'd brain,
The mists of madness fly.

Lyre! companion of my leisure,
Lyre! that I have loved so well;
Say, are these the notes of pleasure,
That I bade in varied measure,
Thy rude and tuneless numbers tell?
Yet well may pleasure wake thee, bringing
Extatic numbers, light and springing,
To sing the friend of human kind;
Who, emulous of doing good,
Where late o'erwhelming mis'ry stood,
Bids gay contentment spring.

SANFORD! through thy lawns extending,
Monumental of thy fame,
Sweeps the lake in graceful bending,
Where tall arches proud impending,
Shall long record thy honoured name.
Thou heard'st the poor, and with employment,
Gav'st life, and health, and best enjoyment,
And bad'st thy fields an Eden grow;
Where (led by fine BENEVOLENCE)
TASTE, sweet Enchantress, charms the sense
With Nature's noblest glow.

Above: *Ode to William Ayshford Sanford by Thomas Browne, 1817, celebrating the new parkland at Nynehead.*

Left: *A bill for a theodolite and other surveying equipment bought by the Sanfords in 1810, but not paid until 1812.*

Below: *'Lower' Nynehead from the south. The River Tone winds its way from top left to bottom right, while the canal is the straight line across the middle of the scene. Nynehead Court can be seen at the top middle and Poole Farm at the bottom left.*

The whole of the labourers employed by W.A. Sanford Esq. at Ninehead Court near Wellington, in forming the canal through his grounds (an undertaking as we have already stated, originating in the sole desire of giving employment to the poor of his neighbourhood) partook of a hearty entertainment of meat, bread, and beer, at his hospitable mansion on Christmas Eve. Upward of three hundred persons were assembled for this purpose. The feelings towards their unwearied benefactor with which they quitted the scene of festivity, may better be imagined than described.

It is not clear who the workers were. The newspaper refers to the poor of the neighbourhood, but 300 seems out of proportion to the population of the area – about 4,000 in Wellington and Nynehead together in 1820. In 1908 the then Mrs Sanford was quoted as saying that the work was provided for soldiers returning from the Peninsular War (1808–14), who might of course have formed part of the unemployed of the area. It might also be significant that in 1809 the estate provided dinner for the 'sarjants' for seven weeks.

An alternative source of labour, in addition to the estate's own employment, might have been work on the Grand Western Canal (as a navvy). Between 1810 and 1814 work on the first stage of the canal was under way only six miles away at Burlescombe, near other land owned by the Sanfords. In 1811 some 300 navvies were working on the canal and work there ceased temporarily between June and December of that year. No evidence has so far come to light of their involvement in the Nynehead project but they might have been available and would have had the skills needed.

Creating a new parkland is a complex operation physically but also requires the involvement of both the landowner and his tenants and someone had to be in overall control. This task would have fallen to the Sanfords' agent Charles Bailey. Whatever his commitment to the project William Sanford himself would not have done this as he had political and social interests which occupied his time in Somerset and elsewhere.

Why he undertook this work is difficult to answer authoritatively because no accounts of his intentions have so far come to light. Providing work for the alleviation of rural distress is one possible motive but another could have been his desire to enhance his estates and keep up with his peers. The creation of new landscaped parks was common in this period and Sanford must have known about the work of the notable landscape architect Humphry Repton. Sanford could have met Repton in Bath but there is no evidence that the latter had a role at Nynehead. It was common at this time for landowners and their stewards to produce home-grown schemes inspired by the nationally known designers.

William Sanford's commission to the young architect Thomas Lee to design the new bridge over the river indicates that this might have been part of his thinking. Thomas Lee (1794–1834) was a Barnstaple man who initially trained in the office of Sir John Soane in London before moving to that of David Laing. He was clearly a young architect of some merit as he won both the silver medal of the Royal Academy Schools and the gold medal of the Royal Society of Arts. His work was to include Arlington Court in North Devon for the Chichester family (related to the Sanfords through marriage). Sanford might have first come into contact with Lee when he won the competition for the Wellington Monument, the foundation-stone of which was laid on 20 October 1817, two years after Sanford put forward the idea. Lee's drawings of the bridge at Nynehead Court were shown in the Royal Academy Exhibition in 1818. There is no documentation about the bridge in the Sanford papers, apart from a letter about an alternative design, a single-span iron bridge proposed by Barnard Dickinson of Colebrook Dale in 1816.

The parkland of Nynehead Court was an amenity much appreciated in the locality. When a big party was held in May 1815 to celebrate Edward Sanford's 21st birthday the *Taunton Courier* was lyrical:

Vast numbers flocked from all parts within many miles of Ninehead Court, the beautiful grounds and meadows of which mansion were literally covered with countless visitors. The interesting nature of the tout ensemble is beyond description. The beauty of the surrounding country – the gaiety of the adjacent meadows, now in the prime of their loveliness – the dancing groups of villagers who formed themselves in happy parties beneath the spreading trees, and the universal joy which beamed on the countenances of all around, – appeared to concentrate every feeling of delight which rural enjoyment can bestow.

The *Courier* made no mention of the way in which the parkland had been transformed, although an earlier report on the visit of the Duke of Cambridge in October 1809 referred to the valley as being 'delightfully variegated with the happy intermixtures of art and nature.' A visitor who did leave a personal record was Thomas Ernst who spent October 1813 travelling through southern England. Having left London on 28 September he reached Plymouth by way of the South Coast. On his way back to London he came through Somerset and recorded the following in his diary for 21 October:

The country level and the road good all the way to Wellington where I put up at the White Hart and after breakfast walked through the lane by the Church across some fields to a place called Nonhead – or some such name – belonging to Mr. Sandford who has a large estate here and has taken some pains in laying out his grounds and making them accessible to the people of Wellington. The best part of them is a shrubbery walk on rising grounds in the midst of water meadows. Mr. Sandford is described as a great benefactor to the poor and a friend to the Royal Family, having received a visit from 2 of the princes 2 yrs ago on wh. occasion a bullock was roasted under a large elm tree before his house.

The 'shrubbery walk' could have been Stedhams Covert, on the south side of the flood plain and on rising ground, although now it has mature trees rather than shrubs. This is preferred to Laurel Covert which abuts the Great River. It consists largely of shrubs but is on the same level as the surrounding fields rather than on rising ground.

The most remarkable tribute came in a letter to William Sanford from Thomas Browne, the proprietor of a classical boarding academy in Fore Street, Wellington. Having referred to 'the service you have rendered to a great number of your fellow creatures' and 'the important addition it has made to the picturesque and architectural beauty of the county', Browne enclosed his own 'Ode to William Ayshford Sanford', the last verse of which praises the new parkland:

SANFORD! Through thy lawns extending,
  Monumental of thy fame,
Sweeps the lake in graceful bending,
  Where tall arches proud impending,
Shall long recall thy honoured name.
  Thou heardst the poor, and with employment,
Gav'st life, and health, and best enjoyment,
  And bad'st thy fields an Eden grow;
Where (led by fine BENEVOLENCE)
  TASTE, sweet Enchantress, charms the sense
With nature's noblest glow.

At the end of the 1810s there were major changes affecting the management of the Nynehead Court estate. In March 1818 William Sanford handed over responsibility for the estate to his son Edward and moved to Lynton in North Devon (where he died in 1833), while in about 1820 the young Charles Bailey succeeded his father Charles as agent for the Sanfords. Twenty years later the landscape here had changed remarkably, partly in response to the building of the Grand Western Canal through Nynehead in the 1830s. Edward Sanford, with the help of Charles Bailey, undertook a scheme with two main elements: tree planting to screen the canal from the Court and a prestigious new entrance to the estate from the south.

SCREENING THE CANAL

The route of the canal through Nynehead was designed to minimise its impact on the Court. It ran at ground level from the Hornshay–Poole road on its way westwards. About 100 yards from the road a lift was installed to raise the canal 25 feet to a higher level, initially on an embankment. After 800 yards it reached ground level and then entered the deep cutting to the

south of Stedhams Covert. The building of the canal required the removal of earlier plantations.

Without screening the canal would have been visible not only from a wide area of the park but also from the gardens of the Court. Two belts of trees were planted to screen the canal – Blackhams and Long Copse, together about 900 yards long and up to 75 yards wide and consisting of a mixture of deciduous and coniferous trees. Between November 1833 and December 1837 the estate spent about £56 on almost 23,000 trees bought from the nurseryman John Young, a nursery- and seedsman of North Town, Taunton. The trees purchased included 8,900 ash, 5,500 oaks, 1,955 spruce, 5,775 scotch fir, 300 holly, 75 turkey oak and 90 English elms.

THE PRESTIGIOUS NEW ENTRANCE

The building of the canal required the removal of the coach road to the Court and the lodge on the Hornshay–Poole road. There is evidence that steps had already been taken to replace this access with a new one close by but it was never completed, presumably because it was also on the line of the canal. However, a new entrance was built in 1833–34 to coincide with work on the canal. It was indeed an impressive approach to the Court, in keeping with Edward Sanford's position in society.

A new public road lined with an avenue of trees was built from the Wellington–Taunton main road at

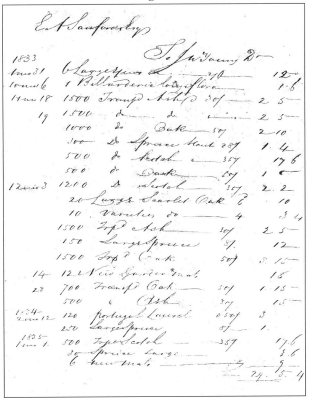

A bill for trees purchased in 1833–35 from John Young, nurseryman, of North Town, Taunton. Note the large number of trees of each variety. These trees were probably used to screen the canal.

Above: *The coach road avenue in 1949, from the three-arch bridge.*

Left: *The 1833 coach road and avenue as it would have looked from the air.*

Poole to Handcock's Corner. Stone gate pillars, still in position, marked the entrance to the new coach road across the fields towards the Court. There was tree planting at the entrance and a lodge which was later incorporated in the bridge taking the Bristol and Exeter Railway over the coach road. It passed under the canal then crossed the flood plain to the three-arch bridge through an avenue of about 140 turkey oaks. The trees were planted by Edward Sanford to celebrate the passing of the Great Reform Act in 1832.

THE PARKLAND AFTER 1840

By 1840 the layout of the parkland was in its final form, except for some minor additions and alterations to field boundaries, although of course the planting was by no means mature. By 1890, although the planting was established and the Great River was becoming a well-known and well-used amenity, there were some changes. The river was already becoming silted and overtaken by vegetation. This probably started soon after the river was widened as work was undertaken to clean it out as early as 1835. The process continues today with the stretch above the three-arch bridge being particularly marked with shoals of fine red sand, the growth of willows on the northern side and the movement of the channel southwards. The turbine house had been built at Hornshay Weir, Home Farm had been rebuilt and its grounds extended and the coach road from the three-arch bridge had been realigned to approach the Court from the north.

The dramatic changes in the park landscape in the first 40 years of the nineteenth century have been matched by equally dramatic changes in the second half of the twentieth century, only in the reverse direction. As a result only fragments of William and Edward Sanford's grand schemes remain. Aerial photographs taken by the RAF just after the Second World War show the planting still relatively intact but with signs of decay, such as gaps in the avenue along the coach road. Because of silting the Tone had diminished to a narrow river rather than the wide 'lake' created 130 years before. Laurel Covert had encroached into the silted area. Since the war major changes have occurred. The River Tone itself, now no longer the 'Great River', is of a normal width and behaving like a natural lowland river over most of its course. Above the three-arch bridge, willow, alder and other waterside trees have colonised the silt and since the abandonment of the 'Tone Struggle' have grown considerably, now overhanging the river in many places. Below the bridge the 'new' channel of the Great River is showing some silting and there is also some erosion on the southern bank which, if unchecked, could lead to increased flooding of the riverside meadows and the Hornshay road.

Many trees have been lost. Since 1887 plantations and copses have been removed and not replaced, and there are now only a handful of parkland trees, most over-mature. The areas lost include Blackham Copse alongside the road to Poole, the plantations along the Back River, the avenue, orchards next to the Court and the belt of trees from the Court to Hornshay Bridge. Long Copse remains and has been replanted twice, in the 1950s and in 1993. A belt of poplars was planted on the north bank of the river in the 1950s.

In contrast to the loss of planting most of the structures are still present, although not all are in good condition. Thomas Lee's three-arch bridge has been 'listed' but is partly covered with ivy, has a major structural crack and is now officially recorded as a Building at Risk. Hornshay Weir was lowered by the River Board in 1987 and the stone superstructure replaced with a steel footbridge. The upper weir has lost its brickwork and the stone wall that formed about half of it is now partly hidden in the adjoining field. The bridges which carried the two coach roads over the 'new' section of the Back River are still in position, although there are almost no traces of the coach roads themselves.

Finally, the parkland has not escaped the needs of late-twentieth-century society. The Tone Valley was chosen in the 1960s for a new 400kV power line whose cables and pylons can be visually overpowering. To the west is the Wellington Waste Water Treatment Works which, with the buildings and chimney of the Fox's Tone Dale works and more recent industrial development, dominates the view upstream from the three-arch bridge. However, despite the fact that only fragments remain of the Sanfords' original schemes, the River Tone and its valley by the Court are still an attractive and popular place for walking, being enjoyed by both local people and visitors at all times of the year. The river also has wildlife interest – to see a kingfisher is not unusual and otters are returning.

MANAGING THE NYNEHEAD ESTATES
The story of Charles Bailey

Large landowners such as the Sanfords and Clarkes depended a great deal on their land agents or stewards to manage their estates while they were away on commercial or parliamentary business, or enjoying the social life of the landed gentry. The role of the land agent on big estates was an important and varied one, specialising in the detailed day-to-day running of the estate in their employers' interest while at times even becoming involved in the more personal lives of tenants. They were essentially practical men, learning on the job, close to the soil. Their theoretical knowledge was obtained from books and from contact with other land agents. During the late-seventeenth century John Sanford at Nynehead and Edward Clarke at Chipley were assisted respectively by Richard Wyatt and John Spreat, but it was in the nineteenth century that most of the significant changes that we can see today took place. Many of these changes were brought about by the most influential of the Sanfords' agents, Charles Bailey.

Charles Bailey was born in Nynehead in 1796. His father, confusingly also a Charles, was tenant of the Home Farm on the Nynehead Court estate. More significantly for the younger Charles' future was that his father was also the manager of the estate and William Sanford's confidential agent, having a close working relationship with his employer and a great influence on the development of the property. As was usual at that time Charles junr learnt his surveying and land-agency skills from his father and was not formally trained, writing in 1845 that:

> ... at the age of ten or thereabouts I began to assist my Father in keeping the books relating to and receiving the rents of the said estate and by that means from that time I knew every part of the said estate.

Charles soon became sufficiently skilled to help on the estate and may also have helped William Sanford with his projects to develop Lynton and Lynmouth in North Devon, including the construction of North Walk in 1817. He was certainly sufficiently competent by 1820 to take over from his father as agent for the Sanfords.

Unlike his father he was not a tenant farmer of the Sanfords. Instead he lived in a cottage on the estate at Heywood Farm and embarked on a career as a freelance surveyor, seeking commissions from other clients as well as managing the Sanford property at Nynehead, Lynton and elsewhere. In April 1820 with another surveyor, Mr Bright of Simonsbath, he organised the letting of the sheepwalks for the Knights who had recently purchased the Exmoor Forest. Four years later, describing himself as a surveyor and engineer, he carried out a 'cursory survey of the different lines for the formation of a new road from Barnstaple to Eggesford Bridge' for the Barnstaple Turnpike Trust. By 1827 he was working for the Blaythwayt estate at Porlock and in contact with the Knights about access to port facilities at Porlock Weir. On 1 January 1828 he married Charlotte Brown of Crediton. Between 1828 and 1837 they produced a family of five girls (one of whom died in childhood) and one boy (Charles Frederick), all living in the cottage in Nynehead.

During the 1830s Charles was increasingly busy in Nynehead and further afield. He negotiated with the Grand Western Canal Company and with Isambard Kingdom Brunel of the Bristol and Exeter Railway, both of which projects required Sanford land at Nynehead. He also became embroiled in a dispute over the commons at Lynton. He was acquiring aristocratic clients, including Lord Sherborne, on whose behalf he went to Dublin in 1832. In April of the following year he was away in London when news of William Sanford's death in Lynton arrived at Nynehead Court.

At the same time Bailey was making his mark on the highest level of government. He gave evidence to a parliamentary inquiry on agricultural improvements and played a part in the review of the tithe system. This system had been increasingly seen as unsatisfactory and from 1828 a number of bills were put forward, culminating in 1836 in the Tithe Commutation Act, which replaced tithes in kind with cash payments. Locally he was appointed a valuer under the Act, making the apportionment for Nynehead in 1837, and he also contributed to the review nationally. Lord John Russell (the Whig Home Secretary 1835–39) was instrumental in promoting the 1836 bill and received advice from Bailey in the form of a pamphlet entitled 'An Honest Mode of Commuting Tithes in England and Wales.' As the *Taunton Courier* reported on 26 March 1836:

> The pamphlet, we are informed, has received the approbation of many noblemen and gentlemen in Parliament, as well as clergymen. The plan appears to us to deserve notice for its simplicity as well as for its strict justice towards both parties. Mr. C. Bailey's manuscript of his Tithe Pamphlet was in the possession of Lord John Russell a month before his Lordship brought forward his measure for the commutation. It was written for the purpose of giving his Lordship information and would not have been published had not what is considered to be the best part been omitted in the Bill now before Parliament.

Precisely how the contact with Russell arose is not known. Edward Sanford, William's son, was Whig MP for West Somerset and a supporter of reform, but it is probably not coincidence that Russell was the brother of the Duke of Bedford who was married to the sister of Lady Caroline Stanhope, Edward's second wife.

The Tithe Act was a great stimulus to the development of the surveying profession, creating a need for the type of valuation expertise that Bailey possessed. By the late 1830s, with his local tithe work over and more clients outside the West Country, he was ready to advance his career. In 1838 he left Haywood Cottage for an elegant Georgian house at 5 Stratford Place, just off Oxford Street and not far from the Sanfords' London homes. Here he and Charlotte added a son and daughter to their family. In addition he was now sufficiently affluent to buy his own country house, Lee Farm just to the west of Lynton, of which he would have known through his contacts there. He bought the property in about 1841 but did not take possession and convert it into the Gothic mansion of Lee Abbey until about 1850.

In the years that followed Bailey combined an active land-agency practice in London and continuing to serve the Sanfords, with his role as owner of the estate outside Lynton. However, his rise in social status did not always please his aristocratic clients. Lord Methuen of Corsham Court in Wiltshire (who married a Sanford in 1844) wrote to Edward Sanford:

Bailey is doing country gentlemen down at Lynton – and cannot come here until next week… However when Bailey's 'company' leave him he will I suppose come here – 'pleasure first, business after' – rather reversing the old adage.

Bailey's professional activities involved much travelling. During eight days at the beginning of November 1856 he went from Lynton to Porlock, then to Dyrham Park near Bath (home of the Blathwayts), to Sherborne in Gloucestershire and then to London. He did have time for interests apart from land management. In the nineteenth century Nynehead Court was a musical household, among both the Sanford family and the servants. In 1810 William Sanford paid for piano lessons for 14-year-old Charles who later became known as an 'organ enthusiast', installing an organ from Nynehead Court at Lee Abbey.

Charles' death on 2 December 1858 at Stratford Place was not unexpected. In 1856 he had had a fall and his sight was poor, and the notices of his death in the Devon newspapers refer to a long illness, as borne out by a letter from Thomas Tanner, vicar of Nynehead, to Edward Sanford on 3 December 1858:

Sad tidings this morning of the death of poor Bailey. I hope he is happy after a toilsome existence in this state of life. He was a truly honest, worthy man. I trust his friends will appoint his son his successor. He is very, very deserving too, and a truly 'simile simili gauditus'.

Four days later Charles' son and inheritor of Lee Abbey, Charles Frederick, also wrote to Edward:

The last sad ceremony of burial took place this morning at Kensal Green Cemetery in accordance with my Father's expressed wish. I should perhaps tell you that I have been most liberally treated by my Father and that I take under his will about £20000.

The wish of Charles, which he expressed in his will, was that 'my remains shall rest at Nynehead by those of my late beloved brother William.' However, there was obviously a change of plan. His tomb in the West London cemetery, which he shares with his wife, contrasts greatly with the modest tombstone of his parents in the churchyard at Nynehead. His father had died only three years before and is buried close to members of the Sanford family.

Charles Bailey left Lee Abbey to his son Charles Frederick. Initially the land-agency firm remained at Stratford Place, with various changes of name, but by the end of the century the name of 'Bailey' had disappeared from the letterhead. Until the end of the century they continued to advise the Sanfords on the development of their land at Deptford in south-east London, but work on the ground in Nynehead was overseen by local men such as John Gidley at Chipley and Stephen Bailey at Hornshay Farm.

Charles Bailey, the Sanfords' agent and owner of Lee Abbey near Lynton, is buried in Kensal Green cemetery, West London. His tomb is pictured bottom middle.

Nynehead Court and Lower Nynehead from the air, c.1970. Hornshay Farm can be seen top middle, with the three-arch bridge and Laurel Covert top right, and the Hollow and the Burrows middle left.

Island Cottage, built c.1740, the blacksmith's shop from 1821. Shown are Mr Baker and his sons Robert and Joseph in about 1880. In the left background is the lower end of the Hollow leading to Higher Nynehead.

Chapter Seven

LOWER & HIGHER NYNEHEAD, CHIPLEY & EAST NYNEHEAD

LOWER AND HIGHER NYNEHEAD

Clustered near the entrance to the Court, 'Lower' Nynehead (once Nynehead Florey) is more of a hamlet than a village and its early history was dominated by the church, the Court and its associated buildings. Apart from these and the farms at Hornshay and Heywood, this part of the parish 200 years ago consisted only of the vicarage and the smith's shop (William Bailey, blacksmith and parish clerk) surrounded by orchards.

By 1830 the village school had been built by the Sanfords and by 1888 what are now known as Forge Cottage (with the slate roof and gable-ends typical of the village at this time) and the Old Post Office had appeared on the scene. On the road to Heywood Farm Court Cottages were built in about 1890 but it was not until the twentieth century that more houses were built. These included Orchard Cottages opposite the school, built by the Bolnore Estates in 1947. The builders were Potters of Taunton, whose worker Archie Priddle was one of the first occupiers. The village Post Office was here, run by Miss Jennings. It survived until after the war. Water for all the houses was provided from a well behind the Post Office (remembered by Jim Lake who lived at Island Cottage between the two world wars) until water was brought from Chipley to the pumping station behind the school.

The island where the road from Hornshay comes into the village was created in the 1920s to make it easier for lorries and large wagons to negotiate the left-hand turn at the bottom of the Hollow. Stones were delivered by traction engines and steam wagons (probably by Kings) to Lower Nynehead. One man, Jenkins, came every day and sat all day on a sack hammering stones into smaller pieces, grading them by size. They delivered very large stones as a base for the road and laid much smaller stones to fill in between. The surface was then steamrolled to flatten the top – no tarmac was used.

The Hollow

The Hollow is the most unusual physical feature in Nynehead and the biggest puzzle. It takes the form of a cutting through the sandstone, carrying the road up from Lower to Higher Nynehead, a rise of more than 60 feet in about 300 yards between vertical rock walls, draped in ivy, up to 30 feet high and sometimes only 10 feet apart.

There had always been a road in this position, probably in a shallow cutting, but the origin of the Hollow as we know it is a mystery that has not yet been conclusively solved. A gradual deepening by erosion of the original road is thought by some to have been the cause, but Edward Jeboult in his *History of West Somerset* (1873) suggests otherwise:

... the owner of this parish generously acted some years ago in providing for the wants of the poor during a severe winter by having a deep ravine cut for a road through the rock. It now forms a most picturesque feature.

The owner of the parish in 1873 was William Sanford of Nynehead Court but no evidence has so far been found of precisely when the Hollow was cut or who cut it. Jeboult's statement is in fact the only known contemporary written reference. The Sanfords were known to be philanthropic and it is likely that the Hollow was cut in the time of William's father Edward who died in 1871. There were severe winters in the middle of the century, in particular January 1855 which was known as the 'Crimean Winter', but so far no link with the Hollow has been found. One suggestion is that it was cut at the same time as the building of the new vicarage in 1867 and the press report celebrating the laying of the foundation-stone does indeed show that it was known as the Hollow by then. The reference to the 'wants of the poor' must rule out a belief long held locally that it was cut by French prisoners of war. There is also no indication of what happened to the material removed, more than 150,000 cubic feet of sandstone. It is likely that it was used locally for building work of a minor nature such as barns and walls.

Whatever the Hollow's origin it has remained a unique and picturesque feature of Nynehead. In 1926 it was described as 'quaint and peaceful with the sand martins flitting in and out of the nearby sandpits.' The sand martins have gone and over the years the Hollow has been widened by natural processes and by wear and tear, particularly more recently with the advent of larger road vehicles. People old and young have etched their names in the soft rock, including American servicemen during the Second World War, and at one

The Hollow in the 1960s.

Above: *The 'plaque' in the Hollow – who carved it and when is not known.*

Below: *A pony and cart in the Hollow before the days of motor traffic.*

An aerial view of Higher Nynehead from the east in 1999. Upcott Farm is middle right, the Burrows and the Hollow top left.

Demolition of the poorhouses in Higher Nynehead, c.1970. No. 1 Farthings Close can be seen in the background. Note the Wellington Rural District Council lorry – a Commer Carrier.

time a plaque with a date was carved, although this has virtually disappeared. The Hollow is a pleasant cool place on a hot summer's day but at night can be somewhat eerie. Not surprisingly it has also acquired its own legend of the ghost of a horsewoman who plunged to her death in the Hollow while out hunting.

Higher Nynehead

From the top of the Hollow the road leads into Higher Nynehead which is even more of a twentieth-century creation than Lower Nynehead. In 1837 there were Upcott Farm on the Milverton road (from which the hamlet's original name of Upcott was derived), the poorhouses, eight cottages and the chapel and its adjoining cottage at Prings. By the end of the century things were little different. The new vicarage had been built on glebe land at the top of the Hollow in 1867/8 and a pair of cottages on land behind the poorhouses in about 1890, all in brick with slate roofs. Glebe Cottage (now Higher Upcott) had also been rebuilt in this style.

Four generations photographed at Farthings Close, c.1925. Pictured are: Alice E. Perry (née Lake) (standing), Ellen Mary Lake (née Morrish, the wife of William Lake) (seated next to her father), with Gerald H. Perry on her lap.

Higher Nynehead developed rapidly between the two world wars with the building of 16 houses by Wellington Rural District Council at Farthings Close. Numbers 1–4 (known first as 1–4 Furzeys – in the opposite direction) were built in 1926, the first recorded occupiers being Ash (No.1), H. Harnell (No. 2), H. Perry (No. 3) and Mrs Garley (the health visitor) (No. 4). The rents were £1.5s. a month. Numbers 5 to 8 followed quickly in January 1930. The first tenants were H. White (gardener), Thomas Cooksley (a labourer in the brickworks), F. Walter Pulman (a labourer in the woollen factory) and Wm Th. Gollop (factory operative). The remaining eight houses at Farthings were occupied in 1939.

Further big changes came after the Second World War. Although the poorhouses were condemned as being unfit in 1936, when it was recorded that the three cottages were occupied by a total of 18 people – the Lock, Elson and Brown families – they were not demolished until the early 1970s. The only part remaining is the stone wall now forming the rear boundary of Penhallym next to the Memorial Hall. The hall had been built in 1950 and it is in this part of the village that new houses have been concentrated – eight additional houses in Roundoak Gardens in the 1960s, seven in Blackdown View in the 1990s, and several detached and semi-detached houses and bungalows.

CHIPLEY

At the far north-western end of the parish lies the often-forgotten part of Nynehead known as Chipley, centred on the large house of the same name. There was a settlement here in Saxon times which developed notable connections in the late Middle Ages through the Warre and Lottisham families (it has also been suggested that the sixteenth-century poet Samuel Daniel was born at a house here in about 1562). It reached its peak in the late-seventeenth century when in 1652 Edward Clarke of Bradford-on-Tone, a widower with three small children (Ursula, Anne and Edward), married Elizabeth Lottisham, the granddaughter and ultimate heiress of Edward Warre of Chipley. She and Edward had no children and she bequeathed Chipley to her stepson Edward, who took over the running of the estate on his father's death in 1679. The younger Edward was to make his mark at the highest level, becoming a Member of Parliament, Commissioner of Excise and Auditor-General to Queen Mary. He was also an instigator of the Bank of England but was too busy to become a director.

After attending Taunton School and Wadham College, Oxford, Edward had married heiress Mary Jepp in 1675, when he was 25, and was keen to make improvements both to the estate and his home. He decided to build a new house at Chipley, perhaps inspired by the example of John Sanford who had rebuilt nearby Nynehead Court four years

Above: *The old house at Chipley built by Edward Clarke in the 1680s, as shown in Buckler's drawing in 1837. It was pulled down only a few years after the drawing was made.*

Right: *Some visitors, or perhaps members of the Chipley household, travelled by horse-drawn carriage. The driver appears to be in uniform.*

Above: *Visitors to Chipley in the early 1900s came by motor car. The vehicle is a 15hp Panhard and records show this to have been registered to the owner of a company in Yeovil. The driver clearly wears a uniform but sadly the other figures remain unidentified. (Grateful thanks to the Librarian at Haynes Motor Museum at Sparkford for his assistance in researching this vehicle.)*

Right: *Bringing transport up to date! Mr William Sanford outside Chipley in October 2002.*

A veteran tree at Chipley, planted in 1760,
probably a London plane but referred to by the
Victoria County History *as an 'occidental' plane.*

earlier. Clarke's new house was to dominate Chipley for the next 160 years. The site chosen was just to the north-west of the present house on a platform looking south across the valley to the Blackdown Hills. At the same time the range (Chipley at the time of writing) was rebuilt. Some believe this used to be the stables but it could well have been the original house.

The new house replaced an older property which, according to the inventory after Edward Clarke senr's death in 1679, was worthy of the landowners preceding the Clarkes – it had a new parlour, a parlour chamber, a chamber over the 'syder' house and a great gallery – but was very old-fashioned.

The new house was clearly impressive but although it was an important building it seems that there is only one illustration in existence, by John Buckler in the nineteenth century. It was a large 'double-pile' house, almost square in plan, measuring 100ft on the north and south sides and 96ft on the other two. It had a basement, a ground and first floor and rooms in the roof with dormers. The doorways or 'frontispieces' on three sides were impressive, as was the cornice. Unusually for a Somerset house of this time, Chipley was built of brick and was faced with white ashlar and with a 'tyle' roof. The bricks were supplied by John Kingston of Taunton, who was paid 6d. per 1,000 bricks for turning the earth, 3s. per 1,000 for moulding and 18d. when 1,000 had been burnt. By January 1681 he had been paid for turning the earth for 100,000 bricks and contracted for a further 50,000. In March 1681 10,000 'tyle stones' were brought in, at a cost of £12 plus 30s. for carriage.

Research has shown that Edward Clarke commissioned a London surveyor called William Taylor, who may have been introduced to him by John Locke or John Sanford, to design and supervise the

building work. Much of the building was done by local craftsmen, their work having to be fitted around the usual seasonal farming activities, and Edward Clarke was responsible for providing the materials. Two limekilns and a saw-pit had to be built specially. Work on the house was started in 1681 and, like most building, took longer than expected.

After Edward's death in 1710 Chipley was inherited by his son Jepp and then by Jepp's son, another Edward, who died unmarried in 1796. The estate then went to the granddaughter of Jepp's eldest sister Betty, but she died childless and John Nurton, a friend of Edward, inherited, upsetting all the remaining Clarke descendants. However, on his death in 1829 he left it to Edward Sanford, great-great-grandson of Anne Clarke, another of Jepp's sisters, who had married Henrietta Langham, the great-great-granddaughter of Molly Clarke, yet another sister. On 3 September 1830 Edward Sanford gave a banquet for 'his Neighbours and Friends, in that antient seat of hospitality, Chipley Hall.' Sanford had recently been elected an MP for the county of Somerset and a song had been written in his honour to the tune 'Liberty Hall'.

So Chipley had come back into the possession of the descendants of Edward and Mary Clarke, but unfortunately the Sanfords now owned two large houses within two miles of each other and the relative merits of improving Nynehead Court as opposed to Chipley were investigated. Edward Sanford was advised that 'Chipley Park and Nynehead Court cannot and ought not, as rival monarchs, be permitted to remain together.' Consequently, it was decided to pull down Chipley, Edward Sanford continuing to live at Nynehead Court while the surviving range at Chipley became the main house there. This was occupied, among others, by John Gidley, one of the Sanfords' agents. In 1902, on the death of his father, Colonel E.C.A. Sanford took up residence and the house has remained in the Sanford family's possession ever since.

Aerial view of Chipley from the west, c.1970.
Heywood Farm and Higher Nynehead are top right.

Life at Chipley 1680–1710

Edward Clarke's new house was designed to suit a new style of living, perhaps matched by that at Nynehead Court, in which landowners went to London for months at a time, employed fewer servants and wished for privacy. On the first floor were modern apartments – bedchambers with dressing-room and closet, and a long gallery overlooking the hall. Corridors gave access to rooms without going through other rooms. A great staircase linked the two principal floors with back stairs serving the whole height of the house, enabling domestic tasks like emptying close stools to be unseen by the family. A new feature was the service basement containing a servants' hall, a 'kitchin', scullery, 'pastery' (with hot oven for baking and roasting), larder (probably dry for spices and wet for meat), a 'greate sellar and beere sellars' and a butler's room. Chipley was clearly well supplied with water, as one of Morland's modern forcing pumps was used. John Locke, philosopher friend of the Clarkes, said 'I have never seen a house that I like better... and suited to all purposes.'

It must have been an attractive home, approached by a flight of steps to add majesty to the house and improve the views, full of light and space, with entrances from the gardens on all sides. Edward, with his gardener John Barber, was continually improving the grounds, and was given trees and vegetables like turnips and red cabbage that Locke sent from his exile in Holland. There was a kitchen and herb garden, a cherry garden, the oval pond garden, apple and pear trees in the orchard, philbert hedges and a bowling-green. There was also a brewhouse, where little Jack was saved from diving head first into the cistern, and a saw-pit. Outside were the deer park and rookeries and ponds where Edward fished for carp on his rare visits from his hectic working life in Parliament and the Treasury.

The most notable thing about Chipley was how young everyone was. In 1683, when Edward was 33 and Mary 28, they had no relatives left alive of an older generation, but they had three small children, with five more to follow, and a household of young servants. These were chosen from the sons and daughters of yeomen and became part of the 'family'. Edward and Mary were responsible for their physical and moral welfare and provided them with clothes, food and a share in any social jaunts. Of the two who stayed for a lifetime, John Spreat was only 25 when he became steward and Eleanor Pike 17 when she arrived at Chipley in 1672.

There was a never-ending hunt to find good servants, Mary preferring local girls – 'I had rather take the trouble of makeing them fitt for that place than be plagued with one that have lived in London long enough to larne all the rogueryes and cheates of it' – but they were not necessarily permanent fixtures and many just worked for a year before seeking pastures new, often annoyingly leaving immediately after they had been provided with their annual suit of clothes. Many of the maids would go to London for a more exciting job or set up as a milliner until they married. Servants turned their hands to various tasks – a coachman or a gardener might also be expected to be able to serve at table. When Mary decided to spend more time at Chipley the servants resented her continual presence which prevented the easy-going ways they had got used to when she was in London.

Romantic problems occurred – nursery maid Nan fancied Gabriel Spreat and pined when he went to London, Isaac Heath (decorator and handyman) flirted with Dorcas and then married Rose, probably bigamously, and John Spreat was divorced in Doctors Commons by his wife Grace. Between 1687 and 1705 six Huguenot refugees came as tutors and they caused other problems, mainly because Chipley was so far from their countrymen in London and they resented 'putting up with the boredom of the most appalling solitude that ever existed.' De la Roque also felt superior to the servants, and Mary had to tell Spreat:

... if he will not be thought a servant, though in effect he is so, let him be thought what he will, it is no great matter but for the childrens supping with him that I dont think at all proper no more than a hot supper to be dressed a purpose for his worshipp it being that which I havent for my self when alone.

Not all the children were there all the time; the babies went to a wet nurse in Thames Ditton until they were weaned. Ward went to school in London for a while, and spent time with Locke at Oates. Nanny went to school in Hackney, while Molly and Jack at different times boarded in Chelsea. Betty stayed for long periods with close friends, the Stringers, near Salisbury, following the custom for girls to gain a little social polish and have some freedom before marriage. But some of them were always there, up in the nursery above Mary's room, playing battledore and shuttlecock, guarded by Eleanor Pike and John Spreat if their parents were in London, and visited by Aunt Ursula Venner, Edward's sister, who lived with her son Gustavus Adolphus at Gundenham.

Chipley was a place of continual activity; food was grown on the estate and preserved for the winter:

... lett Dorcass know I would have her to looke out some of the largest mouthed stone bottles and when they are very dry fill them up with goosberyes full gone and ye blackes and stalkes picked, but the goosberyes must not be grone soft, and when the bottles are full, corke them up very close and put them into a kettle of cold watter and lett them boyle an howere then take them out and lett them stand close stoped as they are till they are cold yn sett them away in the seller.

Food was also sent up to Edward in London; in March 1700 Mary despatched:

... 3 dozen and half of this yeares sider and a little deal box with a gammon of bacon such as you use to love when you was heare in the countrey and in the same box I have put up 7 baking pears which was all I had left.

Best friends like the Bluetts from Holcombe Rogus or Sir Walter Yonge from Escot, neighbours like the Comers, and political allies in Taunton all came to dine in the great hall.

Everyday clothes were made locally but the latest fashions had to come from London, like Betty's topknots from John Locke. A hasty SOS had to be sent to Edward when Queen Mary died in 1694 and not a yard of black cloth for mourning remained in Taunton. Mary wanted a 'black cloth mantua with a train and a black silk apron with bib, mantuas and pettycote with a head and rufles' for the girls and a coat, waistcoat and breeches for Jack.

But it was not necessarily a comfortable or luxurious life. In October 1696 there was great hardship in the area:

... a great many are forst to go a beging that are weavers, tradesmen they say will not give them any work so that a great many goes abeging allredy, and we have had a great robbery committed not far off.

Mary kept a mastiff in the house as a guard. Wood for fuel was so short that Mary:

... had no fire above stayrs this winter; Jenney and all the rest have bin dressed and undressed without it yet for the people of the chitchen will have a constant good fire theare who ever wantes and to spare my fagott wood I have for this last 2 burnings bin forst to live with straw. The beggars of Wellington have got a horne which they sound at theyr apoynted times for a generall meeting and then they go out in bodys with hookes and other conveniencies at noon day and cutt down the wood as if it was theyr owne and nobody dares to control them, for if you touch one you was as good touch them all for they all fall upon you.

Mary and Spreat set about organising a serge-making business to employ the poor, who were also given food at Chipley, particularly at Christmas:

Satterday I disposed of near a hundred loaves and about forty peeces of beefe and now I am in expectation of 5 or 6 and thirty of the poor knaighbours and theyr wifes and when all is over I beleve I must lye a bead a weeke to recover myselfe agen, my 2 daughters was very buisey all day yesterday in makeing of pyes.

There were illnesses to cope with: poor Humphrey, the gardener's boy, died of smallpox; Mrs Burgess, the housekeeper, fell off a horse; Isaac could only hop from his bed to the fire with gout; Mary herself had a life-threatening miscarriage; and little Sammy suffered after a surfeit of wigg (a sort of hot-cross bun). Mary had written to her husband about her children:

... when they are under the roofe with me I love best to be wheare they are night and day, for I find then they doe best; and if they was all at home I beleve I must make my bead in the Great Hall, and have soe many little beads as I have children sett up all round about and then to lye downe in peace and quiettness in the midst of them with a prospectt of theyr all doeing well; who could be more happy then I, espeshally when I should thinke you would be pleased with the sight alsoe.

Tragically, Ward suffered from depression for years and finally committed suicide in 1704, while Jack died the same year in Holland from fever. But Betty married John Jones, Anne married William Sanford, Molly married George Musgrave, Sammy married Sarah Guest and Jepp married Elizabeth Hawker – all of them had children, though Jenny who married Henry Sanford did not.

Although Edward's Chipley has gone, the avenue of lime trees that Locke sent from Holland still stretches into the surrounding countryside. Through the Clarke letters we know that little Jepp and Sammy clattered up the great staircase, Betty wore the flowered silk with silver tabby lining her father sent from London, Monsieur de la Roque threatened to cut his throat, John Spreat evaded his drunken wife, and Mary Clarke continued to look after her brood of children and 'family' of servants.

John Locke

A frequent visitor to Chipley in the last years of the seventeenth century was the English philosopher John Locke, a close friend of the owner Edward Clarke. He was arguably the most influential person ever to be associated with Nynehead.

Locke was born on 29 August 1632 at Wrington on the north side of the Mendip Hills in Somerset, the son of a solicitor and small landowner who fought on the Parliamentarian side in the Civil War. He was a pupil at Westminster School, under a famous Royalist headmaster, Richard Busby, and then a student and don at Christ Church, Oxford. He was the friend, secretary and doctor of the Earl of Shaftesbury, with whom he was implicated in the political manoeuverings of the late-seventeenth century, being expelled from Christ Church and spending some years in exile. He returned to England at the Revolution of 1688, when William III and Mary succeeded James II, and held several minor government offices, being particularly involved with trade with the colonies.

Ill health had dogged him all his life and from 1691 he spent much of his time at Oates in High

The philosopher John Locke (1632–1704), friend of the Clarkes and a frequent visitor to Chipley.

Laver, a small village in West Essex, as the paying guest of the Masham family (at 20s. a week). Damaris Masham, the wife of Sir Francis, was the daughter of Ralph Cudworth, a leading Cambridge philosopher, and before her marriage had conducted a slightly flirtatious correspondence with Locke, who held her intelligence in high esteem. He made Oates (which like Clarke's 1680s house at Chipley is no more) the intellectual centre of Europe, eventually retiring there from 1700 until his death in 1704.

It was probably Mary Clarke who first introduced John Locke to Edward Clarke, as Locke had been a school friend of her uncle John Strachey, but Edward would have heard of him when he was an undergraduate at Wadham College, Locke being part of the intellectual circle at Oxford that included Christopher Wren and Robert Boyle. They all believed that knowledge was discovered through direct observation and that it should be expressed in understandable language.

Locke visited Mary in her lodgings in town when she was confined after the birth of her children and advised on nurses and childcare. As he was a physician the Clarkes consulted him continually about their health and his letters to them are full of advice on dealing with ague and childhood illnesses, with instructions for making medicines and diet drinks. He took a great interest in the new house at Chipley, staying there in 1683, where an apartment – a bedchamber with a dressing-room and closet – was always kept for him. As he wrote to Mary in February 1685 'I could not be so happy anywhere as

at Chipley when you and Mr Clarke are there with your little ones'.

As a lawyer in London Clarke was involved with Shaftesbury's supporters and became a trustee for both Shaftesbury and Locke when they fled to Holland, being entrusted with Locke's manuscript of the 'Two Treatises of Government'. During Locke's exile they corresponded regularly and it was the letters dealing with the education of the Clarke children that became the foundation for *Some Thoughts Concerning Education*, published in 1693 and dedicated to Edward. Although at first concerned with Ward, the eldest child, it was Betty, the eldest daughter, who was the most intelligent and became Locke's favourite, calling herself his 'wife' and whom he often supplied with books. Locke's ideas on child rearing were revolutionary as he thought they should have lots of fresh air, unlaced clothes and a plain diet, and, most important of all, that fathers should make sons their friends and teach by example. He encouraged the Clarkes to employ Huguenot tutors, as he disapproved of boarding-schools, and when it later became obvious that Ward's memory had been damaged by dangerous childhood illnesses he often looked after him at Oates.

All the time Locke was in Holland, he took a continual interest in the estate at Chipley, sending suggestions and plans for tree planting, together with poplar and abele cuttings and lime saplings, and seeds for turnips, carrots, parsnips, sugar roots and blood-red cabbage (plus ideas for cooking them), and jonquils and nasturtiums for the flower garden. He also sent prolific Friesland sheep from Holland in 1688.

Probably the most important things that happened at Chipley were the conversations that Edward, the prospective politician, and Locke had about the theory of government. Edward succeeded in becoming an MP in 1690 and was able to give a voice to Locke's ideas in the House of Commons. Later, with barrister John Freke (1652–1714), the three of them formed the 'College': Locke wrote pamphlets, Clarke

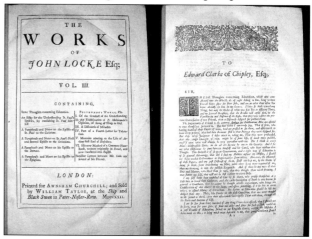

The frontispiece and first page of John Locke's Some Thoughts Concerning Education, *dedicated to Edward Clarke.*

made speeches in the House and Freke recorded the opinions and policies of Lord Somers, one of William III's chief officers of state. The recoinage bill and the freedom of the press resulted from this alliance.

As Locke wrote to Edward: 'I placed my greatest happiness in enjoying your company and expressing to you some other way than in bare words the esteem and acknowledgments I owe you.' When he returned from Holland in 1689 he was instrumental in getting Edward appointed Auditor General to Queen Mary. Locke continued to take a great interest in all the family; he sent topknots for Betty to wear and at one point there was talk of a marriage between her and his nephew Peter King, future Lord Chancellor. When this came to nothing a slight coolness developed between him and Mary, but as he wrote to Edward in April 1704:

... whatever it shall please God to do with me I shall always be concerned for you and your family whilst I am in this life, and wish all happiness continued to you when I am gone.

In his will he bequeathed £200 to Edward and £200 to Betty, together with the portrait of Mary he had hanging in the parlour at Oates.

John Locke remained a bachelor, quiet, almost timid, intensely thoughtful, the soul of intellectual and moral integrity, a typical seventeenth-century thinker and Christian, yet in a class with Isaac Newton. One can only wonder how the rectors of the churches that Locke attended – including Nynehead and High Laver – would have felt about preaching to

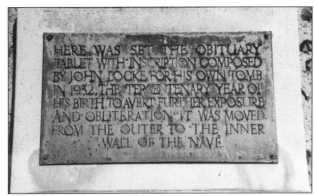

The plaque on Locke's tomb at High Laver.

one of the greatest minds of the time. On his death in 1704 he was buried by the south wall of High Laver church, his tomb simply inscribed 'JOHN LOCKE, ESQ. Died October 28th, 1704.' Above the tomb is a tablet inscribed:

*In grateful memory of John Locke 1632–1704,
who lies buried here.
His philosophy guided the founders of the
United States of America.
Erected by the American and British
Commonwealth Association
of the United States, 1957.*

A memorial inscription in Latin, composed by Locke himself, was moved inside the church in 1932 to protect it from the weather. In translation it reads:

Stay, Passer-by. Near here is placed JOHN LOCKE. If you ask what kind of man he was, he answers that he lived content with moderate means. Nourished in letters, he made so great progress that to truth his service was unparallelled. What else there is about him, learn from his writings which will set this forth in a manner more worthy of your belief than the suspect eulogies of an epitaph. If he had virtues in a lesser degree indeed than what he would set before himself to praise, and before you for an example, let these be buried together with his faults. If you seek for an example of character you have it in the Gospel. For an example of faults, would that nowhere (such is our wish) inhumanity could such be found here or anywhere. That he was born in the year of Our Lord 1632 on August 29, and that he died in the year of our Lord 1704 on October 28, is recorded by this tablet, which itself is soon to perish.

In Nynehead church a memorial tablet, which has been restored, records a well-known verse by Locke:

*A little booke and taper's light
Did solace me in my last night
My taper spent, book closed, I, late
In bed thereon to meditate:
With what improvement thinks I know
Than volumes more, or sunne can show.*

The parish church of High Laver in Essex, where John Locke was buried in 1704.

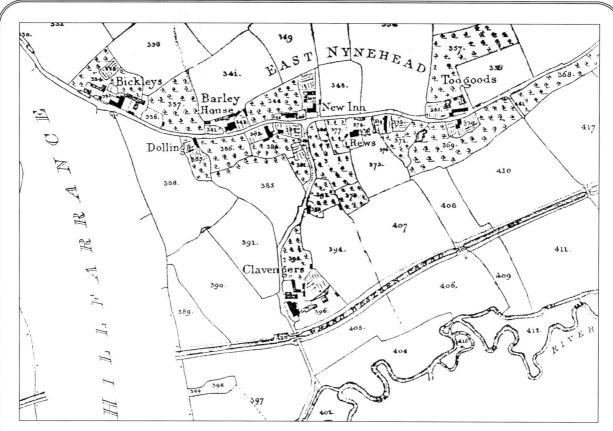

An extract from the Tithe Map, showing how in 1837 East Nynehead consisted of small farms surrounded by orchards. The canal crosses the map. Note the outlying part of Hillfarrance which included Perry Farm.

Aerial view of East Nynehead from the west, c.1970. Bickley fruit farm can be seen in the bottom left, with the railway and River Tone top right.

EAST NYNEHEAD

East Nynehead, half a mile to the east of Higher Nynehead, has always been seen as a part of the parish with its own separate identity. The Tithe Map of 1837 shows a group of small farms surrounded by orchards, a pattern that survived until the 1960s when the building of houses and bungalows markedly changed the hamlet's character. In the past, it supported two hostelries or drinking establishments, one of which also served as a shop. At the time of writing the sole public amenities are a Victorian letter-box and the Parish Council notice-board. Happily for many residents East Nynehead remains small and rural, with no street lighting, mains drainage or gas supply.

To reach the hamlet from Higher Nynehead, one must turn right from the road to Oake towards Bradford-on-Tone. At this corner in 1933 Mr Fred Gollop built the property known as Oak Ridge on land purchased for £60 from Francis Henry Elston of Perry Farm. This was probably the first of the many bungalows in East Nynehead. In 2001, a prospective buyer for one of the oldest houses in the hamlet rejected the property because there were 'rather a lot of relatively modern bungalows in the immediate area.' Whilst ten single-storey properties out of 24 in the hamlet may seem high, many of the other dwellings are of considerable antiquity and interest and have changed faces several times throughout their history.

Mr Reginald Salter aged 78 with his dog in the garden at Dollings in 1988.

The earliest inhabitants have left no dwellings, but evidence of Bronze-Age man was found in the nineteenth century when work was carried out to build the railway bridge over the river at Pickings, to the east of Clavengers Farm. Among the bones and artefacts the most valuable find was a torque, a pliable metal chased necklet, which would have belonged to a chief or leader. Since it was broken in two, the wearer could well have lost it – and his life – in battle. In the Middle Ages East Nynehead was known as Nynehead Monks or Monachorum, being owned by the Priory of Montacute, an order of Cluniac monks. It was said that the original bridge over the Tone at Bradford was built to enable the priory's stewards to visit their land in Nynehead Monks.

The house known as 'Hillside' at the time of writing stands where the monks kept their livestock. They were probably not in permanent residence but came to tend the land on a seasonal basis, they and their animals inhabiting the area of the building, of which only the main chimney piece remains, dating from the 1500s. The home has been enlarged and altered many times and in about 1750–88 was occupied by Thomas Pole, whose name was used to identify the property as 'Poles', later Pules. (This practice of using the owner's name for identification of properties was commonplace and can be seen in the recorded names of many properties.) Very little remains of the original house which, like most houses of the time, would have been thatched. Some of the beams that supported the thatched roof remain, as does a section of the original wall in the middle of the house. Five feet thick, this contains an inglenook fireplace and a bread oven on the ground floor and another fireplace above it on an upper floor. There are also the remains of an eighteenth-century doorway at the end of the wall. In the garden there is a 24ft-deep well which supplied water to the house until 1960. The house was extended four times in the twentieth century and land to the west of the property was sold in 1968 to enable the building of three houses and a bungalow.

Bickley Farm on the north side of the road through the hamlet is more commonly referred to as the 'fruit farm' because of the nature of the crops grown, and it has been farmed for centuries. The house is rambling, with many additions and alterations having been made, the main body being a typical Somerset longhouse, built endways on to the road. The kitchen and scullery which run parallel to the road date from about 1600, with an ancient well in the floor. Like most of the farms in the vicinity, fields have changed hands over the years and the main field in use today, to the west of the house, was sold to Perry Farm and then bought back again. Until 1883 Perry Farm to the south was not in the parish of Nynehead but in a long tongue of land stretching north and south which was a detached part of the parish of Hillfarrance.

Dollings Cottage, a simple farm-worker's cottage on the right of the lane, was not associated with either Bickley or Perry Farms, but was for labourers from Clavengers Farm, on the lane running south to the river. Although a property called Dollings appears on the Tithe Map the present cottage was (re)built in brick and slate in about 1891. Clavengers, a fine brick house, used to be a working farm with some 63 acres in 1861 but is now a private dwelling.

Barley House was the only off-licence and shop in the village, run by Herbert and Margaret Williams. In the summer of 2003 new owners changed the name back to 'Barley House' from 'The Bush', as it had been known for many years.

Havilands Farm, burnt down c.1968. It was a thatched and whitewashed building, once common in Nynehead, but of which few remain.

The Bush was once the village shop and off-licence and the house still retains the original flag-stone floors. The Tithe Map shows that barley was grown, possibly for brewing, but the property also had an orchard and until the mid-twentieth century cider was made here, as recalled by Joy Stone, née Gollop, who as a girl lived in 'Rosadene'. This small cottage was demolished and replaced with three bungalows:

Rosadene was once thatched, Dad had a new roof put on not long after moving in. [This was probably in the late 1930s/early '40s as Joy was born in 1936 in Farthings Close before moving to the cottage.] *Quite a few of the houses in the area were thatched, 'Havilands Farm' opposite 'Rosadene' and 'Clematis Cottage' (now 'The Old Granary'). Rosadene was demolished and the bungalows were built in our old orchard.*

My mother's family, Margaret and Herbert Williams, lived in 'The Bush', correct name 'Barley House'. The 'Bush' got its name, not because of a bush, but when my grandmother bought the house in 1918 it was owned by a Mr Holloway and his daughter Rosy. Rosy helped in the shop. Mr Holloway was a very short man and sported a long bushy beard almost to his boots. Because of his appearance he was known by the locals as 'Bushy Holloway'. This resulted in 'Barley House' being eventually known as 'The Bush'. Gran ran the shop until 1948. It was the only shop and off-licence in the village. I remember the men from Poole brickworks covered in dust sitting on the hedge outside with their cider. Also during the war Gran allowed Americans to have their drink in her sitting room behind the shop. My grandfather made the cider in a huge cider press in a shed to the left of the house. Our orchard at Rosadene was part of Gran's orchard and it was given to Mum and Dad as a present when they bought the cottage. My father's parents Thomas and Maria Gollop lived at 'Hillside'. They also had an orchard and a field. Dad's brother Fred had 'Oakridge' built and lived there for many years.

Mrs Williams outside The Bush.

Havilands Farm today bears no resemblance to the thatched farmhouse remembered by Joy Stone as a child, the original building having burnt down in 1967. Most of the extensive outbuildings remain intact and there is one section of the wall of the original house at the side of the large bungalow that now occupies the site. Havilands was part of the Belmont estate and was sold to the tenant in 1949 for £2,400,

comprising at that time 41 acres, including New Barn and its surrounding land half a mile to the east. Today Havilands has just two acres of land, a bungalow ('Ploughshare') having been built on land to the west and 'Barnstone' having been converted from a two-storey barn into a single-storey dwelling to the east. The name of Havilands Herb Farm reflects the present use of the property.

In his book *The Changing Scenes of Local Life* Frank Webber records that a family called De Havilland from East Nynehead owned Gundenham Farm near Langford Budville at the end of the nineteenth century. They gave their name to a smaller farm at East Nynehead. One son was more interested in machinery than farming and he left the area for Hatfield in Hertfordshire. His exceptional interest and knowledge enabled him to start an aeroplane-building company and he was involved in the development of the Mosquito plane in the 1940s and the Comet in 1950, which was the forerunner of Concorde. The road through East Nynehead used to be called Havilands Lane.

Langham Farm is situated at the centre of East Nynehead, in a commanding position, facing due south down Ash Lane at the head of the T-junction. Seemingly a typical country farmhouse with barns for cattle and other livestock, a part of the house has also been the New Inn and is shown as such on the 1836 map. It was to ease access to this hostelry and the nearby Barley House that one Mr Sanford arranged for ashes and clinker from Nynehead Court to be strewn on the rough roads during bad weather. Perhaps the construction work on the canal also brought increased custom to warrant the existence of this establishment. The oldest title deed in existence is an enormous hand-scribed document on parchment, much overwritten. It lists the property as having several cottages with gardens, two orchards, three fields, a meadow, the flax shop and field and the New Inn with garden and barton. The first orchards lay to the west between New Inn and Barley House and contained the cottage known as Rosadene. The other orchards lay to the south on both sides of Ash Lane, the one to the west probably being the site of the cottage now known as Bluehills and the one to the east becoming 'Mon Vue' in 1976.

Although the New Inn may have prospered at the time of the canal building, the names Bluetts and

'The Bush', formerly the off-licence run by Mr and Mrs Williams. Cider was made in an outhouse.

three sons. The 13 acres were very much the same as they had been in some of the previous records. When the Barrows moved across the road in 1976, active farming ceased at Langham.

The cottage known at the time of writing as Bluehills was recorded in the 1861 Census as Miltons Cottages 1 and 2, named after the owner William Milton who died in 1853 leaving the property to his widow and sons. The deeds of the house state that he had recently rebuilt the cottages but there is no evidence of a building here on the Tithe Map. The cottages were both two rooms up and two rooms down and in 1861 two unrelated families lived in each cottage – a total of 11 people in what is now a four-bedroomed house.

The Miltons were absentee owners, the properties being let to James Sparks and Thomas Seward and occupied by agricultural labourers. Thomas Seward's cottage was the one used for independent worship after 1870 when the Independent Chapel in Higher Nynehead was converted into a cottage. The property was sold in 1886 to a Mrs Thresher – a widow who later married a Milton, thus keeping the cottage names the same. It remained as two tenanted cottages until the 1920s when 'Postman' Hodge purchased it. In 1945 it was sold as one property and the subsequent purchaser named it 'Bluehills'. Four owners later, in 1977, it was purchased by the Locks who are still in residence.

Rews Farm was the dominant property to the east of the T-junction on the south side of the road through the hamlet, alongside which a long brick barn with distinctive rounded corners is a prominent feature. There used to be an Elizabethan barn adjacent to the farmhouse but sadly this has gone. The earliest record of Rews seems to be tax returns of 1782. In 1837 the farm comprised some 37 acres – a house and yard with paddocks, orchards close to the farm, arable and meadow down by the river – with the land divided by the recently built Grand Western Canal. The Jacobs family featured amongst the tenants and owners of Rews, also with an interest in Bluetts.

In October 1929 a Mr T. Maynard owned and occupied the farm but was giving up farming and thus selling the grass of the farm each year. The contents of the farm were sold by auction by W.R.J. Greenslade and Co. on Thursday 10 October 1929. For the auctioneers it was an important dispersal sale of 'Home Bred Dairy Cattle and Young Stock'. The stock included 26 home-bred cattle including a Devon cow with her two calves; a black poll cow with her third calf; a red poll cow with her third calf; a black poll cow in milk and in calf; a roan shorthorn heifer in or with calf; a blue roan shorthorn heifer in milk; a red poll heifer in milk; a black poll barrener in milk; one prime maiden heifer and one very fleshy barrener fit for the butcher; a pair of two-year-old grazing steers; four rising two-year-old

Langham later entered common usage and the land continued to be farmed. As late as 1939 the flax field to the east and north of the house was being used for the linen crop, as well as for teasels. The various owners of the farm have come and gone with many names repeating from other properties in the area. The Jacobs (who sold to the Gidleys, who in turn sold to the Bryants) had to relinquish an annual financial interest in the property before the sale could be completed. This resulted in an interesting document from one of the 11 children who was living in Melbourne, Australia. It included a cheery and informal greeting in the legal document which gave up his right to the hold on the property. The sale to James Bryant the younger was from Robert Gidley of Kentish Town, London.

The Barrows moved to Bluetts in 1964 and settled the name as Langham. The house comprised a sitting-room, a dining-room with a stone floor, a kitchen, larder and dairy. There was a good barn for cattle and, in addition to a dairy herd, Tom kept pigs. There was plenty of room for improvement in the house and much was achieved in making this a comfortable family home for the couple and their grazing maiden heifers; six promising yearlings; an eight-year-old upstanding cart mare called 'Violet', of 16 hands, a quiet and good worker in all gears; a pedigree large black sow and pigs; and one seven-month-old gilt. Among the farm equipment offered for sale were trace, breeching and black-trap harnesses; a 'N.W. Wagon with lades'; a 'B.W. Tip Putt'; a governess cart; a Nicholson's hay rake; a Blackstone's swath turner; a Bamlett's mower; a flat segment roller; a Hornsby's plough; a set of heavy duckfoot drags; a set of chain harrows; an iron sham; and a cake crusher.

Rews has remained a private dwelling and an extension was added to the north side in 2000, making it a substantial family home.

The house now known as The Old Granary was part of the Nynehead estate, like so many of the other properties. In 1949 it was described as being built of brick with a thatched roof and housing a Mr Clapp, who enjoyed a rent-free tenancy. The house then comprised a kitchen, a pantry, a storeroom and three bedrooms and, like most other houses in the hamlet, it had water from a well. An orchard of nearly three-quarters of an acre was part of the property and at the time of the estate sale the then tenant of Havilands Farm had the grazing rights free of charge. The name has changed with many different owners – Clematis Cottage, Maple House – and a large extension was added at the eastern end in 1998.

Toogoods, the most easterly farm in East Nynehead, was linked in the past with land known as Bramble Close or Little Buckland and Ponters Place, which had been the site of 'an old decayed cottage and dwelling'. As a working farm in the nineteenth century it covered $35^3/_4$ acres, along with a further six acres at Ponters Place, both at that time being tenanted by one William Gater. The terms of the lease of the property were set out in 1765. Like many of today's houses Toogoods was formerly two smaller cottages and before extensive renovations in the latter part of the twentieth century had very sloping floors in the bedrooms, sufficient to cause occupied beds to make their way across the rooms!

East Nynehead was the site of two mills – Ash and Pickings – both using the power of the Tone to grind corn for local people, neither of which now comprise more than the remains of a few stone walls.

Lift Cottage is the most easterly house in Nynehead as it served the Trefusis lift on the canal which ran across the northern front of the building. The cottage – or cottages, since it was originally two dwellings – was the home of the lift keeper. In the 1861 Census they were listed as Lift House and Lift Cottage but by 1886, 20 years after the demise of the canal, the maps show them as Mountstephens Cottages, after the owner who lived in Milverton. There is no firm record of when they were originally built but there was probably a

dwelling there before the coming of the canal, since parts are built of cob, which is hardly the material of choice of the canal builders. The cottages were probably reached from East Nynehead by a path across the fields but from an early account it is clear that much more movement of the inhabitants was in the direction of Bradford-on-Tone.

There is an intriguing picture of life at Lift Cottages in the early-twentieth century given by an old lady who called on the owners Keith and Louise Haslam some years ago. She and her nine siblings had lived in the two cottages, their mother taking in washing from the 'gentry in Taunton'. One of her brothers collected the loads and they all had their part to play in the routine. This would explain the large number of flat irons that the Haslams found around the garden, including a round one that the old lady remembered using on starched collars. She pointed out the very old, very basic, bread oven in one of the main fireplaces, which had no door, so was sealed with dough when cooking. The pick of the faggots was kept for this oven. Self-sufficiency was very much the order of the day. There were no trees in the garden, which is now pleasantly green and shady, as all available ground was used for produce. There were numerous traps for rabbits and some of the animals caught were taken to Taunton market to trade for other meat. Her father was a haulier and was often away from home with his horse and cart. He also liked a drink, and no doubt there were occasions when the horse found its own way home.

At this time the bridge taking the old canal under the railway was still in existence and was used by the children going to school in Bradford-on-Tone. The bridge, once known as Trefusis Bridge, has now gone and the railway embankment, much raised over the years, now stands high above the end of the garden. Now one house, the cottage has been sympathetically adapted to today's requirements, but although electricity was installed in 1978, water is still pumped from their well – albeit no longer by hand.

'Rosadene', home of the Gollop family, now demolished.

An early picture of the Wellington fire brigade outside the gates to the coach drive to Nynehead Court.

Workers at the Poole brickworks, mid- to late 1930s. On the right is Fred Pullman (father-in-law of local builder Brian Hardacre). In the background is Windwhistle Cottage, formerly the home of a railway signalman.

Chapter Eight

LIVING IN THE VILLAGE

The population of Nynehead has varied little over the past two centuries. Before the first national Census of population in 1801 it is impossible to say accurately how many people lived in Nynehead. The Lay Subsidy Rolls of 1601 list 106 people but this cannot be compared with the total population of 353 recorded in 1801. The population hovered in the low 300s until 1901 when it dipped below 300 for the first time for over 100 years.

The 1841 Census shows that there were 349 people (177 males and 172 females, 194 adults and 155 children) living in the parish, while the Register of Electors for 1999 records 249 adults (156 men and 148 women). This of course does not include the under 18-year-olds but there were no more than 30 children at that time, bringing the total to 324, less than in 1841. Then there were 68 houses in the parish whereas at the time of writing there are more than 140. Thus, despite boundary changes enlarging the village and the considerable number of houses – including 16 houses built by the council in the 1920s and 1930s and approximately 40 other new houses since – the population has remained relatively static, reaching only 354 in 1991, largely because of the dramatic decrease in the size of the average household.

Most of today's residents were not born in Nynehead. This is not a new phenomenon. The 1861 Census shows that three out of four heads of household were born outside the parish, as was the case with the females. In fact only two couples were both born in the parish. In 1891 the trend was even more marked, with only one in five women and one in four men born inside the boundary, but there were three couples who were both born within. According to the records of the Parish Church there were just over 100 marriages between 1813 and 1900. Of these 46 per cent were of couples with one living in another parish.

The greatest change seen is in the occupations of the male population as the village was once provided with many and varied tradesmen/craftsman. In 1861 two thirds of the male heads of household were workers on the land, directly concerned with farming. There were also gardeners, gamekeepers and shepherds, while the village offered the services of a wheelwright, a thatcher, a shoemaker, a carpenter, a blacksmith and seven carters. There were 11 farmers and only one person was recorded on the Census as 'living on his own

means'. In the next 30 years men found jobs on the railway, at the Poole brickworks and in Fox's textile factory in Wellington. The Poole works made a difference to employment prospects in the area, especially as 11 cottages in two rows were built for workers.

By 1891 the village, partly through natural wastage, lost the shoemaker, carpenter, blacksmith and all seven carters. Although these craftsmen disappeared there were still two sawyers, two laundresses, three shepherds, a gamekeeper, a wheelwright, a mason and a thatcher living in the village in 1891. The carters only disappeared for a few years because by about 1930 two more had begun to trade at Hornshay Farm – Messrs Scadding and Broome. The blacksmith also made a return to live at the smithy in Round Oak Gardens. One sawyer lived at Saw Mill Cottage at Chipley and the other at Lift Cottage in East Nynehead. Doug Lentell remembers Jimmy Langford who worked at Chipley:

Jimmy Langford was a notable character. His wife was an invalid and he pushed her in a bath chair – not a usual sight round here. He was very fond of his cider and did odd jobs around the farms.

When trees were blown down (frequently in winter) men from Chipley Saw Mills came and removed the main trunk leaving behind the roots and branches. Jimmy used

*Winifred Pugh sitting outside her cottage,
now No. 1 Roundoak Gardens, in the autumn of 1965.
Her father was the village blacksmith and his forge
is the modern-day garage for this property.*

77

A group of workers at Poole brickworks at what looks to be a political canvassing meeting in the late 1950s. Partially shielded by the speaker's hand is Bill Lake and to the right leaning against the bricks is Guy Broom. Douglas Parsons (wearing cap) stands with hands in his pockets. The building is the large round kiln, now demolished, which adjoined the loading platform for rail trucks and later for the lorries run by the Sparks family.

Left: Policing in the twenty-first century. The mobile Community Policing Unit based in Minehead visits the village monthly and gives residents the opportunity to meet the officers.

Right: Gwen Fletcher, who ran riding stables in Nynehead, riding Tom, with a pupil on Nona in 1987. Mrs Fletcher was one of the first members of Nynehead's Local History Society.

to blow up the stump and roots with gunpowder and sell the other wood for kindling. He lived in the now-demolished farm cottage opposite Heywood Farm.

In 1851 there were 12 farmers, one more than a decade before and three more than in 1891. At the time of writing the village maintains six farms, though not all of them have livestock. Some have diversified, one into agricultural contracting and another has become a fruit farm. Many of the smaller farms have become houses with large gardens and paddocks while the land has been sold off to other buyers, often to adjoining farmers.

Like all large country houses Nynehead Court had a range of staff from the village and elsewhere. In 1891 20 people were resident in the Court (by contrast, in 1999 there were 22 residents on the electors' list). The Court employed seven gardeners under James Doble, the head gardener who lived in Court Garden Farm. Francis Jenkins was in charge of the ornamental gardens, while Messrs Sharland, Bowyer and Stevenson were the vegetable growers. There were, of course, indoor staff – the butler, the housekeeper, maids and a land agent. The gamekeeper lived in one of the former Lynch Cottages, although in 1881 he lived in Kiln Cottage. The wheelwright lived in Crossland Cottage, the thatcher in Chapel Cottage (now Prings) and the shepherds were at Chipley and Heywood.

Today there are no tradesmen living in the village and plying their trade here, but in the early 1930s there were several delivery men who called at Nynehead. Three bakers supplied the village, Shaplins, Moores and Chaples (later to be Husseys). Mr Kelland delivered fish once a week and there were two or three travelling butchers. Groceries were delivered by Mr Sully after he had taken the orders earlier in the week, and milk was supplied by Gundenham Dairy, although many people had it untreated from Nynehead Court's Jersey herd. Mr Trickey from Cornhill used to purchase all the fruit and vegetables grown in the Court Farm Gardens but later Mr Greenslade owned the property and ran it as a market garden, father and son delivering fruit and vegetables to the village in a horse-drawn cart. At the time of writing the few services that the village has are a daily postal service, two milkmen selling potatoes and other farm produce and a travelling library van that comes every fortnight, but very little else – no Post Office, shop, public house or off-licence. Taunton and Wellington serve most needs although increasingly vans are seen delivering goods ordered over the internet.

WEALTH AND POVERTY

In any society there are always extremes to be found and Nynehead was certainly no exception when it comes to wealth and poverty. There have always been pockets of people who are financially disadvantaged for whatever reasons, whether by their own fault or as a result of unlucky circumstance. As the national population began to rise in the 1500s, poverty and unemployment became serious problems. The system that required each parish to be responsible for its poor meant that men travelling in search of work would be moved on as quickly as possible to another parish before they became a liability. To overcome abuses of the system the Poor Law Act of 1601 distinguished between the sick and incapacitated poor (who were to be assisted from the parish rate), the able-bodied (who were to be provided with materials and work) and the wilfully idle (who were to be branded and whipped). In 1662 settlement laws were introduced to limit migration.

To date no records have been found of such happenings in Nynehead but the village seems to have been very generous in its charity and must have been on a walking route between Taunton and Exeter. There is a dole table in the churchyard from which charities were disbursed. Thus we find in the churchwardens' accounts that in 1673 the sum of 2s.0d. was paid to 'poore travellers viz a man his wife & family who had sustained great losses att sea by certificate appeareth ', 1s.0d. to 'a poore crippled traviler y had a pass' and in 1678 16s.9d. to 'seafaring men and travellers at severall tymes having passes'.

Presumably payments were made only if the travellers had the correct paperwork. The poor were sometimes transported back to their parish of origin, as in 1780 when 'Mary Cross was carried to Taunton and from thence on to London – fares 13s.0d. and road expenses likewise 13s.0d.'

The owners of Nynehead Court and Chipley took their own action to support the poor of the village. From 1685 to 1696 25 parishioners from Nynehead and 41 from Langford Budville each received one loaf of bread weighing 6lb and one piece of beef weighing 3lb, dispensed on Christmas Eve at Chipley by Edward Clarke. Eleven of the people from Nynehead also got an extra 3lb of beef, 'there being so many pieces left' and in all 28 stone of bread was given out. By 1696 the bread had increased to 8lb and the beef to 4lb per recipient. We don't know whether this generosity was in response to the aftermath of the Monmouth Rebellion in 1685, whether Edward Clarke was attempting to gain support to become Member of Parliament for Taunton (which he achieved in 1690) or whether there had been a good harvest. Extra money was paid out during 1685 to the church bell-ringers, presumably in connection with the Rebellion. From 1731 until at least 1796 a later Edward Clarke gave needy parishioners a shilling every Christmas, numbers fluctuating from 27 in 1731 to 37 in 1796.

Farmers and other landowners in the parish who were deemed rich enough also contributed to the Poor Rate. The 1601 Act had authorised the

Left: *Schoolchildren enjoying the snowfall of 1996.*

Right: *Heavy snowfall in the village is now rare, but can seriously disrupt travel, such as here, in 1978.*

Left: *Mrs Cynthia Lock on Ash Lane near Clavengers Farm in early 1978.*

Right: *Ash Lane and Clavengers without snow in 2003 – the same view as above, which reveals the depth of snow in 1978.*

appointment of parish overseers to raise a rate (i.e. to get money from landowners) according to the value of property. In 1773 the contributors to the Poor Rate in Nynehead were assessed at:

John Sanford (for his many properties)	£1.11s.0d.
Edward Clarke for Chipley	2s.6d.
Edward Clarke for other properties	9s.3d.
John Jacobs for Westons	1s.0d.
John Jacobs for Pixton	1d.
William Palmer for Burge	1s.0d.
Others	14s.2d.
Total	£2.19s.0d.

This figure of £2.19s.0d. was a single-rate income, which was collected from the landowners in the parish. If it was insufficient for the needs of the poor a further rate would be levied, rather than the poor turned away. The Poor Rate levies did vary, the single rate income for the following year (1774) raising only £2.17s.4d.

Gifts to parishioners were provided in two categories. Firstly there was a regular monthly payment of a standard sum to parishioners in need, with additional payments for keeping a 'baseborn child' (an unmarried mother), keeping someone else's child (fostering or adoption) and schooling. There were 15 recipients of cash ranging from 8s.0d. for older children to 4s.0d. for younger children and the total monthly sum was £4.1s.4d. This sum was very much the same for the whole year. Presumably these included widows and single ladies.

The second category of payments were extraordinary disbursements made for such things as unexpected debts, sickness, shoe repairs or clothing, as in 1773:

May 6th   Pd Mr Broadfoot for 4 yds of nap at 1s 10d per yd to make Susan James a coat, plus thread and tape 6s 10d

May 15th   Gave James Cording having a bad hand 2s 6d

May 16th   Gave James Pearce, he and his wife both sick 5s 0d

May 20th   "   "   more in sickness 3s 6d

June 12th   Pd Mr Widiecombe for 2 pair shews for Sarah Bodley and Webber boy 6s 6d

September 18th for aprinding and taking Edward Ottery and bringing him to Nynehead 17s 7d
for a gard to carry Ottery to Justice 1s 6d

The same family names occur repeatedly, such as Blackmore. Overall there were 182 entries for 1773 totalling £60.0s.9d. plus the monthly parish payments of £54.14s.6d., making a total expenditure of £114.15s.3d. The rate income fell short by £26.5s.3d., which was raised by a further levy of 12 rates at £2.19s.0d. giving £35.8s.0d., the balance of £9.2s.9d. being passed on to the overseers for the following year.

The amounts varied from year to year. Some overseers might have been more generous than others while people's needs also varied with more required in harder winters and less when harvests were better.

Sometimes other monies or goods were available. In December 1685 an agreement between the churchwardens, the overseers of the poor in the parish and Edward Clarke of Chipley promised to:

... have placed and bound out a poor child Richard Barbar of Nynehead until he shall attain the age of 24 years in husbandry work, funding and providing for him sufficient:- meat, drink, apparel, washing, lodging, hosen and shoes.

Nynehead had its own parish charities, the Wyke and Honniball charities. In 1622 Richard Wyke left £2 per annum for the use of the poor. The parish poor book of 1693 reads:

... the Sunday after the feast of Saint Thomas the Apostle (July 3rd) in 1682 we Robert Jacob and Robert Kington – Churchwardens and overseers of the poor in Nynehead, have seen and do well approve the distributing of 20 shillings to the poor of the parish, the gift of one Mr Wyke and according to his Will.

The following year it was raised to 40 shillings which was paid repeatedly until at least 1741. After 1748 the actual amount received by the poor of the parish was £1.2s.0d. and not £2, it being believed that the reduction was equivalent to that claimed in land-tax. Known as Weeke's Money it came to the churchwardens from John Daniel, the tenant of Wykes Farm that was formerly owned by Richard Wyke. The same amount was also given to the neighbouring parish of Milverton. It was to be given to the poor who did not receive parochial relief and payments were made on Christmas Eve and Good Friday. In the year 1779 the giving totalled £4.16s.0d.: one wonders where the extra money came from.

The Nynehead parish charities survived into the late-twentieth century, the Parish Council being responsible for administering them, although the money available declined in real value and eventually they were wound up.

THE POORHOUSE

In about 1700 the Nynehead churchwardens (Nicholas Gale and John Roberts) and the overseers of the poor (Christopher Mountstephens and James Parsons) contracted with Anthony Bicknell, a carpenter of the parish, to build a Parish House. The contract specified that the property should be:

... of Oak and Elme, sound good and fit for building. It is to contain four under rooms and four chambers over them with six chimneys therein, the whole building to

The River Tone in flood at Hornshay, January 1998.

Right: *Reflections of Nynehead – the village sign at Hornshay Bridge.*

Left: *Floods outside the village school are a common sight.*

Left: *Snow in Nynehead Hollow, 1978.*

Below: *Ash Lane in flood, January 1999. Flooding two or three times a year makes it impassable to traffic and can also lead to structural damage to the tarmac surface.*

be fifty foot long from east to west & 19ft wide... 8 three light windows in ye south side and four staire windows, all oake.

In consideration of all the work to be performed in a substantial and good workman like manner by the appointed time, the churchwardens and overseers promise to pay £45.

The contract is not dated but Anthony Bicknell was paid in 1685 for the repair of bells and other services to the church and died in 1737. This and other evidence indicates that the building was constructed between 1695 and 1700. Bicknell was also allowed the timber and thatch of the 'old house' for his own use, suggesting that this was a replacement for an earlier building of which details have not yet been found.

In April 1774 John Sanford was paid a rent of £3.0s.0d. but the house that Anthony Bicknell built survived only a few more years. From April 1777 the house was rebuilt for a second time, in stone with a thatched roof at a cost of £175.15s.9¹/₂d. which included: 'drawing' of building stone £12.8s.3d.; timber £14.17s.0d.; digging foundations and building walls £11.1s.11d.; bricks £14.5s.6d.; and reed for thatching £1.13s.4d. The payments for goods and services took from April 1777 to 18 April the following year, the last to receive payment being William Bird for supplying bricks.

It was built on land in Higher Nynehead owned by John Sanford who 'claims to have found the stone for the building and contributed his fair quota of the other expenses attending its erection.' Sixty years later, in July 1837, the Sanfords' agent Charles Bailey had to point out to the Clerk of the Wellington Poor Law Union (which was building its workhouse) that Nynehead's building was a poorhouse and not a workhouse. Bailey outlined the arrangements made in 1777 saying that since that date parishioners had used it for their poorhouse without paying ground-rent to John Sanford or his successor. The letter sets out an agreement:

... that Mr E.A. Sanford... shall pay the quota of the parish towards the erection of the Union House amounting to one hundred and seven pounds in consideration of which the parishioners shall release to him any right which they may have in the premises.

The agent goes on to say 'the £107 is the full, if not exceeding the fair value of the house, but this is unimportant to Mr Sanford.'

The 1891 Census shows that the original four cottages had become five, the occupiers being Samuel Evans (farm servant) in No. 1, Samuel Coram (agricultural labourer) in No. 2, James Cooksley (shepherd) in No. 3, Thomas Taylor (agricultural labourer) in No. 4 and William Wood (agricultural labourer) in No. 5.

Thomas and Ann Taylor at No. 4 had been married in 1838. He was described as a husbandman (ranking between a yeoman farmer and a farm labourer) while Ann was a domestic servant employed at Nynehead Court or at one of the larger farms. Thomas was later described as a 'labourer' but also, in the 1861 Census, as a 'carter'. They had ten children, five boys and five girls: James (baptised 1838), Mary (1840), Jane (1845), John (1847), Emma (1850), Harriet (1852), Thomas (1856), William Hill (1858 – died aged six in 1864), Elizabeth (1862 – died aged five days) and Henry (1863). Thomas and Ann Taylor are recorded in the 1891 Census as still working, as a labourer and a laundress respectively.

The poorhouse of 1777 survived well into the twentieth century and was occupied until 1936, when it was officially condemned as being unfit for human habitation and its occupants re-housed by the Rural District Council.

NYNEHEAD IN THE RECORDS OF THE PARISH COUNCIL

One perspective on the life of the village in the twentieth century is given by the records of the Parish Council. In the 1890s local government in England was radically overhauled, with the introduction of county, district and parish councils under the Local Government Act of 1894. The new arrangements replaced a system that had developed over eight centuries or more. The new legislation was soon put into effect in Nynehead. On 4 December 1894 a meeting of the parish of Nynehead was held for the purpose of electing a chairman for the new Parish Council and the parish councillors. On the proposition of Mr J. Kidner, seconded by Mr R. Ash, William

Tree-cutting in the Hollow in May 2003. Robin Darby of Hornshay Farm is standing by the tractor. Fallen trees are a perennial problem in the Hollow.

Ayshford Sanford of Nynehead Court was elected chairman for the meeting.

Six candidates were proposed for the five places on the council: Mr R. Ash, Mr J. Kidner, Mr A. Phillips, Mr Redstone, Col E.C.A. Sanford and Mr H. Taylor. Col Sanford offered to withdraw to avoid a ballot. This was allowed and after the 'prescribed ten minutes' the five remaining candidates were pronounced by the chairman to be duly elected. It is interesting to note that in contrast to today the election took place at a public meeting with no secrecy and only men were allowed to vote.

The new council soon got down to work, holding its first meeting in the schoolroom nine days later on 13 December 1894. The meeting, convened by William Sanford, had as its main business the appointment of its chairman and clerk and other officers and the setting of the parish rate. Surprisingly, because he had not been elected to the council, Col Sanford was elected chairman and William Ludlow of Blockhouse Farm became the Parish Clerk. Mr Miller of Stukeys Bank in Wellington and Mr Ash were appointed treasurer and waywarden respectively. A parish rate was set of halfpence in the pound.

The business of the next meeting, on 8 January 1895, gives a flavour of the matters that dominated the council's activities for many years, largely because parish councils had very few powers. Firstly, the council had taken over the task of distributing moneys from the two parish charities – the Wykes and Honniball – and agreed to give 2s. to each eligible cottage. This distribution took place every other year – in January 1897 47 applicants received 2s. each.

The other matter discussed at this meeting was the condition of the footpath across Mr J. Bailey's land from the poorhouse. It was agreed that Mr Ash and Mr Taylor would inspect the path, with the result that three months later Mr Bailey was asked to do the necessary repairs. The state of footpaths has been a recurring item on Parish Council agendas ever since, with certain paths – for example along the old canal and the path from the school via the three-arch bridge and Stedhams Covert to Wellington – appearing frequently.

Until the First World War the council met infrequently, only occasionally considering other matters, such as the polluted state of Blackham Brook which was the subject of a strongly worded letter to the Wellington Urban District Council in February 1898. In 1903 discussion at the annual parish meeting resulted in a letter about rail services:

It was resolved that the Divisional Superintendent of the GW Railway in Exeter be informed that this council considers that the stopping of a Motor Train at the Bradford Level Crossing to and from Taunton at least once a day would be of extreme convenience to the Parish of Nynehead.

A presentation by John Sparks (chairman, right) to Capt. Neville Upham, Clerk to the Nynehead Parish Council, on his retirement in 1999 after 17 years' service.

Making representations on behalf of the village has always been a role of the Parish Council but in this case as in many others there is no record that the recipient of the letter took any notice, always a source of great frustration to parish councillors.

After the First World War the character of council business changed significantly. A flavour of what was to come appeared in 1913 when an abortive scheme to bring mains water from West Buckland was considered but during the hostilities the only significant matters appeared to relate to food production. In February 1916 it was decided to buy for villagers 13cwt of seed potatoes from the County Agricultural Secretary, at a cost of £4.4s.6d., and in 1917 to carry out a survey of garden cropping on behalf of the County Agricultural Instruction Committee. This interest continued after the war when in January 1919 a further supply of seed potatoes (Arran Chief or King Edward) would be ordered from the Somerset Fruit and Vegetable Society Ltd, if any parishioners wished to buy them. That autumn it was agreed that no action was needed in response to National Rat Week as it was felt the pest was under control in the village.

On 16 December 1918, scarcely a month after peace was declared, the Parish Council met to consider a letter from the Wellington Rural District Council about the provision of housing in the village. The council clearly agreed that there was a need for housing for villagers and replied saying which sites it would prefer, all in Lower Nynehead – two opposite or near the new cottages at Heywood, two on the orchard near Chauffeurs Cottage and two in or near the bend of the road between Hornshay and the Post Office. This was the first of many such consultations and the sites favoured by the council changed from time to time. In February 1919 it was felt that three houses should be built in the orchard opposite the Court and three on or near the potato patch at

Hornshay Farm, while five years later a site for four houses in Higher Nynehead next to the poorhouses was proposed for an RDC scheme.

The provision of housing was tied up with the need for local services, especially water and sewage disposal, two matters which exercised the council for many years until it was resolved after the Second World War. On 14 May 1934 a special meeting was held to discuss sewage from the council-houses. Also on the agenda was the problem of household waste which, at the time, was not collected. That a small amount of waste was produced is shown by the fact that Mr H. Winter agreed to collect it once a quarter, while Mr A.B. Richards and others would provide the horse and cart needed. A charge of 3d. per house would be levied. Finding a place to put the waste was not easy. Mr Sanford was asked if it could be dumped by the vicarage but permission was refused.

The council's minds were not always solely focused on the needs of the village. In January 1930 the floods in the levels around Athelney on the Somerset Levels were particularly bad and at the council's instigation £14.4s.6d. was raised in the village for the relief fund.

During the Second World War matters of food production and civil defence came to the fore, although the discussions as recorded in the minutes do not give much detail. After the war the amount of business dealt with by the council increased remarkably and more-frequent meetings were needed. This is shown by the minute books of which there are four, covering the period from the inception of the council in 1894 to the present day. The first book runs from 1894 to 1971 while the last three span only three decades.

The reconstruction of the country after the war and the improvement to the quality of life in rural areas is reflected in the Parish Council work. From 1945 the council campaigned for improvements in water-supply, sewage treatment, housing and postal services, as well as giving a view on proposals for development under the new planning system introduced in 1948. The running down of some local services was also beginning to happen, especially bus services. The council did not always have an easy time representing the views of the village and confusion sometimes arose. The minutes for 3 October 1949 reveal that Mr Baker, the chairman, was forced to announce that:

... the principal reason for the meeting was to end a rumour in the village that the council was responsible for the curtailment of the bus service. It was unanimously decided to circulate the reason given by the Bus Co. which was that the service was being run at a loss.

On 30 November 1949 the council held its first meeting in the new Memorial Hall, moving there from the school. The main item discussed was, not surprisingly, footpaths. The County Council had asked for the parish's assistance in carrying out the survey of rights of way required by the National Parks and Access to the Countryside Act 1949.

While the Parish Council had or came to have a role in providing facilities for the village – the Jubilee Playing Field, the Memorial Hall – over the last 50 years it has largely had a campaigning role, representing the views of the village and trying to get other public bodies to do the right thing for Nynehead, whether in looking after the roads and footpaths, dealing with flooding, or making decisions on planning applications. There have been some successes and probably more failures while other aspirations take time to achieve. In the early 1970s the Post Office was asked to replace the letter-box in Higher Nynehead with one with a larger aperture. It appeared 25 years later.

In its 109 years 20 different people (but only one woman – Mrs C.J. Lock) have served as chairman of the council, the longest spell being W.T. Baker's 21 years from 1952–73, while there have been 15 Parish Clerks. Revd H.C. Launder, vicar of Nynehead, combined his church duties with that of Clerk for 23 years from 1896 to 1919, although for the last year Mr Tipper the headteacher took his place. In more recent times Capt. Neville Upham served as Parish Clerk from 1982 to 1999, having initially agreed to do to the job on a temporary basis.

At the beginning of the twenty-first century the council continues to deal with the 'nuts and bolts' of village life, while trying to cope with an increasing load of legislation and other changes in the way such public bodies have to operate.

CALAMITIES AND DISASTERS

Nynehead has not been without its calamities and disasters. Some of these have only reached the local papers, such as the flooding experienced most winters, the effects of the 1976 drought and the subsequent 1977/8 snowdrifts, and the fire which destroyed Ash Mill in 1873. Others, however, have made the national press, such as the earthquake in 1863.

One such incident which had a major effect on the village was the Gulf Oil train derailment which happened at Trefusis on the parish boundary in 1991. At about 4.15a.m. on 16 May a train carrying fuel from the Gulf Oil refinery at Milford Haven to a depot in Bovey Tracey in Devon left the rails at the level crossing between East Nynehead and Bradford-on-Tone and exploded. The sound of the explosion reminded local residents of experiences during the Second World War. As the oil ignited, a cloud of thick, black smoke rose from the railway line and was visible from quite a distance, spreading towards the A38 and M5 and lasting quite a long time. It was indeed fortunate that the fuel was light diesel and not heavy fuel oil, because the pollution would have

The perils of driving in narrow country lanes.

been so much worse. Large quantities of fuel oil poured down the road on the Bradford-on-Tone side towards Trefusis Farm, going down the drains only to rise again because of a blockage there. This ignited and burned out a police car that was parked near the drain from which the oil emerged. The roadside hedges caught fire, igniting the creosote-soaked telegraph poles, which severely disrupted communications with the telephone exchange at Bradford-on-Tone. Oil also poured into the nearby field and rendered the field unusable for a season.

First on the scene were the residents of Hillside in East Nynehead, who went to check on their neighbours at Lift Cottage and ensure the safety of ponies grazing in the orchard. Fire appliances arrived from Wellington and were directed to the nearest water-supply – a hydrant and the River Tone. The ground was too soft to take the heavy fire appliance so two small pumps had to be used to pump water from the river. Extra hoses had to be used to reach the seat of the fire. British Rail uncoupled and removed those trucks not damaged in the accident. One great asset the fire-fighters were able to draw upon was a large supply of foam kept for fire-fighting at the Royal Naval Air Service station at Yeovilton and the Hinkley Point nuclear power station. This foam is invaluable when dealing with a large oil fire as it is used to smother it and thus reduce the supply of oxygen, thereby extinguishing the fire. Water may then be applied with a spray nozzle to cool the hot metalwork and prevent reignition.

Access to the scene was mostly from Bradford-on-Tone (the Taunton side of the line) but police closed access to the road at the junction of East Nynehead and remained there most of the day. Forces came from all over Somerset and from Devon and many of them had never heard of Nynehead before. Villagers were very hospitable to them and the rail crews, supplying them with frequent refreshments and offering the use of their toilets.

Film crews arrived and Nynehead was on the television, though it was always referred to as the Bradford-on-Tone oil derailment. As soon as the fire

had been extinguished, equipment was assembled by British Rail, Gulf Oil and others to salvage and gas-free the damaged oil wagons.

Meetings were held to place contracts for the work and to get the up-line back in working order as quickly as possible. That side of the track was not so badly damaged as it was on the down-line where the derailment had occurred. Within a week Taunton-bound trains proceeded to use the line, travelling at reduced speed past the working crews, but it was about two weeks before the southbound line was opened. It was fairly quickly established that the incident was caused by excessive wear on a wheel bearing due to a lack of lubrication.

A heavy crane had to lift the derailed wagons onto the field at the side of the track. It was found that the crane was too large to go under the railway bridge on the Nynehead road at Poole, too high to go up the Hollow and too wide and heavy for Trefusis bridge (on the Bradford-on-Tone side). The bank of the Milverton to Higher Nynehead road was trimmed back at Luckham Farm and it was brought in to the accident site that way. Large trucks were used to remove the rail ballast impregnated with fuel oil and transport it away to a suitable disposal area. Fresh ballast had to be brought in while the British Rail crews cleared the broken rails as they were cut up. A company from Newport was responsible for freeing the gas and cleaning the carriages of oil. When they were clean they were then transported by road away from the site.

The road from East Nynehead to Bradford-on-Tone over the railway was closed for about three months, which caused some closer residents to travel quite a few extra miles to reach Taunton. In recognition of this inconvenience to parishioners, Gulf Oil made a donation to the village, the money being used to tarmac the surrounds of the Nynehead Memorial Hall. Other incidents, like the death of a large flock of sheep that strayed onto the railway line, didn't even make it to the local newspaper.

The re-tarmacing of the Memorial Hall car park, funded by Gulf Oil.

Left: *The Trefusis Gulf Oil rail disaster on 16 May 1991. Smoke rising at dawn from the crash, probably the first sign that most Nynehead residents had of the disaster.*

The crash site.

Left: *Removing a tanker by road through East Nynehead.*

Right: *Clearing up after the crash.*

Chapter Nine

CHURCH & CHAPEL

THE PARISH CHURCH

The village church, dedicated to All Saints or All Hallows since at least 1531, is surrounded by trees next to the manor-house of Nynehead Court and overlooking Lower Nynehead. From the church tower are panoramic views of the Blackdown Hills to the south and the Brendon and Quantock Hills to the north.

While the main body of the church dates from the fourteenth century it is possible that there had been a church of some sort in Nynehead since before the Conquest. In the early-nineteenth century a carved stone head was found during some restoration work on the church, which some suggest shows that the present church was built on the site of an earlier one. Parts of the present church – the foundations of the nave and the piscina – are thought to date from the thirteenth century, but the first recorded change to the church was the addition of the south aisle in 1410 under the will of John Wyke, whose family also provided the rood-screen in 1480. The position of an early-fifteenth-century door can be seen on the west wall of the Sanford chapel.

The fourteenth-century tower is built of the local red sandstone. Because this stone is porous the churchwardens had to pay for protecting the tower with 'ruf cast' render in 1682:

It for fower Hogs heads and a halfe of lyme to ruf cast the church £1 1s 4d
It for six burshells of Heaire and fetching it 4s 8d
It for 2 harffes and a man one day to fetch graiville to ruf cast the church 2s 6d
It for fower scoare and five foots of boarde to make a cradle to ruf cast ye tower 10s 7d
Beare for the workmen ruf casting 2s 6d

The whole church may have been roughcast at one time, a small amount of roughcasting still existing on the outside of the east wall of the south aisle.

The original roof might well have been thatched but by the late-seventeenth century it was tiled. In 1674 John Buryman was paid £1.10s.0d. for re-tiling the roof, a job which took him three weeks and three days, while John Fursland received £1.6s.3d. for tending and working the stones and a boy 13s.9d. for 15 days for making mortar and carrying stones.

A survey by Edmund Rack in the 1780s gives a full description of the church, much of which we would recognise today. There were, however, some differences. Inside the church there was a singing gallery at the west end under the tower, and a pulpit and reading desk, all of 'neat pannelld wainscot'. The church was not kept in good condition. The communion table was covered with 'an old wormeaten blue cloth fringd white', while the floor, composed of mixed bricks and stone was 'not damp but kept dirtily'.

A century later the church looked very different. The gallery had been removed and an organ had been installed in 1821. Other major changes followed in 1869. An extension to the north transept was built to house the Sanford memorials and the sculptures brought from Italy by Revd John Sanford. Another addition, on the north side of the chancel, allowed the organ to be moved from the back of the church to its present position. A vault for the remains of the early members of the Sanford family was built under the south aisle. What is distinctive about the changes is that William Sanford designed them, and did so in a very satisfactory way, as members of the Somerset Archaeological and Natural History Society were told on their visit to Nynehead in 1912:

In the additions made by the late Mr. Sanford nothing of importance was sacrificed except a three-light window in the former short transeptal chapel and the small window in the north wall of the chancel. Mr. Sanford was a very able amateur architect and personally designed the

The church in the 1840s, before the 1869 additions designed by William Sanford.

The Sanford chapel, showing the carved angel
(a male) and the carved bust of Revd John Sanford.

Restoration work being carried out to the Clarke
memorial by Sue and Laurence Kelland, July 2000.

Left: *The church interior in
the early-twentieth century.*

Right: *The church as seen from the south
in 2003. In 1869 the Sanford chapel
was added to the north transept and
the tall new vestry was built.*

additions to the church. There were two very pretty rose windows, and altogether the addition showed a refinement of taste which put this work quite above what any amateur architect was supposed to be capable of.

The full story of these changes has yet to be told. The foundation-stone of the new north aisle and vestry were laid in June 1869 by Mr Sanford's grandson and the work was so substantial that the church had to be closed during the work. A celebratory service was held on its reopening. This was not the end of the changes – later work included the rebuilding of the north aisle wall in 1912, visible with its different stonework.

The interior of the church is one of the gems of the county, reflecting the influence of the successive owners of the Court and of craftsmen and artists from the locality and further afield. There is too much of interest to be covered in great detail here but the following are of particular note.

Memorials are an important feature of the church, of which those to the Sanford family have already been mentioned. The family crest of the Wykes can be seen at the top of the arch in the rood-screen, while a memorial tablet to the family is in the wall on the north side of the altar:

Heere liethe interred Richard Wike of Ninhed in the county of Somerset, esquier, who died 17 of June, 1590 being then of the age of 65 years and Margaret his wif, daughter of Georg Role of Steventon in the county of Devon esquier who died 12 of August 1578, being then of the age of 41 years and parents of 17 children, vic. 6 sonnes and 11 daughters.

There is a tablet from the seventeenth century commemorating the philosopher John Locke who wrote much of his work at Chipley and, in the corner of the east wall of the south aisle, a large memorial to the Clarke family dated 1667.

As well as the memorial tablets in the Sanford chapel the chancel in particular has a rich collection of fittings, furniture and glass, much dating from the

Tony Lock, churchwarden, inspecting the bells.

1869 restoration and later. The Sanfords also donated many other fine examples of work by famous sculptors and artists including Sir Joshua Reynolds, Della Robbia, Costoli and many others. Of local interest under the tower is the nineteenth-century stone carving of Elijah by William Giles of Wellington.

Among the many monuments is an unusual one to a Chipley servant. Eleanor Pike, born in about 1650, had asked in her will of 1719 to be buried with relations at Bishops Lydeard, but a codicil requested burial at Nynehead. Inside the church is a memorial flagstone, a rare memorial to a servant from an employer found inside an English church rather than in the churchyard.

Here lyeth the body of Eleanor Pike, spinster, who departed this life April 8 1722, aged 72, having lived a true and faithful servant above 50 years with Edw. and Jepp Clarke of Chipley Esq., to whose memory this stone was placed by Mrs Anne Sanford, widow, one of the daughters of the said Edw. Clarke Esq. May 18 1722.

At the back of the church there is the church chest. In 1559 Elizabeth I decreed that every parish should have a church chest in which to keep all important parish documents. The parish chest had to have three locks which were all different and, for security, one key was held by the vicar and the other two by each churchwarden, so in order to open the chest all three persons had to be present. The present chest was purchased in 1778 from William Cox for 10s.0d. (50p), the three locks cost 2s.0d. and the clasps 7s.6d.

THE BELLS

In the tower there are six bells. The oldest is a pre-reformation bell cast in about 1500 by Thomas Geffries of Bristol, 44 inches in diameter and weighing about three-quarters of a ton. The inscription reads 'SANCTA MARIA ORA PRO NOBIS TG'. At the time of the reformation bells like this were broken up, but it is said that the villagers removed this bell and buried it in the churchyard. After the reformation it

The church's oldest bell, the tenor, cast c.1500 by Geffries of Bristol.

was returned to the tower. The bell was rung three times at the Elevation of the Host in order to let the people in the village know that the most important moment in the Mass had arrived.

Four more bells were added in the seventeenth century, one being recast in 1894, and the last, a treble, in 1907. This is inscribed 'THE WORSHIPPERS IN THIS CHURCH PUT ME HERE 1907/VICAR: HC LANDER MA/CHWDNS JAMES BAILEY ECA SANFORD C.M.G.' Unfortunately it has not been possible to ring the bells since the summer of 1989 when it was found that the beams supporting them were unsafe.

THE CHURCHYARD

The path to the church is lined with large sweet chestnut trees and in the spring the churchyard is covered with snowdrops, followed by a yellow carpet of primroses. Some of the gravestones date back to the sixteenth century. When one paid a fee to have a tombstone erected to mark a grave, one did not purchase the freehold of the plot but merely compensated the vicar for the loss of grass, the keep for his sheep. Today the churchyard is a haven of peace maintained in good condition by the Parochial Church Council, but it was not always so. In 1594 it was alleged that the churchyard, as well as the church itself, was 'in decay' and that the vicar (Anthony Middleton) had taken over part for his own use. In the churchyard three features among many of interest are of particular note – the dole table to the north-east of the Sanford chapel, the base of a churchyard cross and the Chorley family monument, a 'listed' structure in its own right.

In the Burial Register, c.1666, are affidavits stating that corpses had been buried in a woollen shroud to comply with the Burial in Woollens Act of 1666. Under this Act, passed to help the woollen trade which was then in a slump, an affidavit had to be produced at each burial stating that the Act had been complied with. Failure to comply entailed a penalty

The dole table in the churchyard.

of £5. Not all bodies were buried in the churchyard. In 1911 the warrant for the burial of a felo-de-se was found in the parish chest. Because of his crime he had lost the right to be buried in the churchyard. An extract from the document, shown opposite, reads:

The above certificate being signed I do according to mine office condemn ye corps of ye felon to be buried at a cross roads, a stake struck through him and so forth interorem.
Your humble servant John Clarke
Jan. 8th 1734

The stake was driven through his body to pin him to the spot so that he could not haunt the neighbourhood. At which crossroads he was buried is not known.

THE VICARS OF NYNEHEAD

The first recorded incumbent of the parish was Revd Dr Bovett in 1292. A total of 49 followed before the parish became part of the Wellington Team in 1967. Most vicars no doubt carried out their duties faithfully but some stand out, indicating that the life of the rural church was not always uneventful and was affected by happenings in the wider world. In 1554 John Marler was deprived of the living following the accession the previous year of the Catholic Queen Mary, while 40 years later it was alleged that Anthony Middleton indulged in playing unlawful games, especially on the Sabbath. In 1641 Samuel Peryam was dispossessed of the 'little vicaridge' of

The monument to the Chorley family, mid-nineteenth century. The south side is inscribed to John Chorley and his wife Mary, the north side to their son John who predeceased them in 1847. The Chorleys were farmers and part of a extended family well known across West Somerset.

The record of the burial of a felon at a crossroads somewhere, possibly in Nynehead.

Nynehead, not because his loyalty was questioned but because he also held another living, which he was allowed to keep.

Revd John Sanford has been mentioned as spending much time in Italy, when he put in a curate, Thomas Tanner. In 1826 Tanner married Mary, the sister of the Sanfords' agent Charles Bailey, and became vicar of Nynehead in 1834. However, he did not live in the village, being also the vicar of Burlescombe. So when William Waldron moved into the new vicarage at the top of the Hollow in 1867 there was great rejoicing that at last Nynehead had a resident vicar again, a welcome situation which lasted for 80 years.

MUSIC IN THE CHURCH

The church in the late-eighteenth century had a west or singing gallery under the tower arch, where the musicians and singers would sit. No evidence has come to light so far about the instruments, the music or the musicians, but it is likely that they used music similar to that played in nearby churches. An organ was introduced in 1821, being bought from Chipley Park for £87 with money given for the purchase by Alice Weekes. A trust fund was set up to pay the organist, using income from land in the village. It was stipulated that the organist:

... shall during the time he shall continue organist of the said church punctually perform such duties as are usual for organists of churches to perform, such organist from time to time to be elected by the heirs and assigns of the said William Ayshford Sanford.

For much of the twentieth century the church had a choir. In the summer of 1920 30 members plus the vicar and Miss Sanford went on an outing by four-horse brake to the Quantocks and Cothelstone. Jim Lake recalls being a member in the 1920s when it consisted of five or six women, seven or eight boys and two or three men. The organ was manually operated by a blower and the hymns were sometimes led by an opera-singer daughter of the vicar, Revd Catlow. There was a choir in the church until 1984.

During the twentieth century the church has continued to serve the community, although the attendance at services has experienced peaks and troughs. Today the church is an active one, although the number attending services is not large. The church has close links with the residential home at Nynehead Court and the school and for the past 11 years there has been an active Sunday school.

NYNEHEAD'S INDEPENDENT CHAPEL

During the nineteenth century there was also a Nonconformist congregation in Nynehead with its

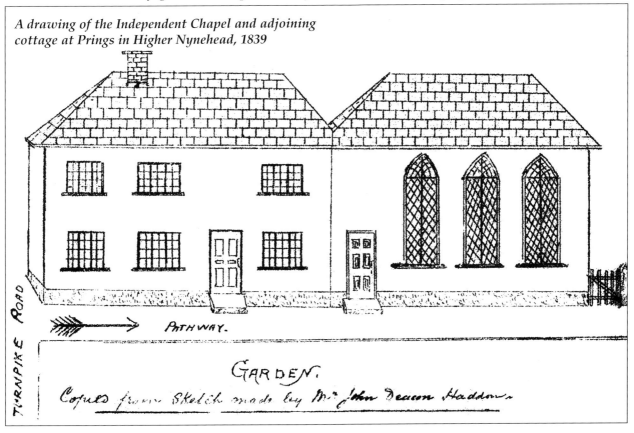

A drawing of the Independent Chapel and adjoining cottage at Prings in Higher Nynehead, 1839

Above: *The church choir and the rector of Wellington, Revd John George, at the opening of the Jubilee Playing Field in 1977.*

Right: *The church choir in the Sanford chapel in 1975, before girls were admitted as choristers.*

Below: *Nynehead School's harvest festival in the church, September 1975.*

own meeting-place. In 1829 'two warm hearted Christian women of some considerable influence and standing warmly supported evangelical efforts in the village.' They were Mrs Rowland of Bluetts House (now known as Langham Farm) and Mrs Honniball of Clavengers Farm, both in East Nynehead, whose husbands were strong churchmen. The two women were instrumental in getting a chapel built in 1839. Prior to this the preaching of the gospel took place in a cottage where Farthings Close now stands.

Mr Cuff, the minister of the Wellington Independent Church, conducted the services with the help of younger members who assisted with the singing (he was reputed not to be able to sing). The services continued in the cottage with some success for several years until Mr Rowland, a well-to-do retired flax dealer, was persuaded by his wife and Mrs Honniball to build a chapel. It was capable of holding 80 people with a cottage attached and is today known as Prings Cottages, at the eastern end of Higher Nynehead – or Middle Nynehead as it was then referred to.

Independent worship continued until the death of Mr Cuff in 1845. With the advent of Mr Winlaw as minister the Independent Friends gave up their services and were succeeded by members of the Wellington Baptist Church who held services in the village on Sunday evenings only while there was no service at All Saints' Church. In 1859 special efforts were made to make the services more interesting and attractive. The chapel was well supported by villagers and the Parish Church choir could often be found assisting with the singing of hymns. Names of note associated with the chapel were J.D. Haddon, W.D. Horsey, John Lock, John Cutter and John Gillard.

With the arrival of Revd W.H. Walrond as vicar of All Saints' Church in 1866, evening services were reintroduced at the Parish Church, drawing the congregation away from the chapel. At the same time Mrs Honniball, a stalwart of the chapel, died

Baptisms in the River Tone, Nynehead's River Jordan, c.1928, by the Poole Mission.

and congregation numbers fell to two or three. Mr Walrond was a popular priest and his preaching was quite evangelical, factors which contributed to the closure of the chapel for Sunday services in 1869/70. However, Revd Pomeer, the Milverton Independent minister, continued to conduct a Thursday-evening service there for some time. Mr Walrond held a night school in the chapel during the week for four years before transferring it the village school.

In 1870/71 the chapel was converted into a cottage by Mr Honniball, who owned adjoining land. This was not the end of independent worship in the parish as services were conducted on Sunday evenings in Thomas Seward's cottage in East Nynehead, now known as Bluehills. The services were conducted by Mr John Burch, a local resident. Thomas Seward's tenancy came to an end some time after 1908 and it is not known if this ended the services.

BAPTISMS IN THE TONE

Religion was not confined to buildings. The River Tone was used for 'total immersion' baptisms from about 1926 for several years. Worshippers from the Poole Mission were part of the Pentecostal Church of the Assemblies of God. The mission was founded in 1926 with Walter Buttle as their minister, who continued to lead the flock until the 1970s. They used to worship on Sundays in a disused room, lent to them by Mr George Hill, situated between the Poole Road and the railway line. When members were ready for baptism, members of the church would walk across the fields to the River Tone on land occupied by Dan Jordan of Wharf Cottage. This was as near as they came to being baptised in the 'Jordan'. Dan would dig out a patch in the river to make it deep enough for immersion. This practice ceased when they moved their worship to the church at Bulford in 1936 after a brief spell in the Temperance Hall in North Street, Wellington.

Baptisms in the River Tone, c.1928.

Above: *Marking the 50th anniversary of VE Day.*
Left to right: *Simon Kemble, Stephanie Hake, Alasdair Ellis, Jessica Harland, David Kerton, Nathan Binding.*

Left: *Miss Andrews, a teacher for the senior section of the school, c.1930. Miss Kick taught the juniors.*

Below: *Pupils dancing at the Summer Cream Tea in 1982.*

Chapter Ten

THE VILLAGE SCHOOL

There is a wealth of material available relating to the school and this section draws on the logbooks of 1870–1910 only to provide examples.

Until the 1860s children's education was dependent on philanthropic or religious bodies, the most notable of which was the Church of England which ran 75 per cent of State schools. Denominational schools were paid by the State when their children were successful in the annual national examinations. The State's role was confined to influencing the curriculum. Board schools were mainly in towns and by the 1870s most people could read and write. This is shown by church marriage registers where people had to sign or make a mark. The last marks in the Nynehead register are those of Sarah Parkman and her two witnesses, dated 19 November 1883.

Various Education Acts had been passed to bring in compulsory attendance, decent buildings, teacher qualifications, etc., but these only applied to board schools. Country areas often had no school or may have had a 'Dame' school, so the quality of education was often poor or inadequate. The 1880 Education Act required attendance for all children at a school housed in a reasonable building with a qualified head teacher Other Acts in the 1890s raised the school-leaving age to 12 (rural areas to 11) and required education to be free.

Nynehead School was started in about 1818 by Mrs E.A. Sanford (Henrietta Langham). In *Lewis' Directory* (1830) it is said to have had one classroom and about 30 children. As the number of children increased it acquired a second classroom, later converted to lavatories, and then a third room was added which was subsequently enlarged for the juniors. The building work was financed by the Sanford family, who gave liberally of their time, money and interest in local children's education. Enlargement was essential as *Braggs' Directory* (1840) notes that there were 60 children attending.

Attendance at the school was free for many years and then a weekly charge of one penny was made. This money was returned to the children at Christmas

A school nativity play in the church.

along with a gratuity for regular attendance. In 1891 an additional Parliamentary grant of £10 was given to parishes with populations below 500 to ensure that education was free. However, Nynehead child-ren already enjoyed this benefit before the law required it to be so.

Teachers had no formal training at this early stage. Most trades had formal apprenticeship schemes but the art of educating children lagged behind. Pupil-teachers were introduced in 1846 and this opportunity was open to anyone of 13 and over, but by 1900 you had to be 15 to start training. This involved a five-year programme of teaching in school, private study, out-of-school training and annual examinations. At the end of the programme the student teacher could go on to college, undertake more study leading to a certificate, or remain teaching with unqualified status.

Nynehead's records show that all these happened in the school and you can follow the staff as they took the various options. As late as 1914 a survey shows that 32 per cent of teachers were fully trained and certificated, 27 per cent had certificates but had not been to college, and 41 per cent were unqualified.

The head teacher (Josiah Leat) was absent for one week by permission of the managers from 3 July 1895 to sit for his final B.A. examination. On 15 July he received notice that he had passed the final examination for the B.A. degree at the Royal University of Ireland. Finally, it is noted on 23 October 1895 that:

By kind permission of the Managers of this school I am enabled to absent myself from duty on the 24th and 25th inst. in order to attend the conferring of Degrees at Dublin. It is not improbable that the timetable will be departed from during these two days e.g. some lessons will have to be substituted for singing on Thursday.

By 1870 teachers were paid the following salaries if they were fully qualified: men received £94 per annum; women received £58 per annum.

Mrs Cottey (left) and Mrs Ware, teachers at the school in the 1950s, with pupils including Joyce Howe, E. Broom, Angela Jones, Norman Parsons, Anna Kirby, G. Gollop, G. Lake, Margaret Coles, Thelma Parsons and Susan Bickerstaff.

The school log-books record the following teachers and monitors during the period 1871–1899:

The teachers
1871
Mary Anne Locke – certificated teacher by examination 2nd Div. 2nd year.
Revd C.H. Walrond – visiting and teaching RE.
Mrs Walrond – teaching needlework.
1875
Mrs Blackmore – teaching needlework.
Mrs Taylor – teaching needlework in place of Mrs Blackmore.
Miss Ellen Paul – assistant mistress in place of Mary Locke.
1878
Mrs Hayes – teaching needlework.
1879
Ellen Paul now shown as 'Provisionally Certificated'.
1881
Miss Fanny Corbin – teaching needlework in place of Mrs Blackmore as well as Mrs Hayes.
1882
Ellen Paul now a certified teacher after taking her examination on 9 December 1881.
Miss Cording shown as teaching but no mention of subject.
1884
Miss Taylor – teaching needlework.
1885
Miss Davies mentioned as absent and six days later she left the school.
Miss Vining – no mention of subject.
I.H.M. Stone commenced duties 14 September 1885.
Miss Frances Mills Stone – qualified under Article 84, became the Infant and Sewing teacher.
1887
Josiah Leat appointed 5 September 1887 as master – he was certificated (1st Div.)
1899
John Martin Wale – late of Saltley Training College

became head on 4 September 1899.
Winifred Mahala Coleman – no mention of subject.
Freda Coleman – went to Wiveliscombe.

The monitors
1871
Jane C. Lock; Ann Scott – gave up her duties; Joanna Fouracre – in place of Jane Lock.
1873
Sarah Gillard – had problems attending regularly; Mary Jane Jennings – in place of Sarah Gillard.
1878
Martha Coram – a pupil who was appointed as monitress.
1880
Emma Hannabuss; Christine Williams; Mary E. Fry; Frances Coleman.

The school log-books show that the following subjects were taught at some time during the period 1870–1897:

Reading	Football	Geography
Writing	Cutting out	Cricket
Arithmetic	Colour lesson	History
Dictation	Object lesson	Liturgy
Grammar and	Knitting	Singing
Parsing	(Boys)	Laundry
Copy writing	Needlework	Human body
Multiplication	(Girls)	Scripture
tables	Dressmaking	Cookery
Composition	Model making	Drill

The daily timetable in 1893 was as shown opposite, and provides a great contrast with today's curriculum.

The first time geography was taught was 16 February 1871. Geography and history were combined and taught to the girls for the first time in September 1899 as 'it seems a great pity that they should leave school without any knowledge of that subject. Geography readers do not in any way supply the deficiency.' Knitting had regular mentions, with sessions lasting from 2–3.45p.m. Football matches played by the boys against Langford Budville and the Union children involved changes to the normal school timetable. Drill took place for an hour in the playground in March 1890, whilst cricket was played in the parkland of Nynehead Court. A series of lessons on the human body began on 7 October 1891, but this had to be cancelled only two weeks later owing to the failure to get the subject for illustration – a dead rabbit!

In 1890 Mrs Sanford made arrangements for the teaching of cookery – 'The girls of Standard IV and V are to go to the Court twice a week for a lesson of $1^1/_2$ hours each.' Cookery lessons were also given by Miss Lamport, at the vicarage by Miss Walrond and at a class in Wellington. Dressmaking lessons were started in the neighbourhood and three girls and a monitress attended. Object lessons were required under the Education Act and appear to have been talks

1893	1893	2003
Monday/Wednesday/Friday	Tuesday/Thursday	Typical day
9.00 Scripture	9.00 Scripture	9.00 Registration/
9.40 Home Lessons	9.40 Home Lessons	Numeracy
10.00 History	10.00 History	10.10 Break
10.30 Writing	10.30 Writing	10.25 Literacy Hour
11.00 Recreation	11.00 Recreation	11.25 Service
11.15 Mental Arithmetic	11.15 Mental Arithmetic	11.40 Break
11.30 Arithmetic	11.30 Arithmetic	11.45 Internet Research
12.00 Lunch	12.00 Lunch	12.30 Lunch
1.30 Drawing	1.30 Singing	1.30 Reading/Library
2.15 Geography	2.00 Problems	1.50 Science experiment
3.00 Singing	2.34 Reading	2.40 PE
3.15 Reading	3.15 Arithmetic	3.10 Story/Prayer
3.40 Copying home words	3.40 Copying home words	3.15 Finish
3.55 Finish	3.55 Finish	After-school clubs

aimed at widening the children's experiences; the object lesson on 13 December 1897 was based on slides of American Indians and in 1906/7 policemen, railway stations and bricks and their manufacture were to be studied. Science was a broad heading used to cover a whole range of items. For example, on 21 March 1899 the children were shown a sleeping dormouse and an onion grown in a glass bottle. Frog spawn, growing alum crystals and glass tubing bent to form a siphon were the topics for 23 March 1899.

Children were regularly sent to scripture and School Union exams, which were taken at Langford Budville and Milverton. Her Majesty's Inspectors (HMIs) would also visit and examine the children, a bright spot being the granting of a half-day holiday for those not taking exams. On 4 February 1873 R.F. Boyle Esq. inspected the school. Unfortunately there had been very heavy snowfalls and the children who were to be presented had to be fetched in carts as they were unable get through the snow.

Exact numbers of pupils are hard to determine and reliance has to be made on the average attendance figures recorded in the log-books. In February/March 1871 the average attendance shown was 44.3 pupils but by June/July 1881 this had risen to 58.4. It is also clear that there was considerable movement of families into and out of the village.

The most common reason for non-attendance was the weather. Continuous rain, heavy storms and presumably flooding meant that the children could not walk to school, particularly if they had to cross the river. Children from East Nynehead and Poole were frequently unable to reach the school. At one point the average attendance was 47 but the weather reduced the number to 18 and the following day only 13 pupils made it to the school. In September 1871 it is recorded: 'many children away on account of the harvest not being over.' On 27 June 1881 several children were given leave of absence during the week on account of haymaking. Due to the heat, children were taught in the shady parts of the playground on 15 September 1899, just as they use the 'round house' today.

Common childhood diseases were far more devastating in the late-nineteenth century. Outbreaks of whooping cough, mumps, smallpox, chickenpox, measles, scarlatina, ringworm and scarlet fever reduced attendance levels considerably. These were highly contagious diseases and children were often sent home as a precautionary measure. On 23 January 1885 Revd Hervey sent home all the Burge children as a case of smallpox was reported. The children did not return until 2 February. The common cold makes few appearances as people were used to such a minor problem, but on 11 December 1899 many children were away ill and on 15 December there were 'Many children still away suffering from bad colds.' Measles was a major problem and on 7 May 1891 there was poor attendance, the next day the school closed and it did not reopen until 25 May and even then only half the children were present. Measles made 'some children not quite so sharp as before and they do not work so quickly.' Some illnesses were not clearly defined and one can only guess what the problem was, e.g. William Blackmore, an infant pupil, was 'to be withheld from lessons of a straining character at a Medical Gentleman's request' and Jane Carro was 'suffering in her head and also had to work lightly'.

Teachers were not exempt from sickness and personal problems. January 1880 saw the schoolmistress ill and with the doctor for ten days, and Henry J. Macey took temporary charge of the school until her return on 17 February. The infant teacher, Miss Stone, appeared to suffer an incredible amount of undefined ill health. It is recorded that the 'timetable could not be adhered to' and she 'caused disruption to the timetable'. Mrs Blackmore was absent after the death of a relative and on 2 May 1881 the sewing mistress was 'off due to the sickness of her little girl'.

School terms were not clearly defined as at present. Two days only were given for Easter, presumably Good Friday and Easter Monday. Whitsun was given a week, three weeks for the harvest in August and two weeks for Christmas. The children were often given

The schoolchildren in 1891. This photograph was probably taken near the church.

The schoolchildren with head teacher Mr Tipper in 1908, in a photograph taken at the school.

The school building without its render, showing the stone used for the original building and the line dividing this from the later extension.

either a day or half-day holiday, most of them linked to Church festivals. These were given to allow the children to attend the service, the most regular being on Ash Wednesday, Ascension Day, St John (24 June), St Peter (29 June), St Michael (29 September), St Luke (18 October) and St Thomas (21 December). The children were also involved in the church choir and were frequently given time off to sing, for example in 1896 on 1, 6, 14 and 25 January at 11.30a.m.

Visitors to the school were frequent as both the Sanfords and the vicar brought house guests to see the children; 'The picturesque dress of the girls, with red cloaks and straw hats trimmed with blue ribbons, used to attract the attention of strangers.' In the period 1871–76 some 52 visitors are mentioned, 11 being clergymen. All members of the Sanford family visited and are recorded as hearing the children read, teaching, giving out prizes, hearing them sing, inspecting the needlework, distributing books in commemoration of the Queen's jubilee, giving out clothing and selecting choirgirls. Visitors were popular as they often asked for a day's holiday to be granted! Other holidays were granted for benevolent reasons, for example Miss Rosie Sanford's wedding (18 December 1894), the Band of Hope treat (21 July 1899), Mr Sanford's birthday (2 December 1901) and the annual treat (9 August 1880).

Boys and girls were subjected to the cane. Henry Taylor, H. Walters, Cooksley and Jenkins were punished for disobedience. H. Walters, G. Yame and J. Derbe received the cane for 'kicking the football in the cloakroom after having been warned.' J. Cooksley and Benjamin Hodge were punished for falsehood, Jenkins, Hayes and Warren were lazy, as was Clyde Washer, who was punished twice. S. Chorley used bad language and Edith Cooksley was caught swearing. Hayes called Miss Bowerman names and Ernest Richards was caned for cruelty to a bird. Fred Tottle and William Walters were expelled from the school by Mr Sanford for indecent conduct.

On 2 July 1890 Bessie Hayes was publicly caned for 'stealing the children's dinners.' She was also 'deprived of her position as caretaker of the school for 3 months.' She was caned again on 18 July for 'stealing cake from dinner bags' and was 'deprived of her position of school cleaner for 3 months.' Presumably she was a pupil at the school or the head teacher would not have been in a position to cane her, but if so she was a child trying to get an education and doing two jobs at the same time. Who did the caretaking and cleaning during the three months is not known.

Sometimes problems can be seen to run in families. J. Chorley was caned on 17 June 1897 for insubordination, while it was recorded that:

Sarah Chorley his sister pretended to be faint and made her nose bleed to excite sympathy. She is a very naughty girl. Her sister is detained in a reformatory school for 2 years. The mother says that Sarah is naughty like her sister.

Carrie Chorley was punished on 28 November 1900 for taking two buns from a girl's basket.

The school building had its problems. Revd Walrond asked that the privies should be provided with separate approaches from the schoolroom as this was a requirement under Article 51a of the Education Act. Various works were suggested to improve the buildings; 'the three seats in the Boy's Offices should be separated' (to comply with the Code), whilst HMI Whitehall reported 'the close proximity of an open cesspool which would lead to doubt whether the buildings could be reputed of as being in a perfectly healthy locality.' In October 1903 the entrances to both offices were entirely cut off by water and one of the playgrounds was flooded at the lower end. On 7 January 1915 this note was made: 'the boys offices are completely flooded this morning so the boys will be let out 5 minutes earlier to make use of the girls offices.' The stove in the big room would not burn on 27 February 1905 and it filled the room with smoke. The thermometer at 10.30 read at 40°F.

The School Attendance Officer made visits to the school. On 19 June 1888 they were obliged to send the Relieving Officer to look after one irregular child. Mary Jane Wood was absent for a fortnight and the school was told that her father was ill and that as she was over 14 she was to leave school. The Attendance Officer took the names of all children who had not made 41 attendances out of 47 in 1899. However, Mr Sanford expressed a wish that no case of irregular attendance should be visited by the Officer without consulting him first.

Some children were obviously keen to learn: Lucy Cooksley was 'granted a Certificate of Exemption' as she had 'made the required number of attendances for 5 years since the age of 5'; 'Sent Frank Merry, Elizabeth Richards, Alice Tudball, Sarah Blackmore to the Wellington Board School for examination for Labour Certificate which they all passed.' John Francis Ebdon sat his exam on 30 March 1893 and came 14th out of 2,155 candidates who sat the exam that year. Others

Above: *The pupils and staff in 1988, a far cry from the earlier photographs where the subjects needed to be still. Photographic techniques now allow a much livelier result! Note the unrendered wall and absence of an entrance door in the end wall of the building.*

Above: *A presentation to mark the retirement of head teacher Pam Bailey in June 1989.*

Left: *Pupils hard at work inside the school, early 1990s.*

were not as keen, as the head teacher was 'unable to teach the 'scholarship boy' with any success owing to his frequent absence.' At times there was mass truancy; 'Poor attendance this afternoon probably owing to a menagerie at Wellington.'

The County Medical Officer called to inspect certain children on 25 March 1908. Maude Hitchcock had come with a verminous head and got sent home with a note but when Nurse Reese visited (21 May 1913 and again on 4 and 13 June) she had to exclude six children as 'their verminous condition was detrimental to other students.' Two pupils returned after further inspection whilst the NSPCC visited the others at home. They made five attempts to return, occasioning a visit from their mother, but they could not return until the paperwork was received on 18 July and they eventually made it back to the classroom on 21 July. Reginald Tucker was sent home as he 'was not in a fit state to sit with the other children.' An infant named Tooze was sent home to be washed but did not return. Mary Gillard was sent home 'until a little older because so troublesome in school.' Poor Alfred Wilkinson was passed over to the Church of England Waifs and Strays Society.

It is very hard to determine what standard of education some of the children reached. It was a generally held belief that all children could achieve if they put their minds to it, but evidence in the school log-books suggest that some children had problems. On 2 December 1896, when attendance was low, the opportunity was taken of:

> ... specially coaching dull children in their weak subjects. Reading in the III Standard was found to be weak but special means must be found for Carro, Redstone and Cooksley.

B. Redstone was:

> ... very very slow in learning Multiplication tables; it seems almost impossible to teach him. His reading is also poor. Sarah Blackmore seems to have no ability for subtracting.

In June 1908 it was said that in reading 'the boys are far behind the girls in this subject... it is desirable that special case be given to training in speech in all classes.' The inspector reported that 'the grammar of the older children was weak and they should be taught to speak out better.'

There are a few indications of what happened to the children after they left the school. Tilly Champion left without a reason, Elizabeth Seward and Emma James went into service, Annie Champion and William Corbin left to go out to work and Thomas Mace, 12 years of age, was given permission to work for Mr Ash on the farm for the period of the war. He started there on 10 May 1915.

There were some sad occasions. After school on 16 December 1889 the children, 'who had made a nice wreath', attended the funeral of James Fowler, late a pupil. Consideration was given to other people's feelings as recreation time was moved on 13 May 1910 to avoid 'interfering with a funeral service'.

The log-books also record some events of national importance. School closed in the afternoon of 2 March 1900 to commemorate the relief of Ladysmith; another holiday came for the relief of Mafeking after a siege of 216 days. Illustrations were shown of the late Queen's life and funeral in 1901 and in 1902 the school closed for the morning 'to enable the children to see HM the King's train pass through Wellington.'

SOME SNIPPETS FROM THE LOG-BOOKS

A Penny Bank was opened on 19 February 1889 and allowed deposits to be made on Thursdays. It was still in existence in 1898.

Slates were still in use in 1891.

The children were provided with a Christmas tree on 11 January 1892.

On 8 October 1913 Revd Launder and Mr Maunders of Milverton announced that 'Trespassers in the orchard opposite the school would be prosecuted.'

The school was also used for some after-school and evening sessions; an address on 'Foreign Missions' was given and a series of magic-lantern slides were lent to the master by Messrs Cassell and Co. on 'The Building of an Empire'.

The end of the school showing the gable-end details typical of late-nineteenth-century buildings in Nynehead.

Mr Gollop and white turkeys at Chipley (year not known).

Percy Heal driving a horse and cart.

Chapter Eleven

FARMING

Historically, Nynehead was a parish of small farms run by tenants of relatively few landowners. Although the pattern was always fluid the first complete picture is revealed in the Tithe Survey of 1837. The Tithe Map was the first to show the entire parish of Nynehead on a large scale and was accompanied by a schedule of the owners, occupiers, areas and uses of individual parcels of land.

Tithes had their origins in Old Testament injunctions to devote a tithe (one tenth) of one's produce to the service of God (see Genesis ch.28, v.22). For over 1,000 years up to the early-nineteenth century landowners in England had to pay tithes to the church, usually in kind, such as corn, hay, wool and other crops. The system became increasingly unpopular from the seventeenth century onwards, particularly with Nonconformists who objected to supporting the established Church in this way. By the early-nineteenth century pressure for reform led in 1836 to the Tithe Commutation Act, under which tithes were changed into rent charges based on the prevailing price of corn.

Under the Act a survey of each parish was carried out to produce the schedule and the map. These allocated the monetary value of the tithes to each parcel of land as agreed by tithe commissioners whose signatures appeared on the map. The Nynehead survey was carried out in 1837, the surveyor being Charles Bailey, the agent for the Sanfords at Nynehead Court. Whether such a potential conflict of interest would be allowed today is doubtful.

Because all parcels of land are numbered the map and schedule are a valuable source of information about Nynehead and its inhabitants. They show that the 1,448 acres of the parish as defined at that time (i.e. excluding the parts of West Buckland, Wellington and Hillfarrance later included) were divided between 21 owners, of whom 12 had more than five acres. The dominant owner was Edward Sanford of Nynehead Court with over 1,062 acres, or about three-quarters of the land, far more than the next three largest: John Chorley (61 acres); William Carpenter (50 acres); and John Honniball (50 acres). Interestingly, in addition to the land associated with Nynehead church (just over one acre), other clergymen are listed as owning significant amounts of land – Revd James Cottle (27 acres) and Revd John Boucher/ Revd Thomas Prowse Lethbridge.

However, it was not a simple pattern of a group of landlords and a separate set of tenants, especially in the eastern part of the parish. For example, John Chorley owned and occupied 61 acres at Bickleys, Common Ground and part of Toogoods while also being a tenant of 39 acres owned by John Jacobs at Havilands and New Barn Ground. Chorley thus had an interest in just over 100 acres of land in the parish. John Honniball owned and occupied land at Clavengers and part of Toogoods, but also tenanted land at Steart and Farthings (owned by Revd J. Boucher) and some Sanford land at Whiteheathfield and Stockers Wood on the road to Oake.

The Sanford estate included 11 farms. James Bailey looked after Burge, Ligorsland, Pigsleys and Home Farm, John Hewett had Hornshay, and William Ludlow ran Blockhouse Farm. Cage, Wyke and Biddles, all around Chipley, were occupied by J. and S. Daniels, while William Palmer was the tenant at Upcott and Jenkings.

Tom Barrow outside Langham Farm in East Nynehead with the last milk churn.

William Gollop in the orchard next to The Bush
at East Nynehead.

As was normal practice Edward Sanford as landowner kept for himself the woodland and plantations, mainly around the Court. Woodland made up a relatively small part of the parish, only about 20 acres in all, scattered in 19 separate parcels. Half of these were described as 'plantations', especially around the Court; there were also three and a half acres of copse/coppice and six acres of 'other'. Many of these trees have disappeared, as have the parish willow beds – just over six acres with a cottage by the canal to the east of the Tone aqueduct and two other small beds on the Luckham stream. There were also many very small parcels of land described as 'waste' or 'pits', spread throughout the parish. These have been filled in or remain as ponds, wet patches in fields or have become overgrown.

When the parish was enlarged during the late-nineteenth and twentieth centuries Perry and Poole Farms became part of Nynehead, although most of the land brought in from West Buckland and Wellington was part of Hornshay Farm.

This pattern, although varying in its details, remained essentially the same throughout the nineteenth century and into the twentieth. The big change came in 1940 when the Nynehead Court estate was sold to Kleinwort Bensons whose estate branch, the Bolnore Estates, sold off the farms. The outlying farms were put on the market in the late 1940s, the others following in the 1950s and '60s. In 2003 there are only six farms in the parish (Hornshay, Blockhouse, Heywood, Ash, Poole and the Bickley fruit farm).

ORCHARDS

Until the Second World War orchards were an important feature of the life and landscape of the village. In 1837 44 acres were under fruit trees, usually in small orchards associated with farms or cottages. The largest were Great Orchard of over nine acres to the north of the Court, and Haywood Orchard (over three acres) and the orchard at Goldhill

on Hornshay. Production of cider was an essential part of the farming regime as a worker on the land was normally accustomed to consuming about half a gallon a day. Farms would have their own cider-press and copious quantities were produced. Thus in September 1811 Hornshay Farm was paid £18 by the estate for six hogsheads of cider.

Orchards and cider continued to be important until the Second World War. The Williamses at The Bush in East Nynehead had an orchard and cider-press, while Jim Lake remembers that the orchard opposite the school had not only cider apples but also eating varieties (Morgan Sweet and Russet) of great interest to the boy pupils. Sadly, the orchards have largely disappeared, through neglect or for agricultural reasons, with only occasional rather forlorn and decayed-looking trees remaining.

HORNSHAY FARM

Hornshay Farm was at one time part of the Nynehead Court estate. Today it comprises 382 acres lying quite evenly around the house and with land both on and off the flood plain of the River Tone. Its story reflects all the important aspects of farming in the parish over the last 400 years, while also being severely affected in the first half of the nineteenth century by the Sanfords' parkland scheme and the coming of the canal and the railway.

The Seventeenth Century

At the beginning of the seventeenth century the manor of Nynehead covered about 400 acres. This would have included a large part of the present Hornshay Farm, some of Heywood Farm, the Court Gardens, Nynehead Court and Blockhouse Farm, together with Farthings Close, Calcotts Wood, and Stockers Wood. Pixton was certainly not included, nor Upcott and Chipley, all being acquired much later.

The ownership and occupation of land at that time was a complex business. Records show that those involved in Hornshay included John Wyke Esq. 'who holds Nynehead Mills' and Richard Sydenham, gentleman, 'who holds a tenement with 30 acres of land, meadow and pasture', probably Hornshay. Others mentioned included Robert Washer (40 acres), Samuel Tomes (36 acres) and John Ramster, who gave his name to an orchard. Today his land, opposite the village school, holds Hornshay Farm's four 'service' houses – Orchard Cottages – built in 1947. Robert Blewe held 28 acres and his name recurs in some litigation in 1630, when he is described as the tenant of meadows which were part of Hornshay.

By 1640 Hornshay had been occupied for at least 50 years by the Sydenhams, Walter and Joan and their son George. Their interest in Hornshay had ceased through their deaths and the farm was leased by Martin Sanford (whose wife was also a Sydenham) to his daughter Mary. She also took on an adjoining tenement previously occupied by the late George Sydenham, and another occupied at the time by Robert Harvey, on the usual conditions of sending extra help to the Court Barton at harvest, and capons at Christmas. The rent was 42s. a year.

Mary Sanford married Thomas Gorges, lived at Hornshay and had three children – Thomas, Susan and Ferdinado. They were happy and prosperous for a while, but Mary died and was buried in the church at Nynehead. Thomas remarried and the children went to live at Heavitree in Exeter, where their stepmother Rose brought them up. The younger Thomas studied at Oxford University but died as a young man in an affray in Fleet Street. Ferdinado prospered in America and Susan married a relative of her stepmother. Their interest in the farm presumably ceased. In 1671 Thomas Gorges senr left a will in which he requested:

If I die by Nynehead to be buried by my first virtuous wife Mary. The demesne of Edbrooke and little Manor of Brooke which I purchased of my honoured and beloved nephew John Sanford of Nynehead Somerset and of London, Esq. Merchant, to my son Ferdinado Gorges.

The next occupier was Martin Greenwood of North Perrott, near Crewkerne. Under his tenancy between 1667–87 Hornshay was mostly pasture, some eight and three quarter acres, but he also had two and a half acres of arable land. This was in plots varying in size from an eighth of an acre to four acres, mostly near the house but but some the river. Haldren and Horsewell are mentioned, by which names the fields are still known.

Under a lease of 1675 Martin had to pay John Sanford a rent of £2.2s.4d. a year, help at one harvest day on the Court Barton (or pay 2s.8d. instead), and provide one fat capon at Christmas. On taking up the lease he had to pay a 'heriot' in the form of his best beast or money in lieu 'at the Lord's election'. Although described as 'Gentleman', Martin made his mark in the form of initials instead of a signature. He had a wife Anne and a son Giles who are both mentioned in the lease. (The churchwardens' accounts show that Martin Greenwood 'Junior' was elected as a churchwarden in 1675 – so maybe there were two men of the same name).

In 1686 changes were made to the deed relating to the surrender of a quarter of an acre of Haldrens by the river – 'ground whereon earth hath been dug to make brick walls'. These might have been linked to entries in the Nynehead estate accounts, for example the entry on 4 May 1681 for paying for 30 bushels of coal brought from Watchet for the kiln. There is evidence of considerable brick building in the parish at this time. Among other work the Court had been rebuilt in 1675, the churchwardens' accounts show that about 200 bricks being used to build an oven for the Church House, and the new house at Chipley was put up in the early 1680s.

At the beginning of the seventeenth century Hornshay was emerging from the mists of time with a Saxon name, probably referring to the 'Home Close'. By the end of the century the house had become a substantial property. The front walls of the present house, the inglenook fireplace in the lounge, some of the foundations of the house and buildings, and the front door, all probably date from these years.

The Eighteenth Century

In 1730 Ann Sanford leased the tenements called Hornshay and Waterhouse to Matthew Haviland, at a yearly rent of £174.10s.0d. The Church Registers show that he married Katherine Stevens in 1720 and that their daughter Joan was baptised the following year. His father, John, of Langford Budville and Runnington, made Matthew his executor and residual legatee in his will and mentions that he is in possession of Peyton Farm. Matthew's brother, Alexander, the curate of Nynehead at that time, had received his share of land and tenements at Runnington on his marriage and was to keep the two large books in folio and the silver 'bowle' that he had. Two more brothers, John and Edward, their wives and the grandchildren were all provided for generously in the will as well as Katherine, Joan and various nephews and servants.

Matthew Haviland farmed a larger acreage than Martin Greenwood, including Haldren Mead, Little Haldren, the two Blackham Moors, Farthings, Kingstones, Coggans Meadow, and Ox Barton adjoining Mary Lake. As well as noting the rents paid – 'received of Mr Haviland by his wife one quarter's rent due Lady-day last part £29.7.6.' – the estate accounts show a variety of activities. James Cross was paid 8s. for laying 'an hundred of reed' on Waterhouse, and 13s.4d. for 80 sheaves on the small orchard at Goldhill. In 1741 John Corner and his man were paid 2s.8d. for work about Mr Haviland's bridges (Hornshay and Ash bridges?) and later 6s.8d. for work at 'ye pownde at Havilands.' The same man 'lofted Waterhouse Barne' and William Peters and his man earned 10s.6d. working on the same barn.

In 1737 Humphrey Burd, miller, leased from the Sanfords two grist-mills and one malt-mill with the house, stables, outhouses, 'courtlages' and gardens, one field called Quarry Close and the hay from part of Mill Meadow called the Cowleaze.

Eight years later Humphrey, now spelt Bird, was occupying Hornshay, the mills and one acre of the Common Meadow. He was collecting land-tax and window tax by 1751 and sales of malts and grindings are also recorded. After his death in 1765, his son John continued his work of tax collection and running the farm and the mills. He signed his name in full, whereas Humphrey merely made his mark of an 'H'. At this time the farm was called Hornshay Barton, the largest in the manor, and John took over part of the Court Barton as well.

Humphrey Bird was married twice, firstly to Elizabeth, by whom he had Mary, baptised in 1730, and John (I), 1735. His second wife Sarah bore him a daughter, Grace, who was baptised in 1737. There were many grandchildren, confusingly with the same names being used in succeeding generations. One day in 1785 John (I) and his wife Martha took their five children, aged 8 to 16 years, to be baptised. His son John (II) married a Mary and also followed the family tradition by bringing his children to be baptised jointly, John (III) and Elizabeth in 1798, and Mary and Ann three years later. John II's sister Mary married James Hellings in 1794, but Ann died aged 29 in 1804. There are other entries of Birds in the registers, including John Bird senr's burial in 1807.

The Nineteenth Century

In 1804, John Hewett, probably from Burlescombe, brought his large family to Hornshay, but continued to farm Holbrook Farm at Burlescombe as well. He and his descendants kept the tenancy for the next 110 years, until 1914. His son, John, was 12 years old when they came to Nynehead and eventually took over the tenancy from his father but, although he married, he had no children. John junr's brother became a builder in Cornwall and had a daughter, Elizabeth, who was living at Hornshay in 1851. John senr had five daughters. Mary and Elizabeth were teenagers when they came, Sarah was five years old, Grace Talbot a baby, and Jane was born at Hornshay.

Mary Hewett was married in Nynehead to John Rowe of Dunkeswell, needing her father's consent as she was under age. Seven years later Elizabeth married Henry Pring of Bradford, a yeoman. Sarah married John Bailey and they lived at Blockhouse for ten years and had a large family. In 1830 they moved to Gundenham Farm, Langford Budville, where a son, Stephen, was born. As a boy or young man he came to live with his grandfather and uncle John Hewett at Hornshay, taking over the tenancy on his uncle's death. Jane Hewett was living at Hornshay when she married Richard William Atton of Taunton, a draper, in 1827. Grace Talbot was the last to be married, in 1841, to Edward Torr, yeoman of Devon, when she was 'with her Father at Hornshay Farm'. It seems that John Hewett senr died some time in the 1840s.

In 1812 the rent was £700 but had dropped to £550 when Stephen Bailey took over in 1856, perhaps partly because of the decline in the area of acreage of the farm – 249 acres in 1823, but only 220 in 1851. In 1823 there were 36 separate plots or fields, varying in size from an eighth of an acre to 21 acres. The eighth was the Bridge orchard, showing that it had been re-planted since Martin Greenwood's time. Home Close, the Haldrens, Haldren Meadow, Long Rews, the willow bed, Blackham and Lears, as well as Waterhouse, Kennel Orchard, Goldhill Orchard, Burrows, Crosslands and Twinainger, and also Harris's Moor, are all recorded.

The Tithe Map of 1837 shows the boundaries of the fields at that time and the outlines of the house, buildings and cottages. From this we can see that since then the house and buildings have been enlarged and some structures erected on new sites. The fact that rents were so high in the Hewetts' time would indicate that some money was spent then, but from the Tithe Map one can see that much of it went on later. Certainly the stable block was rebuilt in 1860 (in Poole brick) as indicated by the plaque on the north wall. The garden, too, was greatly extended, a large piece of Home Close was enclosed by a wall and laid out with paths and borders, and a tennis-court was installed at the back. All these changes are shown on the OS map of 1887.

The farmhouse contains a variety of doors, door and window fastenings, and a cabinet of bell indicators, which is still in use for the outside doorbells. The inglenook fireplace was covered in and a small grate used instead until the 1940s when it was restored and converted to modern use, burning wood. A parlour was built with a bedroom over and the whole of the east wing was rebuilt on a new site. The parlour, now used as a farm office, has a wooden floor but until about 1940 the rest of the house had stone floors, flagstones and quarry tiles.

The 1851 Census shows that the farm then consisted of 220 acres and John Hewett, aged 59, employed 11 labourers. His wife Mary, niece Elizabeth Hewett and nephew Stephen Bailey, aged 21, lived in the farmhouse, as did their maidservant and three unmarried farm workers. The two farm cottages (Waterhouse Cottages, since demolished) were occupied by the Upham and Scott families. The church registers had previously recorded people living at Crab's Hole, in Burrows, near the road. A William Ball lived there until 1823, followed by a family of Blackmores. One of them was sexton and verger for many years. There was another cottage on the withy bed.

Stephen Bailey took over the farm at Ladyday 1856 on a lease of eight years from Edward Ayshford Sanford, at a rent of £550 a year. A few days later in Nynehead church he married Mary Ann Warren, his Uncle James' stepdaughter, of Haywood Farm, whose father 'was the late John Warren of Taunton, a butcher'. Thomas Tanner, the vicar, officiated and was assisted by his son, T.C. Tanner, who was Stephen's cousin. In the course of time, Stephen and Mary Ann had a family of six daughters and a son James.

During the 1860s Stephen became agent to Mr Sanford. He had to sign the Garden Book in which it is noted that six people were employed. Their wages were listed together with plants and materials bought. During the 1870s Stephen organised the Chelwell water-supply, piped from near Chipley to the Court and later extended to Hornshay, where it is still in use. William Sanford, Edward's son, was now in charge, but was often at the family's house at Woody Bay, Lynton, for the whole summer. Stephen had to write to him with builders' estimates, mentioning other news and problems on the estate. Once, Mr Bailey went down to discuss matters with Mr Sanford and enjoyed a sail in his yacht. In the early 1880s, he was engaged in building a cascade at the weir – in late October he was having trouble there because a lot of soil had been removed in the flood. There is also a letter of thanks to Mr Sanford from Lizzie Bailey who was out when he had called in with a wedding present. She married Thomas Boucher of Wiveliscombe, yeoman.

At this time new farm machinery was being introduced on the Sanford estate, but this did not receive everyone's blessing. The vicar, Revd W.H. Walrond, wrote to Mrs Sanford one April between 1868 and 1891:

Mr. Sanford will be interested... to hear that we have had some horrible engines cultivating his great fields, smoking and whistling and puffing. I am a liberal and all for progress, but for all that I don't like it close to my own door: but it must be borne – one good thing they make short work of the business and soon go away again to torment somebody else.

Hornshay was farmed with Upcott for a number of years, which would help to explain how Stephen was able to give so much of his time to his work as agent to Mr Sanford, perhaps leaving the day-to-day management to his relative at Upcott. The farm continued to

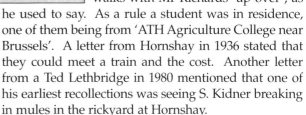
Mr and Mrs E.A. Richards and their dog at Hornshay Farm.

develop, however, and in 1882 a flock of Dorset horn sheep was established at Hornshay by the purchase of ewes bred or sold by J. Kidner of Nynehead, and rams by the same breeder. The flock was replenished by the purchase of ewes bred or sold by S. Kidner and Jasper Culverwell and rams bred by the same three breeders and by J. Farthing. In 1892, the *Dorset Horn Breeders' Association's First Flock Book* was published, recording that the flock then consisted of 240 ewes and 150 ewe lambs, with two rams. Cider was sold from the farm at £2 a hogshead and some went to Lord Methuen's troops in Wiltshire where it was greatly appreciated. Cider-making equipment is still to be found in the buildings. Wheat was grown and sold.

At Christmas 1893 there were two weddings. Florence Bailey married a yeoman's son, Thomas Barrington of Tiverton, a surveyor, and Jane, the youngest of the family, married Edward Corner, a merchant and the son of William Corner of Wellington School. The following September Stephen Bailey died and was buried in Nynehead churchyard, his cousin T.C. Tanner, vicar of Burlescombe, taking the service. His son, James, took over the farm and after he died in 1909, aged 42, Mrs James Bailey farmed Hornshay until giving up the tenancy in 1914.

Hornshay from 1914

Mr Edward Richards came to Hornshay on Michaelmas Day 1914, bringing his stockman, William Lake, and regularly employing up to eight men and a boy, some of whom may have come with him from Ide near Exeter. Presumably they occupied the five cottages mentioned on the tenancy agreement. It is recorded in January 1921 that Mr Richards had put in a new turbine at the river and had installed an electric system. It was mutually agreed that the turbine should be taken off at valuation. About this time, Mrs Richards was entertaining paying guests and electric light was one of the advantages she advertised. Other attractions for guests were a hot bath (1s.), a river boat, tennis, a car garage, 300 acres (mostly park), and cream, honey and butter made on the farm, all at 7s. per day.

Former residents of Nynehead, Mrs Gwen Fletcher and Mrs Ash, remembered that there was a long table in the dining-room with a copper bowl packed with flowers and the guests always had raspberries for tea. There was also a winter guest who, with his wife, came for some of the winter because of his health. In a letter to the Darbys, the owners at the time of writing, his granddaughter recalled how she and her younger brother thought it paradise riding on the cart-horses bringing in the harvest, and going for walks with Mr Richards 'up over', as he used to say. As a rule a student was in residence, one of them being from 'ATH Agriculture College near Brussels'. A letter from Hornshay in 1936 stated that they could meet a train and the cost. Another letter from a Ted Lethbridge in 1980 mentioned that one of his earliest recollections was seeing S. Kidner breaking in mules in the rickyard at Hornshay.

Mr Richards was very active in the National Farmers' Union (NFU) in Somerset right up to 1942, the year he died. He was also involved with the Young Farmers' Clubs and had been elected to represent the county branch of the NFU in 1934 at a meeting to consider the formation of a Somerset Federation of YFCs. Away from farming he had a good voice and would sing when invited on social occasions.

The Farming Year in 1937

Mr Richards' desk diaries have survived from 1937. These are carefully written up in pencil for all days on which work was done – i.e. not Sundays or bank holidays, although someone must have attended to the stock. For example:

January 1937
1st Friday dull and rain
Three men threshing Barley in yard

Mr Steve Ling's Simmental cattle at Heywood Farm.

Below: *William Lake with Devon cattle by the River Tone, just downstream of the canal aqueduct, in the 1920s. Poole can be seen in the background, top right.*

Above: *Mr Clifford Bryant of Ash Farm taking his cows down the lane for milking.*

Right: *The 'Jews' herd of Holstein Friesian cattle at Hornshay Farm and the last surviving apple trees, 2003.*

One man feeding sheep and helping threshing
One man one boy feeding and cleaning cattle in yard
One man sick
Four extra men threshing

On the pages headed 'Memoranda' are listed the sales and purchases: 'January 5th Wellington Market 18 hogs 2 ewes, January 6th 10 pigs to Taunton Institution.'

The work done each day is listed in the same way, giving a good picture of how hard farm work was at that time. A full day was apparently worked on Saturday to allow for no work on Sunday beyond milking and feeding – no entry was ever made for Sunday. Each day he recorded one man with one horse feeding store cattle outside and hauling cabbage (Mr Richards used the word 'halling'); one man with one horse hauling cabbage and winnowing barley; one man feeding and hurdling sheep; and one man and one boy feeding and cleaning cattle in the yard. On one day four of the men helped with hare coursing after their usual jobs. They went on winnowing barley for a couple of weeks which then had to go to Wellington station, hauled by one man and two horses on two days in January and two more days in February. When the cabbage was finished it was replaced by swedes.

Other jobs in winter were pruning apple trees and tying wood, as well as cleaning swedes. One day in January one man and two horses went chain harrowing at Chipley. Dust (from the threshing-machine) had to be taken up to the arable field to cover the mangolds. All of these jobs continued, with a visit from the vet on a couple of days to attend to the store cattle and dock the lambs' tails. Manure was hauled up to the arable field making one heap, and chain harrowing was done in Lower Lears. The same work was carried on all through March, with no work on Good Friday or Easter Monday. Ploughing started on 30 March with one man and two horses for the first few days and then two men and two horses all though April and May and the first week of June.

From 23 April the outside stores were no longer fed, freeing the tractor driver who had been spring harrowing for several days after feeding these

Champion cattle bred in Nynehead, at the Bath and West Show when it took place at Hillcommon in 1962.

Mr Lewis Sparks with one of the Haywood Farm prize-winning Devon cattle.

animals. The tractor was used for harrowing or cultivating every day until 15 May and on the 18th and the 20th. The horses were harrowing as well in April, one man with two horses and another man with three horses. A third man has one horse to light harrow. There were other things to do such as drilling barley, rolling, sowing fertiliser, hailing and spreading manure from the yard. The weather turned dry and warm at the end of May and beginning of June so the knives were sharpened and two men and four horses were cutting grass, the hay being carried ten days later. Most days crops were weeded and hoed and two hours' overtime was worked on several evenings, this becoming more frequent as the month went on. Several ricks were made and the thatcher came to roof them.

In July the arable work continued, harrowing and rolling the ground with horses for swedes, spreading fertilisers and then sowing the seeds. Other men hoed the cabbages already growing in the same field. They went on hoeing mangolds and potatoes by hand after feeding the sheep and cattle and cleaning the yard each day. They were trimming hedges and did some more haymaking in Lower Lears and Harris's Moor. One man was cutting weed at Chipley for over a week.

At the end of the month the binders were prepared for the harvest, starting with the beans, which took three days to cut and stitch (arranging the sheaves upright to dry out.) On the last day of the month grass was cut by two men and four horses and, as it was a bank holiday, no work was done until 3 August, when knives were sharpened and the resulting hay picked up. That day and the following the sheep were dipped. Other work at this time included weeding potatoes, cleaning sheds, hauling and spreading yard manure, hoeing swedes by hand and horse hoeing.

Cutting wheat started on 6 August and the beans were re-stitched. Cutting and stitching the wheat

Left: *Mr Ian Darby at Hornshay Farm with his dogs, Badger and Rover.*

Right: *The face of modern farming – round bales at East Nynehead.*

Below: *Harvesting maize, another aspect of modern farming with implications for wildlife.*

One of Mr Lewis Sparks' cattle lorries at Heywood Farm. For the photograph Mr Sparks poses with one of the prize-winning Devon Herd.

took two more days and then the beans were hauled and made into a rick. Each time it rained there was re-stitching to do. Overtime was worked on ten evenings in August – eight men and one boy for two hours each night and four hours on the last night. Overtime was also worked in June on 16 evenings between 9 and 28 June. All the men and one boy (sometimes two) spent two or three hours each evening working. The jobs were weeding corn on six evenings, hoeing mangolds on four evenings and working on the hay harvest on six evenings. As before the cattle and sheep were fed each day, the yards cleaned and manure hauled and spread. The weather was dry and warm most days.

In September arable work was resumed with harrowing and chain harrowing with horses and the tractor. Vetches and trifolium were sown. The potatoes were dug and straw left in the cornfields was picked up. The kale was weeded and hedges trimmed. On 17 September two colts were prepared for work and help was given in working them. The next day three men were working the two colts, chain harrowing with two other horses. Ploughing was started on the 15th and went on most days into October by two men and four horses. One man and the tractor went over to Ruggin for three days' cultivating and picking up stubble.

In October they started picking up apples, the threshing-machine came for four days to do the barley and mangolds were hauled. The last day spent picking up apples was on 2 November. Wheat was sown on 6 November and on four further days. The sheep were hurdled in December and the work became similar to that in January. The yearly cycle then began again.

Hornshay Farm, 1967–2003

In 1967 Hornshay Farm was sold by the Bolnore Estates to Ian and Joy Darby from Jews Farm, Wiveliscombe. It is run at the time of writing by their son, Robin, and his wife, Carole. It has traditionally

been a mixed farm with a dairy herd, sheep flock, and perhaps some beef cattle. Wheat, barley and potatoes were grown. The 'Jews' herd of Holstein Friesians has expanded from 60 cows in 1967 to 160 in 2003. This number has been static since 1984 because of the introduction of quotas. In addition, 100 followers are kept.

As a result of a series of dry summers, notably 1989 and 1990, the maize acreage has been expanded. First grown at Hornshay in 1975, it now accounts for more than half the winter diet. The acreage was increased in the early 1990s when improved varieties and high-output forage harvesters became available. To allow for this expansion, the acreage of the cereals has been much reduced, potatoes are no longer grown and sheep are kept only in the winter months to graze off surplus grass.

In 1981 a new herringbone milking-parlour was built beside the existing Atcost barns which were converted into cubicles for the milking herd. This parlour was replaced again by a larger herringbone parlour in 1999. The cropping at the time of writing is only 20 acres of wheat. In addition 100 acres of maize are grown and made into silage for the milking cows. The number of men employed has steadily dropped from five men and casual workers in 1967, to help with potatoes etc., to the normal staffing level of just two men.

By direction of Fenchurch Nominees Ltd.

With Vacant Possession at 25th March, 1967   Freehold

SOMERSET
IN THE FAMOUS VALE OF TAUNTON DEANE
About 6 miles from the County Town of Taunton and 1½ miles from Wellington.

HIGHLY IMPORTANT SALE OF ONE OF THE FINEST

AGRICULTURAL PROPERTIES
in the West of England, known as

"Hornshay Farm"
with charming well appointed PERIOD RESIDENCE, extensive and well equipped FARM BUILDINGS, 4 MODERN POST-WAR COTTAGES and extremely rich VALE LANDS intersected by the River Tone, extending to about

382 Acres
also

THE VALUABLE BLOCK OF

RIVERSIDE ACCOMMODATION LANDS
AT RUNNINGTON

extending to about

42 Acres
which will be SOLD BY AUCTION IN 2 LOTS, (unless previously sold) at the

WYNDHAM HALL, CASTLE GREEN, TAUNTON

on Tuesday, 28th February, 1967
at 3 p.m.

Chartered Auctioneers	*Solicitors:*
Messrs. W. R. J. GREENSLADE & CO.	Messrs. BISCHOFF & CO.
2 and 13 Hammet Street	City Wall House
Taunton	79-83 Chiswell Street
Telephone: 7131/4 lines	London E.C.1
	Telephone: Metropolitan 9111

The cover of the catalogue for the sale of Hornshay Farm by Bolnore Estates in 1967.

The aqueduct carrying the canal over the coach road to Nynehead Court, early 1900s. The former avenue of trees can be seen through the arch.

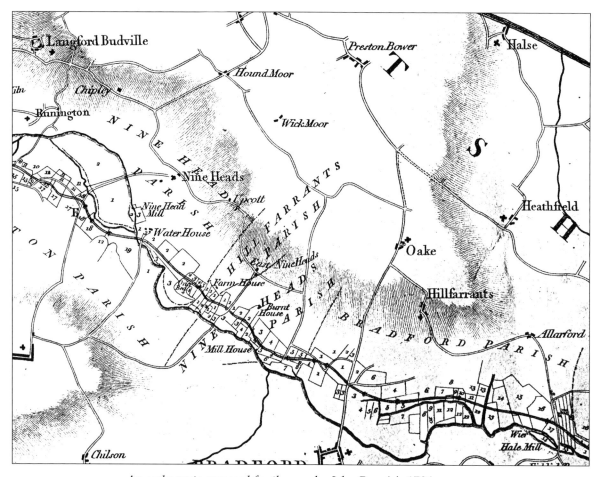

An early route proposed for the canal – John Rennie's 1794 survey.

Chapter Twelve

TRANSPORT, TRAVEL & TRADE IN THE PARISH

The earliest inhabitants of the land evolved ridge-ways and tracks, generally on high ground, but when necessary developed ingenious solutions to cross low-lying wet areas, such as the famous 'Sweet Track', a timber causeway on the Somerset Levels. It is possible that similar tracks crossed the Tone Valley near Nynehead, as the pre-Roman occupiers of the area must have had tracks and paths for communication.

Road building was a priority for the Romans, to serve the military and to facilitate commerce, through long straight stretches of carriageway directly crossing the contours rather than following them. The main route to this area was the Fosse Way, the southern part of which connected Bath with Ilchester, with a further connection to Exeter, while Roman roads in Western Somerset must have existed to serve the forts such as that at Wiveliscombe. An earlier network of roads was probably used and improved following the higher ground above the Tone flood plain.

After the Romans withdrew, their elaborately constructed system fell into decline. During the next 600 years or so the Saxon and Norse invasions leading up to the time of the Norman Conquest changed the culture and needs of society. There was much international trade from the various ports around the country fed by navigable rivers, but inland increased agriculture created a network of new roads and tracks to connect outlying farms and villages with the nearest town, market and fair.

The completed canal west from the Nynehead lift as it might have looked from the air.

Movement of goods, largely agricultural, became localised and the significance of local roads increased.

From the Conquest onwards historical records begin to improve and in medieval times it is almost certain that a network of roads crossed the area and that there was in existence a major route approximating to the present A38. Roads and tracks were of a very low standard with little attention paid to construction methods; regular use by packhorses and heavy carts made them almost impassable in wet weather. Maintenance was the responsibility of the manorial courts through which the roads passed and in accordance with common law local labour was used to repair the 'rights of passage'.

Increased usage and a breakdown of the manorial system in the sixteenth century made maintenance more difficult. A new tenant recently freed from his traditional manorial duties would not wish to carry out additional work mending roads so, to ease the problem, an Act of Parliament 'for the mending of highways' was passed in 1555. Each parish was to

The aqueduct carrying the Grand Western Canal over the River Tone. The water was carried by an iron channel which is visible under the arch.

elect a 'Surveyor of Highways' to enforce the new law and each man was required to work for four, later six, days per year on the parish roads. The surveyor's position was unpopular and priorities were often affected by personal relationships. Unskilled and reluctant workers usually carried out the repairs under the supervision of the surveyor.

The system worked after a fashion but the situation slowly worsened and in 1691 the appointment of surveyors was taken out of the hands of parishioners and made at the Quarter Sessions. Further regulation took place. Some Quarter Sessions increased tolls for loads over a ton and in 1662 the Highways Act limited the number of horses that could be used to carry a single load to seven and required that all carts should have wheels not less than four inches wide at the rim. From 1663 the new turnpike system had a slow start but increased rapidly throughout the eighteenth century, reducing travelling times significantly as the century progressed.

The eighteenth century also brought with it great changes in the country's social structure. A healthy economic climate, developments in ironworking and increases in demand for manufactured articles brought an unprecedented expansion of industry. Initially manufacturing was done in small workshops all over the country producing items for domestic consumption. As demand increased a factory system was established and people began moving into the towns. Coal became an important commodity for domestic heating in newly built accommodation for factory workers and to power the new steam engines driving the factories, but its transportation from mine to consumer along the existing road system was expensive and tedious. Most of the coal for this area came by boat from South Wales to Bridgwater, where it was transhipped into barges for carriage up the Tone

The Tone aqueduct before the vegetation was removed by Canal Trust volunteers.

Navigation to Ham, east of Taunton. Final distribution was by cart or packhorse.

THE GRAND WESTERN CANAL

In 1776 the Duke of Bridgewater opened a canal from his mines in Worsley to Manchester, marking the beginning of the canal age. Eight years before the opening a group of Taunton businessmen, also seeing the advantages of waterways, proposed a canal linking the Bristol and English Channels to provide an alternative to the hazardous voyage around Land's End and attract the lucrative coal trade between South Wales and South West England. The route proposed included a link from the River Exe to Taunton via Wellington, thence via the Tone Navigation and another new canal to Uphill at the mouth of the River Axe near Weston-super-Mare. It would have passed through Nynehead.

The scheme was shelved and others proposed and dropped, until in 1794 a route surveyed by John Rennie was accepted which passed through Nynehead, crossing the Tone just to the west of Hornshay Bridge. Parliamentary approval was obtained in 1796 but the uncertainties created by the looming war with France prevented the scheme from commencing. In 1808 the near completion of the Kennet and Avon Canal prompted a resurrection of the scheme, as it would provide part of an inland waterway between Exeter and London, avoiding French privateers in the English Channel. Work commenced on the section between Holcombe Rogus and Tiverton to take advantage of the lime trade between the Whipcott quarries and the kilns at Tiverton. Lime had become an important land improver and it was hoped that this trade would help finance the remainder of the route. Thus the Grand Western Canal was born. Unfortunately, because of major engineering problems brought about by changing the proposed water-level, the company ran out of money and construction stopped in 1815. Only the 11 miles between Lowdwells Lock near the Devon/Somerset border

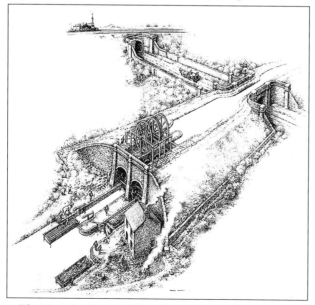

The Nynehead canal lift as it might have looked from the air in the 1840s.

Wharf Cottage and the canal as they might have looked in the 1840s. It was then known as Horsey's Wharf.

and Tiverton were completed and trade turned out to be not as brisk as had been hoped.

In 1827 the Bridgwater and Taunton Canal was opened, and completion of the 13-mile link from Lowdwells Lock to Taunton again seemed financially viable, but there were still problems. Both the Devon and the Bridgwater and Taunton sections had been built as broad canals to take barges, but the 262ft change in level between Taunton and Lowdwells would have required about 30 locks, making construction expensive and water consumption prohibitive. The reservoirs planned for Rennie's scheme to supply water for the locks had not been built, as springs at Lowdwells provided an adequate water-supply for the summit section.

In 1829, James Green, an engineer of some note in the South West, proposed an alternative scheme – a tub-boat canal. Tub boats were designed to carry five to eight tons of cargo and up to eight boats in line could easily be towed by one horse, giving a total cargo capacity equivalent to the barges on the Bridgwater and Taunton Canal. Their small size enabled the canal dimensions to be minimised, reducing construction costs and water consumption. This also had advantages when the route had to pass through the areas of rough terrain and irregular water-supply as found at the western end of the proposed link. Used with inclined planes or canal lifts, as alternatives to locks, the tub-boat canal was an ideal solution, just about within the engineering capabilities of the day. Green's proposals were accepted and a survey conducted producing a route similar to Rennie's, but with some deviations. The final design included one inclined plane, which employed proven technology, and seven canal lifts. These were new and experimental, never having been used for more than four years in a commercial operation. It was a brave venture.

Green divided his tub-boat section into eight lots for contracting purposes and proposed the use of cast iron for the numerous bridges and aqueducts along the route. Nynehead included lots four and five, with much of lot five across Edward Sanford's land. They included a major river crossing, three road crossings, culverts, accommodation bridges to connect fields broken by the line and two new canal lifts, one at Trefusis (38$\frac{1}{2}$ft) and one at Nynehead (24ft). The contracts for the Nynehead lots were awarded to Messrs Houghton & Co., a company experienced in canal building, but problems were already beginning to emerge.

The early canals followed contours as much as possible, reducing the number of embankments and cuttings but making them tortuous and longer than necessary. As business increased and time spent in transit became more important, engineers learnt how to straighten a line by arranging for the spoil from a cutting to match in volume that required to build an embankment, a method known as 'cut and fill'. They also learnt how to build impressive aqueducts and bridges across rivers and roads, sometimes in an ornamental style to satisfy the whims of a local landowner. These lessons were to be applied on Mr Sanford's land.

Work started in 1831 but a delay occurred at Nynehead due the 'difficulties of arranging the line with landowners', work here not getting under way until 1833. Edward Sanford was objecting to the proposed route (along with other landowners) and the lift sites, as it was stated that 'a large Embankment in Ninehead Park and a proportionate quantity of deep cutting, with 3 lifts form the principle obstacles to be surmounted.' James Green met the Sanford agent Charles Bailey to discuss a change of line. The logical route would have been to cross the flood plain from near the Tone aqueduct to Stedhams Covert where the lift could have been built into the hillside, so following Rennie's line of 1794. Earthworks would have been considerably reduced but the canal would have crossed the parkland, against Mr Sanford's wishes.

While negotiations were taking place with Mr Sanford, construction started along other sections of

A conjectural interpretation of a lift on the Grand Western Canal.

117

The old Girdle Bridge over the former canal at Stedhams Covert, before the cutting was filled with Wellington's rubbish. The canal was a popular place for walks.

the canal. One can only wonder what effect the arrival of several hundred navvies had on the local community. There would have been a requirement for bricklayers, stonemasons, blacksmiths and labourers to move earth. The skilled artisans reputedly moved around the country in gangs as work demanded and set up camps at convenient points along the line. Life was tough, with drunkenness and brawling endemic. The navvies were shunned by polite society and classed as itinerants, their presence remaining largely unrecorded. Labourers were recruited locally as much as possible, which must have created friction with local landowners as much of the labour would have come off the land. The canal was dug by hand using pick and shovel, the earth being moved with the assistance of wheelbarrows and horse-drawn tubs running on cast-iron plate rails. Local people would have watched progress, marvelling at the undertaking while complaining about the inconveniences it caused. Letters to the *Taunton Courier* reflect these different attitudes:

The bill... for uniting the two canals, and destroying the navigation of the Tone appears to me to be an iniquitous and monopolising measure... The Grand Western Canal will never be used for conveying corn to Taunton; the farmers will always prefer sending their produce direct to market; and avail themselves of the great advantage of loading back with coals.

The carting to and from the Canal is an insurmountable objection to the Canal being used for this purpose.

(26 February 1832).

These fellows [coal-cart drivers] on the Wellington Road, are perfectly remorseless, and defy the law, or rather confide in the supineness of those who ought to enforce it... The inconvenience, alarm and positive danger attending this shameful carelessness, to persons in carriages may be easily imagined. The opening of the canal may ere long put an end to this nuisance; but in the mean time what frightful mischiefs may intervene unless some proper examples be made of the offenders!

(3 September 1836)

By the summer of 1835 the canal was open as far as Wellington and, after difficulties with the inclined plane at Wellisford, achieving through-passage to Tiverton in June 1838. Problems continued until about 1841 due to bad management and poor operation of the innovative canal lifts. Captain Twisden, an officer of the company since 1815, recorded problems arising between 1836 and 1840, including four breakages at Trefusis and one at Nynehead. Inexpert lift keepers were not controlling the descent of the caissons containing the boats, allowing them to crash into the bottom of the lift chamber. William Horsey, an eminent Wellington tradesman who occupied Horsey's Wharf, Nynehead (later known as Wharf Cottage), complained in August 1838 about the resultant loss of trade:

I think it right you should be immediately informed an accident occurred at the Trefusis Lift which stops the passing on the canal and will do so until it is repaired. The shaft and chain are broken and both Cradles Shattered – It is hardly necessary for me to say how very unfortunately this happens at the precise juncture of time when we are laying in our stock [presumably coal], for the winter. I have not a weeks consumption on hand and Mr Trude but little more.

In October 1840, newly employed lift keepers were instructed to meet at White Ball to receive training, and other efforts were made to improve the situation, for example:

John Burridge (Nynehead Lift) being absent from his Lift half a Day when more than 40 Boats waited to pass – generally an attentive Man – to pay a Fine of one Weeks Wages of £0 16 6 only, in Consequence of his previous good Character – to attend the next Meeting (Canal Company, Minutes, 8 July 1841).

There is evidence that, initially, trade along the canal was quite good, the majority of cargo being coal for domestic use and culm and limestone for the limekilns. Cargoes landed at parish wharves in August 1842 were as shown on p120.

The impressive wall of the Nynehead lift chamber.

Volunteers working at the Nynehead lift, 1999.

Left: *An archaeological investigation of the canal by Wharf Cottage. The road from Nynehead was carried over the canal by a bridge which was demolished in about 1870.*

The restored stretch in water, April 1998.

Restoring the canal – dredging by the Nynehead lift in April 1998.

Goods	Horsey's Wharf		East Nynehead		Trefusis	
	From	Tons–cwt	From	Tons–cwt	From	Tons–cwt
Coal	Taunton	649-0	Taunton	83-10	Taunton	60-0
Timber	Taunton	0-10				
Sugar	Taunton	1-10				
Bales	Taunton	0-5				
Salt	Taunton	7-0				
Rails	Taunton	13-0				
Deals	Taunton	11-15	Taunton	4-0	Taunton	4-0
Bath Stone	Taunton	17-10				
Building stone	Whipcott	31-10			Whipcott	26-0
Casks	Taunton	0-5				
Slates	Taunton	2-10				
Lime Stone	Whipcott	14-0				
Lime			Tone Dale	7-0		

The wharf at East Nynehead was on the west side of Ash Lane where an aqueduct crossed it below Clavengers. Horsey's Wharf was purpose-built on land purchased from Revd Jarrett, vicar of Wellington. Charles Fox was the first owner after the purchase and William Horsey occupied the site. The massive foundations and vaulted ceilings indicate that the original building was purely a warehouse and a spur from the canal was cut into the site for transhipping goods for local distribution. The Tithe Map shows an extensive range of buildings. Mr Sanford became the owner in 1846 and Robert Peach, a drainage-pipe maker, later occupied the site, and it was probably during this period that it was converted from a warehouse to a residence. An estate map of the Poole brickworks dated 1866 shows the wharf and buildings still intact but the canal was closed in 1867 and the 1886 Ordnance Survey map shows that the adjacent canal and spur had been filled in and many of the buildings removed. Peach later moved to Wellington and started his own brickworks. Bricks bearing his name have been found when old buildings have been demolished. Dan Jordan and his descendants lived there from about 1875, the ownership later passing to the Alderman family when an Alderman married a Jordan daughter.

The Canal Company provided accommodation for the lift keepers. Lift Cottage at Trefusis is older than the canal and would have been acquired and utilised when the land for building the canal was purchased. The accommodation at Nynehead was purpose-built by the company and the Wawman family, whose name predominates in the Census records of the cottage during the life of the canal and who had long associations with the waterway. Information kindly provided by Mr Keith Wawman, a direct descendant of William and Sarah Wawman of the Nynehead lift-keeper's cottage, shows that two brothers, William and Thomas Wawman, moved from Northamptonshire to Devon and were described as yeoman farmers and canal contractors. William Wawman of the lift-keeper's cottage was the son of Thomas Wawman and was probably employed at the Trefusis lift before moving to Nynehead.

William and Sarah Wawman eventually moved to Bristol as warehouse owners and a photograph of their golden wedding anniversary in 1888 exists in New Zealand. Evidence suggests that the cottage was built by 1839 and demolished about 1900. It was certainly occupied from c.1842 to 1881 and probably occupied before and after those dates.

The Coming of the Railway

It is possible that the canal, efficiently managed and well maintained as it later was, could have produced more dividends for the shareholders than it did if it had not been for the advent of the railway. The appointment of H.J. Smith as manager of the canal had led by 1846 to a reduction in expenditure and an increase in trade, but the canal's days were numbered.

In 1841 work was well under way on the Bristol and Exeter Railway for which I.K. Brunel was the engineer, assisted by William Gravatt. The line of the new railway passed through Sanford land at Nynehead and construction materials were already being ordered in 1836 for this section. Between 1836 and 1843 six million bricks were supplied to the railway company by W.D.

The Nynehead canal aqueduct and, through the arch, Brunel's bridge carrying the railway over the coach road, as seen c.1960.

Steam locomotives are still seen from time to time on the railway through Nynehead. 5029 Nunney Castle and 5081 Earl Bathurst hauling a 'special' at Harris's Moor on 3 May 2003.

Left: *Jack Reed, the level-crossing keeper at the Bradford level crossing in April 1947 with his cousin Marion and nephew Philip. In 1967 the barriers were electrified, prior to which the gates remained closed between 10p.m. and 7a.m. (except in an emergency). This meant that one road to Nynehead was unavailable for part of each day, requiring a considerable detour.*

Brunel's broad-gauge railway and the Grand Western Canal meet at Trefusis (an interpretation by Simon Bowditch).

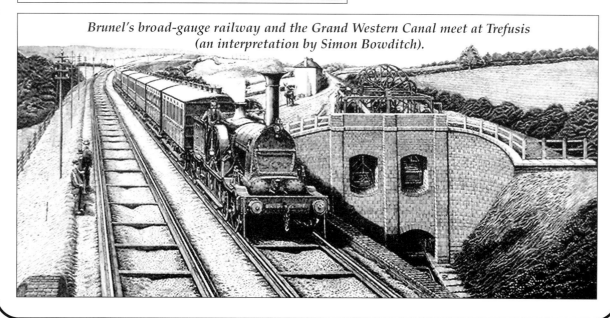

Horsey, mostly for the White Ball Tunnel, but also for other structures along the route. On 1 May 1843 the first train called at Wellington on its way to Beambridge where passengers were transported by road round the still uncompleted tunnel at White Ball and thence to Exeter, again by rail. The line through to Exeter was opened on 1 May 1844, heralding the beginning of the end of the canal.

The link between London and Exeter was completed in a remarkable 12 years from conception to completion, using the same construction methods as employed on the canal. Once again the arrival of navvies with their riotous way of life would have upset Nynehead's rural tranquillity. Brunel's drive to complete the railway at the lowest possible cost and in the shortest possible time while attending to the utmost detail is illustrated in a letter to Edward Sanford dated 11 January 1836:

When I had the pleasure of seeing you at Ninehead Court on the subject of the Bristol & Exeter Railway, you expressed a very natural anxiety to know the manner in which it was proposed to construct that part of the railway which passes through your property, more particularly where the line crossed the private road to your house, and the period during which it was likely that part of the work would be expected.

In reply to these inquiries I should propose on the part of the Company:

1st. That the line of railway should not be varied from that shewn in the Parliamentary plan more than 10 yards. It is necessary to reserve some small power of deviation to cover any accidental inaccuracy in the survey.

2ndly. That the bridge over the private road to Ninehead Court shall be a Stone bridge of the same style of architecture as the existing Canal bridge, but superior in every respect of proportions, materials, and workmanship. – That it shall be substantial and well built, and that it shall if desired include a lodge in the abutments or wing walls, and the design be subject to your approval.

That dwarf walls shall be built on each side of the road between the two bridges, the banks of the railway planted, and such other arrangements of a similar nature adopted as you may suggest to render the space between the two bridges and the embankment of the railway at that part, as little objectionable in appearance as the case will admit of.

3rdly. That the period of execution shall be limited – That the bridge and work immediately connected with it should be commenced in the month of April following the passing of the Act, and completed by the end of the Month of July of the same year.

These arrangements will I think secure you from the annoyance which you might otherwise fear, and I can safely undertake on the part of the Company that they shall be strictly attended to.

Further conflict between canal and railway companies occurred at Trefusis where the railway had to cross the waterway. Brunel, with his characteristic opportunism and lack of regard for things insignificant to him, wanted to build the railway over the lift. The canal company naturally objected and suggested the railway company either pay to move the lift or alter their proposed line, threatening to take out an injunction if a satisfactory solution was not found. The railway was finally built crossing the canal by a brick bridge just below the lift. British Rail later filled in the bridge when the curvature of the track was altered for high-speed trains in the 1950s.

So the railway arrived and brought with it the demise of the canal as trade transferred from water to rail. The canal struggled on for a few years until leased to the Bristol and Exeter Company in 1853. Trade continued to fall until maintenance costs exceeded income. An Act of Parliament was obtained in 1864 to sell the canal to the railway company for £30,000. The Act gave the railway power to abandon the Somerset section and required it to sell the land and works not required for railway purposes within three years, offering it initially to those with land adjoining the canal. Compensation also had to be made in respect of roads crossed by the canal as legally the pre-emption included all the machinery, masonry and bridges etc. Robert Dymond & Sons, Surveyors of Exeter, were engaged to deal with the transactions. All landowners were contacted and requested to claim or abandon the right of pre-emption. Several claimed and some declined the right but most abstained from replying, hoping that the land would eventually pass to them gratuitously. The problems were eventually resolved and the company agreed to sell the land less the machinery and masonry, which it reserved the right to sell itself. However, particular reference was given to Mr Sanford who claimed the right of pre-emption but wanted it to be selective and the land sold at a nominal price, claiming that the canal company had never paid him the full cost of the land he originally sold to them. He also wanted to keep the two aqueducts over the River Tone and carriageway intact. Eventually an agreement was reached whereby Mr Sanford purchased the land, retaining the aqueducts and the lift-keeper's cottage, the company to dispose of the remaining machinery and masonry.

However, the railway company had retained ownership of the bridges and culverts and had probably not maintained them very well, so from 1867 the newly constituted Milverton Highways Board took over the maintenance. Over the next few years the removal of several humpbacked bridges and aqueducts from local roads and footpaths was carried out.

The first local work was the removal of the aqueduct over Ash Lane by Clavengers. The company removed the ironwork and disposed of it, but left the

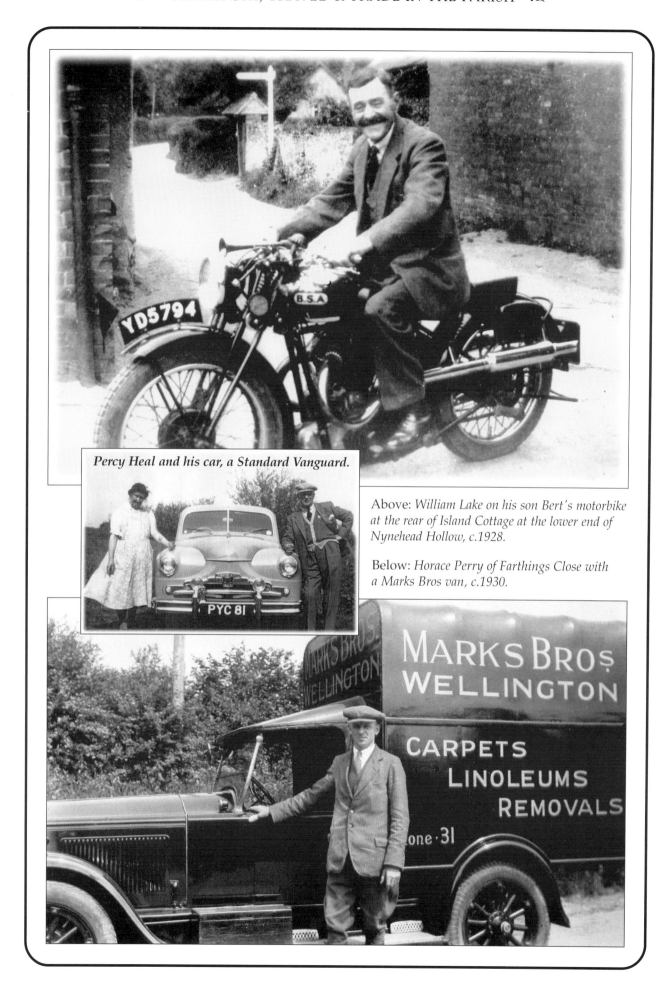

Percy Heal and his car, a Standard Vanguard.

Above: *William Lake on his son Bert's motorbike at the rear of Island Cottage at the lower end of Nynehead Hollow, c.1928.*

Below: *Horace Perry of Farthings Close with a Marks Bros van, c.1930.*

A Commer 8 tonner fitted with custom bodywork. This vehicle was used for stock haulage by Mr Lewis Sparks from 1962 and is seen here at Heywood Farm.

Left: *Commer Cars Ltd of Luton used this photograph of a Sparks' lorry in advertisements for some years. Interestingly, the Sparks' signwriting on the vehicle was progressively airbrushed from the photographs as the years passed.*

An early lorry belonging to Mr Lewis Sparks' haulage business. An Austin 5-ton model from 1948.

road and fences in a bad condition. Eventually it was put right and the road lowered by three feet. Next was the Longforth to Nynehead footpath bridge over the canal cutting by Stedhams Covert. William Bishop, iron founder of Wellington, was commissioned to provide a footbridge with masonry and approaches over the cutting at a cost of £12. This was followed by the removal of one of James Green's unusual cast-iron road bridges over the canal by Wharf Cottage, the road being widened and lowered by about six feet. The bridge by Trefusis Farm is the only remaining example of the original design and is protected as a listed structure.

The second half of the Victorian period heralded great changes in transport. The Bristol and Exeter Railway was absorbed by the Great Western Railway in 1876, Brunel's broad-gauge line succumbing to a mixed gauge and then finally dying in 1892 when a three-day conversion to the standard gauge of 4ft 8$\frac{1}{2}$ins took place. The battle of the gauges nearly brought the GWR to its knees, but from the 1890s improvements took place and within 20 years it was running fast services to the South West including mail and boat trains between London and Plymouth in competition with the London and South Western Railway. The LSWR had the shorter route and attempted to lure rich Americans from the Atlantic steamers, but the GWR had the mail service. Speed was of the essence and both companies tried to prove themselves to be the best. On 9 May 1904 the 'City of Truro' reputedly reached a speed of 102.3mph, the first recorded incidence of a steam locomotive exceeding 100mph, while descending the Wellington Bank with a five-coach mail train bound for Paddington. We can only guess at what speed it passed through Nynehead. The recorder was Mr Charles Rous-Martin who would not initially publish the record for fear of alarming the public and upsetting the GWR. Later, the accuracy of the recording instruments was questioned and others suggest that the locomotive could not have stayed on the track at speeds over 80mph because the driving wheels were poorly balanced. However, the record still stands as a tradition in railway circles.

THE COMING OF THE MOTOR VEHICLE

The end of the Victorian era saw the advent of the motor vehicle, although it was available to relatively few people before the First World War. The railway companies must have realised the significance of this new form of transport and the more progressive ones sponsored their own motor passenger services to outlying towns and villages away from the railway. It is likely that these first road motors, or omnibuses as they became known, led to the introduction of 'halts' as stopping places along the line. In 1903 the GWR introduced its rail motor car in the Stroud Valley. Although described as motor cars they were actually powered by small steam engines. It was an attempt to reduce operating costs on lightly used services and rapidly spread throughout the system servicing the new halts located at convenient places along the line. In 1904 the Nynehead Parish Council tried without success to have a rail motor car halt built at the Bradford level crossing.

The First World War brought with it dramatic social changes and advances in technology and manufacturing methods, and after the war the motor car came within the reach of many more people. Several local villagers purchased cars in the 1920s, including the Good family and Mrs Pugh, who owned an Austin 7. By the 1930s most local farmers had cars. Mr Richards from Hornshay had a Lanchester, Mr Luxton from Blockhouse had a Rover and Mr Ash from Upcott had a V8 Ford Pilot. Mr Sparks started his transport business carrying sheep and animals to market, apples to the cider factories and sugar beet to Wellington station. The railway companies ran their daily goods trains, trundling from station to station dropping off and picking up goods, providing a countrywide service for all. Road transport steadily increased. Charabancs and coaches served local outings but railways retained their lucrative holiday passenger traffic throughout the 1930s and up to the Second World War.

As the country slowly recovered from that conflict, rationing finally ceased and the economy improved. Increasing use of motor transport was causing congestion on roads designed for a more tranquil era and the government of the day decided to develop a new road system, at the expense of the railways. Under Dr Beeching's drastic plans for rail rationalisation in 1963 many stations closed, including Wellington. A national motorway grid was planned and the M5 to the South West opened in 1976, but road traffic through the village remains a major topic of conversation, especially the inconvenience of speeding traffic passing through to join the motorway.

For the foreseeable future the motor car will be with us as the main local transport used by Nynehead residents to get to work and services. The oft-talked-about Wellington distributor road would help relieve the village of rush-hour traffic passing through from the north. Proposals for a new station (or 'halt') for Wellington are included in the Local Plan, but without supporting infrastructure to get people to and from the station efficiently, such as the GWR instituted in Edwardian times, it will fail. Reliance on the car causes congestion and pollution problems and does little to enhance the viability of a public transport system. At the time of writing there is talk of reinstating the old Grand Western Canal. Not only could this provide a tourist attraction but also an alternative motor-free route for walkers and cyclists linking Wellington and Nynehead with Taunton and Tiverton.

125

Above: *A charabanc outing. A day-trip to the Wellington Monument in the mid-1920s, including Herbert and Margaret Williams of The Bush, East Nynehead (5th from left standing and 7th from left sitting).*

Below: *Gillian Sparks and Father Christmas.*

Gerald and Brian Perry in fancy dress at Nynehead Court, c.1936/7.

Chapter Thirteen

RECREATION & CELEBRATIONS

At the Bishop's visitation in 1594 it was alleged that the vicar of Nynehead, Anthony Middleton, indulged in playing 'common table' and other unlawful games, especially on the Sabbath. This was probably the earliest reference to games and pastimes in Nynehead but we do know that rural communities had traditionally engaged in a wide range of recreational activities. In the Elizabethan age church services were followed by all sorts of activities – dancing, sports, bull baiting, quoits, bowling, shooting at butts, cudgel playing, tennis playing and many others. In which of these the inhabitants of Nynehead, and the vicar in particular, indulged and where are not known but by the end of the sixteenth century the attitude towards such activities was beginning to change. In 1594 and 1596 decrees at Quarter Sessions in Somerset flatly prohibited church ales, reflecting similar action in other counties such as Devon where Sunday plays and May games were abolished. How this applied specifically to Nynehead is unknown but it is interesting that the leading advocate of abolishing such 'licentious' events was Sir John Popham of Wellington. This set the trend for the next century and the Puritan attack on such public activities.

The Restoration of the monarchy in 1660 brought relaxation and a revival of village events. The Nynehead churchwardens' accounts show that the bell-ringers received special payments for performing on certain secular occasions. In 1674 they were paid 11s. for ringing on 5 November, 23 April (St George's Day) and 29 May (Oak Apple Day), when no doubt various activities took place. During the eighteenth century the normal pattern of village recreation must have continued. While the Sanfords and other well-off residents were able to go further afield, for most people this meant doing things within the village or at most in the neighbouring towns and villages. However, from 1800 this began to change, particularly due to improvements to transport.

Nynehead Court was the centre of many activities, for which the Sanfords often paid. In April 1802 Mr Sanford bought £10 of fireworks from Mackland of Southwark, Artist in Fireworks to the Royal Family, but we do not know if this was for an event in the village or in London. At this time singers visited the Court each Christmas, being paid a guinea (£1.05) in 1811 and half a guinea two years later. The accounts do not say who the singers were but it is likely that they welcomed the payment in the middle of winter when work was much harder to find. Some very fortunate people had the opportunity to indulge in new activities. On 25 October 1814 Charles and John Bailey were given a ticket (£1.6s.) for admission to 'the Cathedral and Balloon' at Exeter.

The coming of peace after the Napoleonic Wars gave rise to village celebrations in 1814 and Mr Sanford donated £6.3s.11d. towards the cost. In the following year the parkland at the Court was the venue for the celebration of the 21st birthday of Edward Sanford. The park was frequently used for such events – for example the visit of the Duke of Cambridge in 1809 when, according to newspaper accounts, all and sundry seem to have been invited. The birthday celebrations were recorded in the *Taunton Courier* and the estate accounts. Ringers from Taunton, Wellington and Burlescombe received £4 between them, while musicians were paid a total of £2. Beer at 'the farm' (presumably Hornshay) cost £2.16s., while a bullock was roasted on the lawn – 'by estimation 28 score @ 13/ per score £18 4s.' Does this mean that there were at least 560 people present? The opportunity to make the most of the event was not missed as the hide and tallow from the bullock were sold for £2.10s.

The coming of the railway radically broadened the leisure opportunities available to the ordinary villagers, assuming of course that they had the money and the time, which was not often the case. However, it was the beginning of village outings for which the train was the ideal form of transport, even if in Nynehead's case it meant a two-mile walk to the station. In the 1850s, only a few years after the railway arrived in Wellington, Edward Sanford paid for the schoolchildren and his workers to go by train for a day at the seaside.

Other groups also took advantage of the railway. The late-nineteenth century saw the spread of the temperance movement to such an extent that the *Wellington Weekly News* ran a column headed 'Temperance Notes', with brief reports about what was happening nationally and closer to home.

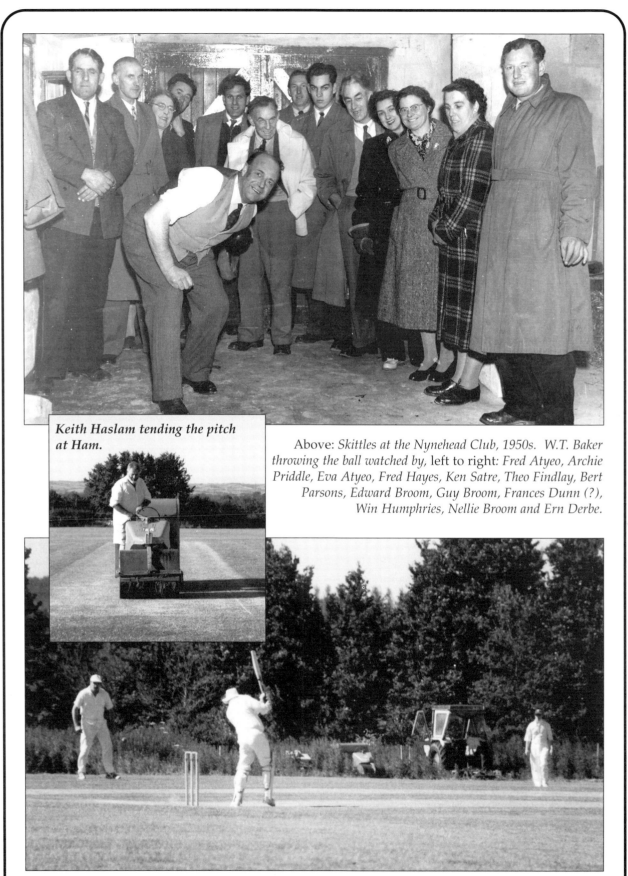

Keith Haslam tending the pitch at Ham.

Above: *Skittles at the Nynehead Club, 1950s. W.T. Baker throwing the ball watched by,* **left to right:** *Fred Atyeo, Archie Priddle, Eva Atyeo, Fred Hayes, Ken Satre, Theo Findlay, Bert Parsons, Edward Broom, Guy Broom, Frances Dunn (?), Win Humphries, Nellie Broom and Ern Derbe.*

Cricket at Nynehead CC's home ground at Ham, just to the south of the parish. Cricket started here 30 years after it ceased on the ground at Nynehead Court.

The Nynehead cricket team, 1950s. Pictured are: Sid Jones (Umpire) with, left to right, back row:
D. Fudge, R. Rowe, Frank Hayman, Alf Hayman, Alan Scholney;
middle row: *Ken Hawkins, Bert Hodge (Secretary), Mrs Tucker (scorer ?), Brian Chaplin, Maurice Quick;*
front row: *Stan Broom, Eddie Darch, Darby Ash.*

The Nynehead 'Reds and Blues' football team, 1927/28. Left to right, back row: ? Mortimer, Revd Catlow,
Ern Lake, Jim Lake, Fred Pulman, ?, ?, ? Parr, Guy Broom, Bill Gollop, Ben Hodge; middle row: Bert Hodge,
Alf Jenkins, Stan Jenkins, Ivor Palmer, ? Jackson, ? Jones, ? Hawkins; front row: Fred Gollop, Francis Jenkins.

Nynehead did not escape, with a public meeting being held in the schoolroom in October 1889 to set up a local group. However, it should not be assumed that temperance meetings were dull affairs limited to the promotion of the virtues of abstinence. The Nynehead Temperance Society, like other village organisations, was a place where local people could meet and enjoy themselves and was certainly popular for a time. Thus on one summer day 33 members went on their annual outing to Weston-super-Mare, catching the 9.35a.m. train from Wellington and enjoying a picnic lunch in glorious weather on the beach by the pier. They returned home on the last train. They also enjoyed themselves in the village. In the schoolroom during May 1891 Mr W.S. Price 'showed a capital series of pictures through his magic lantern, which gave general delight' and the entertainment included a dialogue, 'How would you manage him?', by Misses F. Stone and E. Jenkins and Messrs W. Griffin, J. Merry, W. Wood and S. Jones.

By the end of the nineteenth century, while Nynehead residents were going further afield, people were coming to the Wellington area as tourists. In August 1891 Toser & Gregory exhorted them to inspect at their shop in South Street the stock of photographic views of the town and its neighbourhood, including the church, the avenue and the bridge at Nynehead.

List of Matches.

Date.	Opponents.	Where Played.	Result.
June 1 ...	Wilton	Away	*Won.*
„ 15 ...	Rockwell Green ...	Away	
„ 22 ...	Bishop's Lydeard ...	Away	
„ 29 ...	Trinity, Taunton ...	Away	
July 6 ...	P.A.S.L. Infantry ...	Away	
„ 20 ...	Bishop's Lydeard ...	Home	
„ 24 ...	County School Wellington	Home	
„ 27 ...	Cotford	Away	
Aug. 3 ...	Milverton	Away	
„ 10 ...	P.A.S.L. Infantry ..	Home	
„ 17 ...	Wilton	Home	
„ 24 ...	Trinity, Taunton ...	Home	
„ 31 ...	Rockwell Green ...	Home	
Sept. 7 ...	Milverton	Home	

The latter part of the century also saw the widespread growth of sports clubs in the area, notably cricket and football, both of which were played in Nynehead on a seven-acre field to the north-west of the Court, given by William Sanford. A cricket club was established in Nynehead by 1891 which, in 1902, joined forces with the neighbouring village of Langford Budville to form a team. Although initially having mixed fortunes they improved during the summer. On 24 May they lost away to Rockwell Green by an innings and three runs, the team consisting of C.H. Luxton, E. Merry, H. Davies, F. Jenkins, A. Taylor, H. Merry, W. Pike, A. Kidley, W. Braddick, G. Canley (?) and J. Wood. On 21 June they lost away to Wiveliscombe 47–98, but a week later beat Norton Fitzwarren away 61–52 and on 2 August won against Bishops Lydeard away 71–54. On 29 August a keenly fought match at home against Wiveliscombe ended in a draw. The visitors were set 64 to win in 35 minutes but the home team's bowling and fielding were too good and they reached only 31 for 8.

Twenty-five years later the Nynehead football team was sufficiently well established to have its own nickname – the 'Reds and Blues' – and Saturday 19 February 1927 saw a home match against Oake. Although the local paper reported there was little to choose between the teams, Nynehead were victors by five goals to three. Both clubs were thriving and many fund-raising and social events including dances, socials and whist drives were held in the school, the only facility available. Jim Lake can remember having to remove all the desks on a Friday after school and replace them all on Sunday whenever the school was used. Revd Catlow's daughter used to teach the youngsters to dance. In 1953 the cricket club were top of the Westford Cup League – players included K. Hawkins, E. Coram, F. Hayman, D. Fuge, R. Rowe, M. Quick, V. Boobier, K. Hayman, D. Ash and B.W. Chaplin. The ground at the Court was used until 1958, ceasing when Bert Hodge, secretary of the cricket club, died. A Nynehead cricket club restarted in 1990 but now plays on a ground at Ham, just outside the parish. Sadly the village no longer sports a football club.

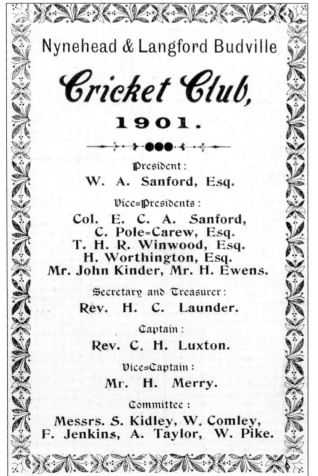

Nynehead & Langford Budville

Cricket Club,

1901.

President:

W. A. Sanford, Esq.

Vice-Presidents:

**Col. E. C. A. Sanford,
C. Pole-Carew, Esq.
T. H. R. Winwood, Esq.
H. Worthington, Esq.
Mr. John Kinder, Mr. H. Ewens.**

Secretary and Treasurer:

Rev. H. C. Launder.

Captain:

Rev. C. H. Luxton.

Vice-Captain:

Mr. H. Merry.

Committee:

**Messrs. S. Kidley, W. Comley,
F. Jenkins, A. Taylor, W. Pike.**

Nynehead's first pantomime in 2003, Up the Beanstalk. Performers include Helen Clarke and Abi Howard as the cow 'Pullover' (because she was a Jersey!).

While traditional sports and games, such as skittles and cricket, are still played, others disappeared many years ago. In September 1889 the Wellington Quoits Club visited Nynehead for a match against the village team, beating the home team by 121 points to 75. Playing for Nynehead were ? Phillips, ? Scott, E. Griffin and ? Smith. Tea and refreshments were provided by the vicar, Revd J.A. Hervey (or more likely by his wife).

Since the late-nineteenth century clubs and societies have been important in village life. The people of Nynehead have always been active, and in 1891 the residents supported a working men's club, a Temperance Society, a Band of Hope, a book club, a ringers guild, a Sunday school and church choir, a cricket team and a football side. The book club was based in the school and subscribed to the national Popular Book Club. Books purchased in 1891 included *A Flat Iron for a Farthing*, *Black Beauty* and *For Faith and Fatherland*.

In 2003 the village is just as busy with at least ten different organisations – the church and Sunday school, the cricket club, the Local History Society,

Victoria Westaway (Actiontrack) and Lydia Grant (work experience) building a willow figure for 'Building Up Steam'.

the Women's Institute, the toddler group/under-fives, the Playing Field Committee, the Friends of Nynehead School, the Amateur Dramatics Group and the Nynehead Memorial Club with a skittle alley. These, together with the Parish Council and the Memorial Hall Committee, keep villagers as busy as they wish to be. Even so, between these dates other organisations have come and gone, such as the British Legion and the croquet club.

Music has always played a part in the life of the village for which the school was a favourite venue as well as the Court and, more recently, the Memorial Hall and Club. A typical concert was held in the school on 13 December 1881 for which admission was 1s. The programme started with a trio (composer not stated) played by the Misses Sanford and ended with a part song 'Night', by Blumenthal, and the National Anthem. In the interval Mr James Ball and his sons gave a performance on handbells. Other performers were Messrs E. and R. Pearce, Miss Pearce, Mrs Kidner and Miss L. Bailey (Hornshay Farm).

THE CHURCH HOUSE

The focus for recreation in the village has changed over the centuries. The 1792 picture of Nynehead Court shows a building to the east of the church that is thought to have been Nynehead's church house. Church houses were common in villages

---

Nynehead Amateur Dramatic Society

Presents

Up The Beanstalk

By Darren Vallier

To be performed at:

Nynehead Memorial Hall

Commencing at 7.30 p.m.

Friday 21st March 2003
and
Saturday 22nd March 2003

Produced by arrangement with Jasper Publishing

The Community of Nynehead
in association with
Actiontrack Performance Company and **West Deane way ARTS PROJECTS**

present

BUILDING UP STEAM

a community play

supported by **TAUNTON DEANE**

SATURDAY 9TH JUNE   6.00pm
NYNEHEAD COURT

**VICTORIAN PICNIC
FROM 4.30pm**

Entry by programme - £1 on door
PARKING LIMITED

Above: *The Taunton Deane Morris Men entertaining the audience at* Building Up Steam.

Top left: *A scene from* Building Up Steam *with Richard Crowe as the Duke of Bedford, Mike Briginshaw as Edward Ayshford Sanford and Sheila Rabson as Henrietta Sanford.*

Country dancing at the perfomance of Building Up Steam.

A celebration in the Nynehead Memorial Club.

Right: *The inauguration of the Eva Edwards memorial seat at the Poole turning on the A38. Seated are: Mr and Mrs D. Lentell; standing: Mr J. Sparks and Mrs C. Lock.*

Below: *Walking the village dogs for the millennium, New Year's Day 2000.*

Above: *The group who in the autumn of 1948 travelled to Torquay to purchase the building which became the Nynehead Memorial Hall. Left to right: C.J. Rowland, Mrs M. Sparks, Mrs W.M. Pugh, E. Atyeo, Mrs T. Luxton, L. Sparks and T.H.G. Luxton.*

Above and left: *Sale details of the huts on sale in Torquay in 1948.*

LOTTING

1	Hut No.1	Hut and annexe with 4 W.C.s and 4 lavatory basins.
2	Hut No.2	Hut with four compartments enclosed by framed and wallboarded partitions.
		Two approx. 11'0" x 9'0".
		Two approx. 18'0" x 12'0".
3	Hut No.3	Hut and annexe with 4 W.C.s and 4 lavatory basins.
4	Hut No.4	Hut with framed and wallboarded partitions across centre.
5	Hut No.5	Hut and annexe with 4 W.C.s and 4 lavatory basins.
6	Hut No.6	Hut with framed and corrugated sheet iron covered way to No.7.
7	Hut No.7	Hut and annexe with 4 W.C.s and 4 lavatory basins.
8	Hut No.8	Hut with framed and boarded covered way to No.9
9	Hut No.9	Hut and annexe with 4 W.C.s and 1 lavatory basin.
10	Hut No.10	Hut with framed and asbestos sheeted annexe used as store.
		Hut divided by framed and wallboarded partitions into 4 compartments
		Dining Room approx. 38'0" x 30'0".
		Kitchen approx. 30' x 15' with 4 oven cooking range on concrete base.
		Two 40 gla boilers.
		One 30" x 18" x 10" Belfast sink with draining board.
		Scullery approx. 12'0" fixed with 4 22" x 18" x 10" Belfast sinks with draining boards. Quantity of shelving.
		Store approx. 12'0" x 9'0".
11	Hut No.11	Hut and annexe approx. 11'0" x 6'0" with two W.Cs, also framed and asbestos sheeting covered connecting way to Hut No.10.
		Portion of flooring concreted over an area approx. 12'0" x 12'0".
		1–30" x 18" x 10" sink disconnected.
		2–27" x 18" x 10" ditto ditto.
12	Hut No.12	Hut and annexe approx. 12'0" x 6'0" with 2 W.Cs and two lavatory basins. Hut has two compartments approx. 11'0" x 8'0" enclosed by framed and wallboarded partitions.
13	Hut No.13	Hut and annexe with 4 W.Cs.
14	Hut No.14	Hut as described.
15	Hut No.15	Hut and annexe with 4 W.C.s and 4 lavatory basins.
16	Hut No.16	Hut as described.
17	Hut No.17	Hut and annexe with 4 W.C.s and 4 lavatory basins.
18	Hut No.18	Hut as described.
19	Hut No.19	Hut and annexe with 4 W.C.s and 4 lavatory basins.
20	Hut No.20	Hut and covered way approx. 10'6" x 6'0" leading to Hut No.21.
		Hut has two compartments approx. 18'0" x 11'0" and 11'6" x 8'6" enclosed by framed and wallboarded partitions.
21	Hut No.21	Hut and annexe with 1 W.C. 1 concrete slabbed urinal. 4 lavatory basins.
22	Hut No.22	Hut as described.

(one survives and is still in use at Crowcombe in West Somerset) where they were the centre of village celebrations such as church ales – in today's terms a combination of village hall and public house but under the control of the churchwardens. The church house in 1792 appears to have been of brick or stone with a slate roof, but the churchwardens' accounts of the seventeenth century give a different picture. By 1668 rent was already being paid for the house, and payments then and in future years show that it was thatched with a beaten earth floor with benches and a chamber. By 1674 repairs were required – 'tymber to repayre ye Church House' cost 8s.6d. – and repairs and improvements continued to be necessary, culminating in 1685 in the addition of a thatched oven for which considerable expenditure was incurred:

For nayles about the church house and Keyes and nayles
for the bells   1s 10d
For Rafters Virst and other tymber about the church house
          4s 6d
For a hundred and halfe of Reed, its carriage and watering
alsoe   £1 5s 6d
For ten bundles of spars 5s 0d
For rods and Wythyes   10d
For Reed, spars and Thatching the oven at the Church
house   1s 4d
For laying up the hundred and halfe of Reed to the
Thatcher
For one hogshead and halfe of lymbe and carriage
          4s 7d
For 200 Bricks for the Oven
          5s 0d
For drawing stones making the Oven and footing the
walls of the Church house 18s 0d
For bringing Stones, sand and bricks in place
          4s 0d

The church house had disappeared by 1837 but by then the schoolroom was available for village recreation. Built probably by the 1820s, it provided a centre for many village activities, ranging from meetings of the Temperance Society in the late-nineteenth century, through musical events and wartime dances, to meetings of the local branch of the British Legion in its early days. It continued to be the main venue for village events until the opening of the Memorial Hall in 1950.

THE MEMORIAL HALL

A survey of the village by Bristol University just after the Second World War showed that a committee had been set up to build a village hall. The survey return, by the headmistress of the village school, stated that:

Nynehead is desperately in need of a Village Hall. A Village Hall Committee has been working for two

years and I believe has about £500 in hand. The Committee has had a difficult task as the only room available is the school.

Nynehead's village hall is deliberately named the Memorial Hall. During the war a series of social events, such as dances, concerts and whist drives, was held mainly in the village school. The aim was to build up a fund to assist the families of any members of the Armed Forces who lost their lives whilst serving in the war. Fortunately all returned and when a public meeting was called to obtain views as to how the money raised should be spent it was agreed that, after a gratuity given to each serving personnel, the balance should be put towards a lasting memorial, namely a village hall. In 1995 the Nynehead Memorial Hall was recorded in the National Inventory of War Memorials.

In 1948 the Bolnore Estates, the owners of Hornshay Farm and a large area of surrounding land and property, agreed to donate a site in Higher Nynehead for the hall. On 28 September 1948 a small group – Mr W.T. Baker, Mr and Mrs T.H.G. Luxton, Mr and Mrs L. Sparks, Mrs W.M. Pugh and Mr F.G. Atyeo, together with Mr C.J. Rowland (a Wellington builder asked along to give advice) – travelled to Torquay where a number of timber buildings occupied during the war as offices for Prudential Assurance were being auctioned. It was decided to buy one of these buildings (which cost £310). After dismantling it was brought back to the site where by the spring of 1950 it had been re-erected and equipped. On 15 April Mr Lloyd Fox performed the opening ceremony which was followed by an evening concert.

As a bank loan was needed Messrs W.T. Baker, T. Luxton, T. Stevens and L. Sparks stood as guarantors to meet the eventual cost of £1,580. It was not until 1960 that the loan was repaid in full. In 1964 a trust deed was drawn up and the Parish Council appointed as custodian trustees with the day-to-day running of the hall being the responsibility of a management committee. In the meantime, in 1954, Mr Fred Atyeo, who was then secretary of the hall committee, had the idea of building an extension onto the side of the hall to provide a club and skittle alley. In due course the Nynehead Memorial Club, a private members' club, was formed and occupies this part of the hall building.

Much improvement work has been carried out over the years since the hall was opened. In 1963 a major expense arose with the provision of a new floor at a cost of £278. The toilets have been modernised, a storage area created and a new entrance to the club built. Tarmacing of the car park was completed in 1992 with the help of a gift of £1,000 from Gulf Oil in acknowledgement of the assistance given by parishioners during and after the railway accident in May 1991. Further grants have been received from the Wyvern Environmental Trust.

OPEN-AIR VENUES

Open-air venues have also been important for both organised and informal activities. The use of the parkland by the river as a location for celebrations, such as the visit of the Duke of Cambridge in 1809 and the coming-of-age of Edward Sanford in 1815, have already been mentioned. The gardens of the Court have seen all sorts of events, including the successful Nynehead Community Play on 9 June 2001. This had been displaced from the first choice of location on the canal in response to the national outbreak of foot-and-mouth disease – which in the event never reached Nynehead. Entitled *Building Up Steam,* the play celebrated the coming of the Grand Western Canal and the railway in the 1830s and 1840s. Guided by the Actiontrack Performance Company and financed by the Borough Council and the Lottery, it involved 100 local people and was seen by an audience of 300 on a superb summer's day.

The demise of the cricket ground at the Court left the village without a playing-field, but in 1977, to celebrate the Queen's silver jubilee, a playing-field for informal activities was developed in Higher Nynehead on land which had been acquired from the Diocese of Bath and Wells. In modern times the fields at Hornshay have been used for dog and horse shows and 'point-to-point' events have taken place at Chipley. For informal activities the paths and fields of the parish have always been attractive to children and adults alike, both from the village and from Wellington. In September 1813 T.H. Ernst walked from the church at Wellington to Nynehead on the path which has been used by many people over the years. He commented in his diary that the land belonged to:

Mr. Sandford [sic] who has a large estate here and has taken some pains in laying out his grounds and making them accessible to the people of Wellington. The best part of them is a shrubbery walk on rising grounds in the midst of water meadows.

The path along the former canal has always been well used. The iron footbridge which carried the footpath from Wellington over the canal, even after the latter had been closed, frequently appears in people's recollections. Mrs Liz Darch of Wellington remembers visiting the canal as a girl with friends and smoking cigarettes made from toilet paper and Old Man's Beard.

The river was particularly attractive for boating, fishing and swimming. A boat-house for the Court had been built in about 1810 on the widened river above the three-arch bridge. Later in the century the river was the venue for regattas and boating until its width was reduced by silting. However, the river continued to be used:

Further up the river was the Weir where when we got older we used to swim and have fun, and one of the most happy people on such events was the daughter of Revd McMoren who officiated then at Nynehead and lived at the Rectory. This daughter kept a boat tied at the weir and often when she used it some lads would attempt to turn her out, but not often succeeded I must say. (Edgar Poole)

In the postwar era the Tone Struggle – a raft race – took place on the river but ceased in the 1980s. Fishing was not always welcomed by landowners if undertaken without permission. In March 1816 William Sanford felt obliged with other landowners to put the following notice in the local paper:

The villagers of Nynehead celebrate the Queen's jubilee in 2002.

Celebrations in the Memorial Hall in the 1950s.

Races in the playing-field to celebrate the Queen's jubilee in 2002.

The Sparks family at a coronation celebration at Nynehead Court, 12 May 1937.
Betty and her brother John are in fancy dress.

Children in fancy dress at a coronation celebration at Nynehead Court, 12 May 1937.
Edward Stevens and June Edwards are dressed as the King and Queen.

Notice is hereby given that if any person or persons be hereafter found trespassing upon the Lands of Wm. A. Sanford, John Nurton, Thomas Fox or Robert Gardner esqrs in the several parishes of West Buckland, Ninehead, Wellington, Runnington and Kittisford, for the purposes of FISHING with a fly or otherwise he or they will be prosecuted as wilful trespassers. A liberal award will be paid to any person giving information against offenders; and, to prevent excuses, all persons will be deemed trespassers who may not have obtained permission from any of the above-named gentlemen.

In contrast a rather romantic view of the river (at Hornshay Bridge) was given in the 1930s by the author Arthur Mee:

One winding road leads out of Nynehead through a beautiful deep cutting overhung with green branches; another passes over a bridge where generations of young people have left their names in stone and lost their hearts in love as they have watched the River Tone drop in a waterfall through the meadows.

Some of the carved names can still be seen.

Some Celebrations

During the nineteenth century detailed accounts begin to appear of 'traditional' village celebrations – fêtes, harvest suppers, etc. – which have continued to this day. National events were also celebrated in the village, focussing initially on three venues – the Burrows, the church and the Court. For Queen Victoria's golden and diamond jubilees, at her death in 1901, the coronation in 1911 of George V, his silver jubilee in 1935 and the coronation in 1937 of George VI a bonfire was lit at the Burrows to end each day's celebrations. These bonfires were mostly independent of other areas, but at the golden jubilee in 1887 the blaze was organised in conjunction with other parishes and lit at a signal from the Monument. At the end of the Second World War, villagers gathered together on the hill for an impromptu party. There was food and drink and the violin was played by Mr Floyd, who is still resident in the village at the time of writing.

The Parish Church as expected held services and rang peels of bells to commemorate all of the afore-mentioned festivals. A report in the *Wellington Weekly News* of 6 February 1901 tells of the memorial service held just after Queen Victoria's death:

A memorial service was held in the church on Saturday afternoon. After the opening voluntary, 'O rest in the Lord', during which the congregation stood, the hymn 'O God our help' was sung. The service for the Burial of the Dead was read, the 90th Psalm being chanted. Instead of the committal prayer the Nunc Dimitis was sung. The

remaining collects were read and the thanksgiving for the late Queen's life and reign. This was followed by the hymn 'Now the labourer's task is o'er', a prayer for the King was read and the blessing. The congregation remained standing whilst Mendelson's [sic] Funeral March and Chopin's 'March Funebre' were played. Appropriate hymns were sung at the Sunday Services. A children's address on the Queen was given in the afternoon.

At the coronation in 1937 a fancy-dress competition was held in Nynehead Court and the service from Westminster Abbey was broadcast in the church at 11a.m. and 1p.m. All newspaper reports say that the services were always very well attended, the church holding about 250 people. It seems that the celebrations that took place in the latter part of the twentieth century did not involved the use of the church though, as when the Jubilee Playing Field was opened in June 1977 a service of blessing and dedication was held in the field from a horsebox.

The third focal point for festivities was Nynehead Court, a use that the owners have encouraged. For the golden jubilee of 1887 the *Wellington Weekly News* recorded that:

... there was an excellently provided dinner in the orangery in the Court for those over 14 years of age and a tea for those under 14 years of age; the women being allowed to have their choice.

Ten years later, however, the women were not given the choice but were provided with only tea alongside their children (what happened to equality?). In 1887:

... they held a programme of athletic sports with dancing and other games filling up a most enjoyable holiday, rendered above all enjoyable through the glorious weather from the Provider of all that is good. (Wellington Weekly News, *23 June*).

Celebrations followed the same pattern of events for nearly 50 years, centred around the Court with bands and Punch-and-Judy shows, hat-trimming competitions, fancy-dress parades, baby shows,

William Lake with his four sons dressed for the wedding of his youngest daughter, Doris.
Left to right: *Jim, Bert, Bill and Ern.*

sports, dancing, tug of war and guessing the weight of a leg of mutton. These occasions were facilitated by the lady of the house, but the work of planning, preparation and execution were done by two committees made up of parish worthies, one for sport and one for food.

The first record of commemorative mugs being issued was at the 1911 coronation of George V, when Mrs Lysaght (the wife of the owner of the Court) presented each child in the village with one, while to the women she presented 'a souvenir of the festival' – quite what that was is not recorded.

For George V's silver jubilee in 1935 a play entitled 'The Empire Chains' was performed by the pupils of the village school who had been trained by Mrs Ware and Miss Kick. Miss Dorothy Kick will be remembered by older residents for her notable quote when dispensing corporal punishment: 'This is going to hurt you now but in later years you'll thank me.' The silver-jubilee celebration was not without its tragedy as Mr H. Crowcombe of Blockhouse Farm was taken ill. The doctor was summoned but sadly Mr Crowcombe later died.

Surprisingly, modern residents can remember very little about the coronation in June 1953. Although some people may have been able to watch it on television (by courtesy of the Wenvoe transmitter), we have to rely on two articles in the *Wellington Weekly News* for information about the celebrations in the village. On 25 February it reported that:

The appointment of a 'mayor' to rule the Coronation plans at Nynehead was one of the suggestions put forward at a meeting of the Committee in the Memorial Hall. Other proposals included the hire of a television set, a bonfire and fireworks display and a presentation of a 5 shilling piece to all babies born in the village during Coronation week.

Whether indeed this did actually happen we are unsure because no reports of the festivities appeared in the local newspaper. In May an announcement for a skittle tournament at the village hall was printed. The winner was to receive a live pig and other valuable prizes were offered. The cost was three balls for 6d. (two and a half pence in present-day currency).

The focal point of events in the second half of the twentieth century moved away from the church to the Memorial Hall. At the silver jubilee in 1977, the 50th anniversary of VE day in 1995, the millennium and the golden jubilee in 2002 the pattern of celebration has been largely the same – an afternoon of fun and games, sports, competitions and exhibitions culminating in a village tea party with such activities as a dance or fireworks in the evening. At most of these events, commemorative mugs have been issued to all the children in the parish. In 1995 special £2 commemorative coins were given to the few residents who had spent the previous 50 years within the village. An engraved plaque was also unveiled over the door of the Memorial Hall to mark its 50th anniversary. For both the millennium and the golden jubilee a parish photograph was taken.

THE WORLD PLOUGHING CHAMPIONSHIPS

Nynehead's farmland has always been attractive to the organisers of ploughing competitions. The 18th World Ploughing Contest (and the 21st National Ploughing Match) took place at Hornshay and Heywood Farms in September 1971. Ploughmen came from all over the world and ceremonies started with a service of dedication and blessing of the plough. A Cairn of Peace to commemorate the event was built outside Heywood Farm on the road to Langford Budville. During the three days of the event, which was won by a Dane, 70,000 people were reported to have attended and the cost of staging the event to have been £68,000.

An exhibition of Nynehead's history was mounted by Andrew Bye and others, with paintings provided by the children at the school. There was a seventeenth-century plough, two eight-foot murals of local views, a copy of the 1837 Tithe Map, old plans of Hornshay Bridge, old school groups, parish records and many other interesting items including nineteenth-century plaques which were made at the nearby Poole brickworks. The exhibition was held in aid of the Memorial Hall improvements. Village children had two days' holiday because the school was being used as a First Aid Post. This was another event when 'the Provider of all that is good' sent beautiful weather. Other events to mark the occasion included an auction sale of antiquities and a dance.

It was from that first exhibition that the Nynehead and District Local History Society came into being, which is now in its 32nd year. The Society has about 60 members, some of whom are the main contributors to this book. The Society enjoys a programme of talks each winter and visits to local places of historical interest in the summer months.

A Local History Society outing to Five Barrows on Exmoor, 1 July 1988. Founder members Gwen Fletcher and Eva Edwards are pictured in the foreground.

Above: *Numerous ploughing matches have taken place over the years, giving spectators the chance to enjoy older, traditional farming methods.*

Right: *Souvenir cover from the World Ploughing Championships, held in Nynehead in 1971.*

Below: *Mrs Val Giles of West Buckland prepares her horses at the Wellington Monument match in 1992*

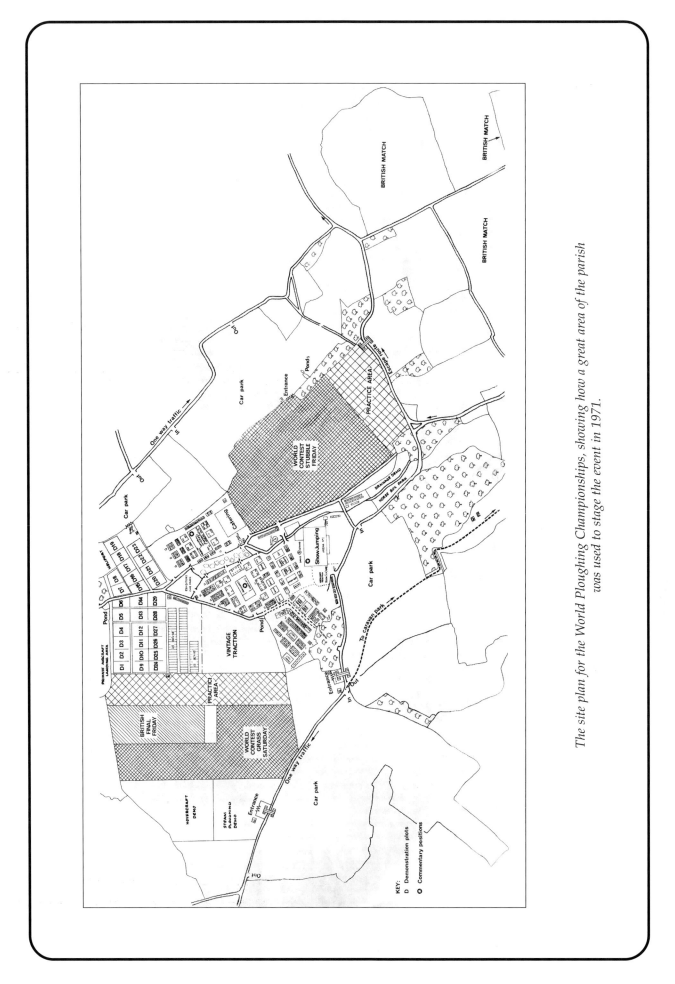

The site plan for the World Ploughing Championships, showing how a great area of the parish was used to stage the event in 1971.

Above: *Building the Cairn of Peace at the World Ploughing Championships, 1971.*

Below: *Dedicating the Cairn of Peace in 1971. Plaques on the cairn show the many nations represented at the championships.*

Tractor ploughing of competition standard

143

The parish church and Nynehead Court, the historic heart of the village.

Right: *The old vicarage in Lower Nynehead, before division into two cottages.*

Cottages at Heywood Farm, typical of the thatched and rendered cottages that have nearly all disappeared. Condemned in 1937 and demolished after the Second World War.

Chapter Fourteen

NYNEHEAD'S BUILDINGS

Nynehead has 23 buildings or other structures officially listed as being of special architectural or historic interest, ranging from All Saints' Church (Grade I), through Nynehead Court (II*) and features associated with the Grand Western Canal, to farm buildings and the Chorley family monument in the churchyard. However, this is not a representative picture of the buildings in the parish and research since the list was prepared has revealed more of interest.

Apart from the larger buildings, such as the church and the Court, little remains of the pre-nineteenth-century 'vernacular' buildings in the parish. It must be assumed that they were on the whole built of locally available materials – rendered stone or cob with thatch for the roofs. Otter sandstone was commonly used, as can be seen at the church and Court both in buildings and walls. On the whole local quarries would have been used but stone was sometimes brought from sources further away, such as Ham Hill in South Somerset. The church reveals a variety of stone types reflecting the importance of the building. In addition to Otter sandstone the builders used Ham stone, especially for windows and doorways, and 'North Curry' stone, which may have come from quarries at Hele towards Taunton. This greyish sandstone was also used in 1817 for the three-arch bridge over the Tone and for the aqueduct carrying the Grand Western Canal over the coach road to the Court.

Brick was used on a significant scale for more important buildings – for example the Court, Chipley, and the houses at Clavengers and Upcott – and at the beginning of the nineteenth century for the ice house at the Court. Nynehead is important in Somerset in terms of its use of bricks. Some would have been produced locally on a small scale in brick pits set up on clay deposits which might not have lasted very long, and others came from further afield. The new house built at Chipley in 1681 required 150,000 bricks and 10,000 'tyle stones', while in September 1800 the Nynehead Court estate paid £12 for 30,000 bricks made and burnt by Thomas Stubbs. There is no indication in the accounts of where the bricks were to be

Interior of the tithe barn at Chipley

used but today this quantity of bricks would suffice to build a fair-sized two-storey house.

The old vicarage next to the school in Nynehead is one of the few remaining examples of rendered and thatched cottages. Although significantly altered, improved and divided into two over the centuries, the building dates from the seventeenth century or earlier. A three-room house with a cross passage, it is built of rendered red sandstone with a gabled thatched roof. It was the vicarage until about the beginning of the nineteenth century when John Sanford became vicar, but remained in the ownership of the church. However, it may not be typical of the ordinary cottages in the village, of which the cottages opposite Heywood Farm were probably a better example. Farm buildings were generally modest, built of the same materials, with the notable exception of the tithe barn at Chipley.

The appearance of the village was transformed in the second half of the nineteenth century with the use of brick and slate on a large scale and the re-roofing or rebuilding of many houses and farm buildings. This stems from the establishment of the brickworks at Poole, on the southern edge of the parish, and the building of the canal and railway which permitted the import of materials, in particular Welsh slate, from non-local sources.

Brick making at Poole began in 1837. Francis Thomas, the owner of Poole Farm, also ran a tannery business and started an interest in clay, which was present on much of his land. He found that the clay near the Grand Western Canal was suitable for brick making and erected an old-style square kiln on or near the wharf, situated where the canal crossed the Wellington to Nynehead road. It was a very convenient site, since fuel could be delivered by canal and the bricks transported afterwards to customers. In the small field bordered by the Poole road, the Nynehead road and the railway line cottages were built for the employees at the brickworks.

When Francis Thomas died in 1842, his son William took over the farm, tannery and brick business. At first he used the old kiln but this was soon

Brickwork cottages at Poole, since demolished. It was said that the occupiers were close enough to the railway to shake hands with the engine drivers.

Poole brickworks in the 1960s.

Court Cottages, built c.1890 in the 'Nynehead' style.

Stables at the Court built or rebuilt in stone with brick details in the late-nineteenth century.

abandoned and he erected others on the site of the first excavations. In all he had to erect five kilns to meet the local demand for his bricks. Pipe drains were also produced to meet the growing demand from farmers wishing to drain wet land. When William Thomas inherited the business, work was already under way on the new railway line that conveniently ran right through Poole Farm, thus allowing his products to be transported further afield.

Although bricks are no longer made here the legacy remains, both at Poole itself where a row of nineteenth-century cottages is dominated by industrial and commercial activity, and in Nynehead which has many brick buildings dating from the late-nineteenth century. These share characteristics which could well be unique to the village – the use of red brick, moulded brick surrounds to door and window openings, a particular form of brick decoration on the gable-end, slate roofs of a 45-degree pitch and no overhang on the gable-end.

The buildings with these characteristics include cottages and barns but so far only two have been accurately dated. The first of these is the new vicarage built on glebe land, at the top of the Hollow. Its construction was so important for the village that the *Wellington Weekly News* gave a detailed report of the celebrations that accompanied the laying of the foundation-stone on 20 June 1867, a report worth quoting in full as it gives a good picture of life in the village at that time:

Stables at Nynehead Court with typical brick gable-end details from the late-nineteenth century.

LAYING THE FOUNDATION STONE OF NYNEHEAD VICARAGE

Thursday last being the fourth natal day of Master Henry John Seymour Sanford, the occasion was deemed a fitting opportunity to lay the foundation stone of the new residence for the Rev. W.H. Walrond, the vicar of the parish. Hitherto Nynehead has not had the advantage of a resident minister and since the rev. gentleman who administers to their spiritual wants has been among them, he has so endeared himself to his parishioners, both young and old, that the determination of E.A. Sanford, Esq. to erect a vicarage was received with great satisfaction. The site of the new building lies about a quarter of a mile from Nynehead Court, and is situated on a fine piece of land at the top of the Hollow. It was in the tenancy of Mr. S. Bailey, and was known by the name of Crosslands. The site commands a most magnificent view of the surrounding country, and

altogether is an excellent position for such an edifice. The erection of the building is entrusted to Mr Davis of Taunton, from the designs of Mr John Hayward, High Street, Exeter, both gentlemen being present at the ceremony on Thursday last. Some members of the band of the 8th Somerset V.R.C. were in attendance, and preceded the schoolchildren from the school house. They were followed by Masters H. and A. Sanford on horseback, with E.A. Sanford Esq., and Mrs. W.A. Sanford in an open phaeton. On arriving at the ground a trowel was handed to young master Harry, who having adjusted the mortar beneath the stone, and tapping it gently with a mallet, assisted by his eldest brother, declared the stone to be truly laid.

After the ceremony, E.A. Sanford Esq. made a few remarks to the effect that they had not had hitherto a resident minister among them, but they had been that day engaged in a work which would ensure them one for the future. He believed that the vicar was beloved by them, and worthily so, and concluded by asking them to give him three cheers. This being effected, the Rev. W.H. Walrond said they had a representative of the State amongst them in the person of Mr. Sanford, as a magistrate of the County, and when he (the vicar) came to reside with them, they would have a representative of the Church, and as upholders of the Church and State, he trusted both would be found doing their best to uphold the higher state of God. He thanked Mr. Sanford and those present for their kind manifestations. Three cheers were then given for the Masters Sanford (the juvenile masons) who had so effectively performed their task, the eldest of whom thanked the company. Three hearty and ringing cheers were then given for the worthy Squire, who said he was always happy to do anything for their benefit, and he knew of no act more gratifying than the one they had that day been engaged in.

The children of the school then sang the Old Hundreth very prettily, and after the band played 'God save the Queen,' the School children proceeded to the lawn in front of the house where tea was kindly provided for them, and likewise for the old people of the parish, who took tea in the conservatory, which had been decorated for the occasion, the initial letters of Master H. Sanford and other devices forming a very pretty effect. During the tea the band played, and subsequently proceeded to the extensive grounds adjoining the mansion, where dancing and various games were indulged in, the Squire lending his presence and seeing

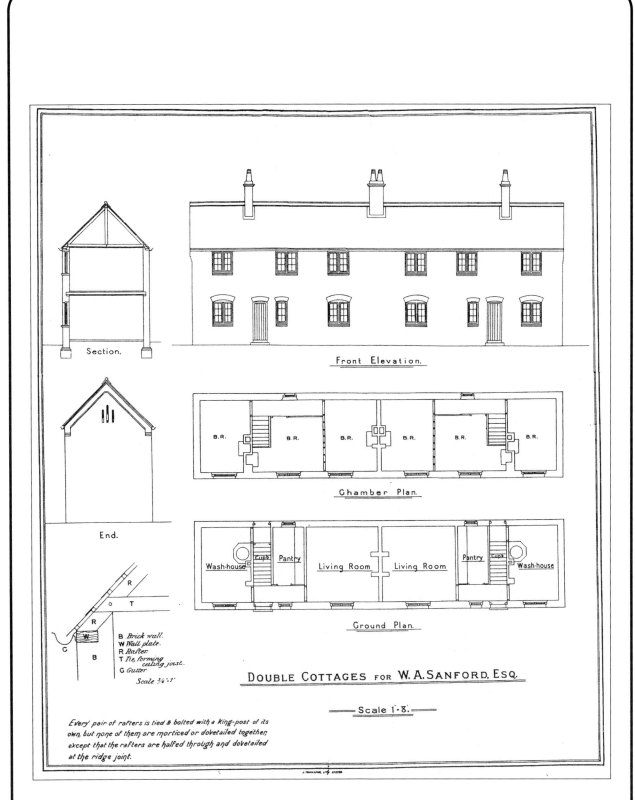

Section.

Front Elevation.

End.

B.R.   B.R.   B.R.   B.R.   B.R.   B.R.

Chamber Plan.

B   Brick wall.
W   Wall plate.
R   Rafter.
T   Tie, forming ceiling joist.
G   Gutter
Scale ¾"=1'

Wash-house   Cupb   Pantry   Living Room   Living Room   Pantry   Cupb   Wash-house

Ground Plan.

DOUBLE COTTAGES FOR W. A. SANFORD, ESQ.

Scale 1"=8'

Every pair of rafters is tied & bolted with a king-post of its
own, but none of them are morticed or dovetailed together,
except that the rafters are halfed through and dovetailed
at the ridge joint.

*A plan of cottages on the Sanford estate. The document is not signed or dated,
but is thought to originate from c.1890.*

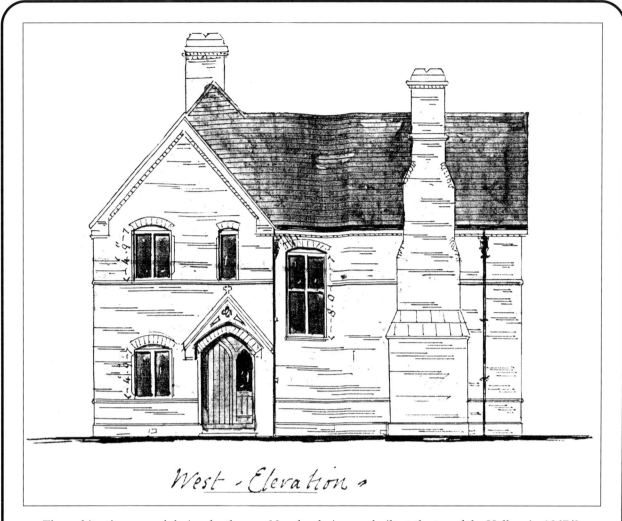

West - Elevation

The architect's proposed design for the new Nynehead vicarage built at the top of the Hollow in 1867/8.

Clearing the latest building site – Higher Nynehead in 2003.

after the wants and comforts of his poor but delighted guests. The amusements were engaged in till day had nearly become night. Among the company present we noticed Mrs. and Miss Goddard, Mr. Ambroise Goddard. Captain and Adjutant Peard and lady, the Rev. W.H. and Mrs. Walrond, the Misses Walrond, the Rev. T.C. Tanner, late vicar of the parish, Miss Warren, besides many members of the Squire's family.

Letters between the architect, John Hayward, Mr Sanford and Mr Walrond show that the original idea was to build the house in stone, like the new vicarage at Langford Budville which Hayward also designed. However, Mr Walrond preferred brick and this was chosen, with Bishops Lydeard stone for the dressings in the chimney and over the front door.

The 1871 Census records that the first occupiers were Revd William Henry Walrond (aged 45, born in Hereford), his wife Patience (38, born in Stepney), a cook Charlotte Tickner (64, unmarried, born in Luggshall) and a housemaid, Sarah Ann Darch (32, born in Skilgate). A survey in 1884 showed that the property then consisted of the vicarage house and offices, a lawn, a partially walled garden, a fowl house, a potting shed, a pigsty, two small stables, a coach-house with a loft over and a tool house. There were also 16 acres of glebe land including a cottage and garden, the cottage 'new brick built and slate covered' (now Higher Upcott). The vicarage was used as such until 1948. It was then let until sold to Thomas's, builders from West Buckland, who in 1958 subdivided the main house, converted the coach-house to a dwelling and built three bungalows in the grounds.

Between the building of the new vicarage in 1867 and 1900 at least 18 more buildings in brick were erected or rebuilt in the same local style. The school extension (1875), Crossland Cottages, Court Cottages and Dollings, among many others, have the same features, as do farm buildings at the Court and Bickley Farm. These buildings are all on the Sanford estate or have Sanford connections and as far as is known the style is unique to Nynehead. At this time it was common for a large estate to develop its own style of building, which raises the question of who designed them. We know that John Hayward designed the vicarage but as no indication has been found that he had direct involvement with the other buildings it seems that his ideas were adopted by the estate. It might be relevant that William Sanford was now in charge, himself an architect who designed the church extensions in the late 1860s. These new buildings had such an impact on the village that in October 1891 the *Wellington Weekly News* reported that:

Visitors to Nynehead during the past summer can hardly have failed to notice the number of new cottages which have been built here in the last few years. Many of these outlook some very pretty views.

There are also later brick buildings, for example Poole Farm and Ash Farm (built 1901), of the different, rather severe style in which the roof overhangs the gable-ends. Buildings of this style occur throughout the Wellington area and many are the work of the local architect E.J. Howard.

The twentieth century saw a considerable amount of house building in the parish, especially in Higher Nynehead, together with individual bungalows on infill sites, in East Nynehead in particular. Of the 40 houses built since the war about half have been erected by local builder Brian Hardacre. Most of the houses are in a style typical of their time and very different from the older buildings in the village.

Although the village has expanded, particularly in the last 50 years, many interesting buildings have been lost. The most significant was the old house at Chipley, while the loss of the traditional thatched and rendered cottages has been mentioned. Some of those shown on the Tithe Map of 1837 have disappeared completely, such as Haywood Cottages and the cottages at Hornshay Farm, while others have been rebuilt. Roundoak Cottages and Glebe Cottage in Higher Nynehead appear on the Tithe Map but were rebuilt in brick in the late-nineteenth century. Other 'lost' buildings of note include the church house, the orangery at Nynehead Court, the lift-keeper's cottage on the canal and buildings at Poole associated with the brickworks.

The building of Roundoak Gardens in 1968.

Militia on manoeuvres by the River Tone, c.1863.

Wartime farming at Chipley including POWs in a view from the top of a hayrick. Both horses and Ferguson tractors were being used.

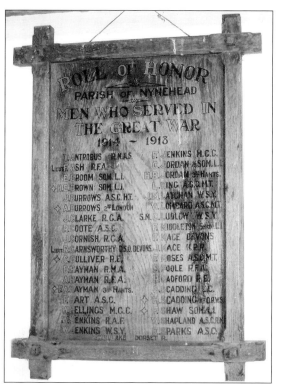

Above: *The Nynehead Roll of Honour for the First World War.*

The Nynehead and Oake Home Guard. Left to right, back row: ?, ?, Jack Hawkins, R. Hartnell, ?, ?, ?, T. Hutchings, F. Pulman, E. Stevens, J. Floyd; middle row: S. Jones, T. Lock, H. Dunn, R. Marks, Bill Winter, Bob Winter, H. Sharland, B. Pavey, ?, L. Stone, E. Derbe; front row: Bill Radford, L. Sparks, Revd Rees Davies, R.B. Hankey, A. Elston, Fred Bickham, ?.

Chapter Fifteen

WARS & RUMOURS OF WARS

Wars and civil strife, or at least news of such events, have never been far away from rural life but what we know of their impact on Nynehead in its early history is limited. In the Middle Ages the feudal system laid certain military requirements on holders of land and some hints of these can be seen. Followers of Simon de Montfort in rebellion against Henry III in the middle of the thirteenth century included Thomas Bramfit of Nynehead who was declared to be a rebel (along with others from West Somerset). In 1266 Henry III decreed that each county should have a 'captain' who, with the sheriff, should have the duty of restraining all robbers. By the sixteenth century communities were required to raise volunteers for national emergencies and in 1569 'muster rolls' were prepared. In the tithing of 'Nynehed' there were eight 'ablemen' and five in the tithing of 'Pyxston'. In Nynehead John Gibbens was a 'light horseman' and there were also three 'pekemen', three archers and a billman. The muster roll also lists the armour and weapons to be provided. Interestingly, Bradford provided only three ablemen while 17 are listed for the tithing of Heale.

We don't know if these Nynehead men ever went into action but in medieval times the village could well have provided soldiers for service elsewhere, maybe even abroad. In 1395 John Wyke served in Aquitaine under John Duke of Lancaster and one can surmise that other Nynehead men might have gone with him.

The domestic turmoil of the seventeenth century did affect Nynehead and the Sanfords, and no doubt others from the village became directly involved in the Civil War on the Parliamentary side. However, the village was not only affected by wars with foreign countries or by civil strife. In the seventeenth century 'Barbary' pirates from the Mediterranean were active around the southern coasts of Britain and Ireland, sometimes making raids and capturing the locals. Even villages not affected directly responded to the captives' plight. In 1680 a collection was made in Nynehead 'towards the release and ransom of the captives in Turkey'. The churchwardens' accounts record that 67 people contributed a total of £3.18s.0d., individual donations ranging from 1d. (Willi Mailes) to £2 (John Sanford Esq. and 'his Ladye').

A century later Nynehead people played their part in the response to the French Revolution and the dangers the new regime were perceived to bring. In 1794 an Act of Parliament allowed the setting up of local volunteer forces, following which a public meeting was held in Wells on 9 May 1794 when the idea of volunteer forces in Somerset was promoted. Among those subscribing £50 or more was 'John Ashford Sanford' (sic) – presumably Revd John Sanford. At the end of 1796 a troop of yeomanry cavalry was formed at Wellington and added to two troops at Milverton. The officers included William Ayshford Sanford. In 1798 a company of volunteer infantry was formed at Milverton, with Lieutenant John Nurton of Chipley as one of the officers.

Sixty years later the threat of invasion by Napoleon III gave rise to the establishment of Rifle Volunteers but little progress was made until after the danger was passed. In 1860 the 3rd (Taunton) Somerset Rifle Volunteer Corps was founded, open to all persons (presumably men only) of 16 years of age and over within 20 miles of Taunton. William Ayshford Sanford (grandson of the William mentioned above) was captain until he resigned in 1867. The Rifle Corps undertook at least one training exercise in Nynehead as reported by the *Wellington Weekly News* on 7 May 1863:

VOLUNTEERS WING DRILL AT NYNEHEAD

The first of these 'wing drills'... took place on Monday afternoon, in the 'Great Meadow' at Nynehead Park, which was kindly placed at the disposal of Capt. Sanford by Mr. J. Bailey (himself a veteran soldier of 43 years experience). A more suitable place could not have been obtained in the neighbourhood. Situated by the margin of the river Tone, affording an excellent view of its miniature falls and feathered spray, and surrounded with extensive plains which gradually undulate towards Wellington and the Blackdown Hills, dotted at intervals with browsing herds and small coppices. The lovers of the picturesque had a beautiful landscape before them. Unrivalled for its natural beauties, which, without any other source of entertainment, would afford them pleasure in being present.

The Mr J. Bailey referred to was presumably John Bailey (1793–1865), eldest brother of the Sanfords' former agent Charles Bailey. It seems that this event was captured by a local photographer, but what caught the interest of the reporter most of all was the quality of the local scenery.

The Boer War in South Africa (1899–1902) had a profound effect on the people of Britain, especially the relief of Mafeking and Ladysmith and the Battle of Rorke's Drift. The war had a particular significance for the Sanfords as Lord Methuen of Corsham Court in Wiltshire who was related to them played a major part in the hostilities. This interest in the war reached the village school in Nynehead as, on the morning of 24 March 1899, there was an extra lesson in geography, possibly to tell the children about South Africa. Half-day holidays were awarded in March and May 1902 at the request of Mr Sanford to celebrate the relief of Ladysmith and that of Mafeking, and yet again on 2 June to celebrate the coming of peace to South Africa.

THE FIRST WORLD WAR, 1914–18

On 13 October 1913 the school was visited by a former pupil, Clyde Washer, who had left the school in 1891 and had reached a responsible position in the Navy. His visit was to encourage the boys to wish to do well, and presumably to consider the Forces as a career. Less than a year later war was declared, but it is not known whether any of the boys took his advice. A total of 37 Nynehead men did serve in the First World War, six of whom did not return, but not all who wished to enlist were able to do so. Mr Tipper, the headmaster,

was one of these, in November 1915 making an unsuccessful application to enlist under Lord Derby's recruiting scheme. In 1917 he went to Taunton to be medically re-examined for the Army but was passed for Home Service only and continued with his duties at the school.

Neither the school log-book nor the Parish Council minutes refer to the outbreak of war in August 1914 but in May the following year 12-year-old Thomas Mace was given permission by the school to work for Mr Ash at Upcott Farm for its duration. 'War boys' are frequently mentioned as being on the school roll, including George Wyatt in November 1915 and Ernest Lake two years later.

The village was active in giving financial help to the war effort. In July 1915 four girls raised £1.12s.3d. in a collection for the French Relief Fund, while more formally a 'Nynehead War Savings Association' was set up, with the aim of encouraging the schoolchildren to help provide money for the war. The head teacher was the secretary and the vicar, Revd H.C. Launder, the treasurer. It was intended that they meet on the second Monday of each month. By 17 October 1918, a month before the Armistice, the progress of the Association was considered satisfactory. There were 53 members and £537.2s.9d. had been subscribed. Other activities were undertaken to stimulate support for the war effort. On 15 December 1915 Lady Tyler of Wellington visited the school, bringing a framed picture of Jack Cornwell, VC, that she had donated. On the second anniversary of the declaration of war the head teacher took as the basis for a talk to the

---

~ Roll of Honour ~
Parish of Nynehead
Men who served in the First World War, 1914–18

T. Antrobus, RNAS	J.M. Latchan, WSI
Lt. F. Ash, RFA	W. Lombard, ASCMT
E. Broom, Som L.Inf	SM C. Ludlow, WSY
H.E. Brown, Som L.Inf	F. Middleton, Shrop. LI
J. Burrows, A.S.C. HT	F. Mace, Devons
A. Burrows, 2nd London	J. Mace, KRR
J. Clarke, RGA	F. Moses, ASCMT
R. Coote, ASC	S. Poole, RE
J. Cornish, RCA	R. Radford, RE
Lt R. Garnsworthy, DSO Devons	G. Scadding, LC
C. Gulliver, RE	H. Scadding, 11th QRWS
D. Hayman, RMA	F. Shaw, Som LI
A. Hayman, RFA	W. Shopland, ASCRM
F.A. Hayman, 3rd Hants	E. Sparks, ASC
F. Hart, ASC	
W. Hellings, MGC	**Six of these died at war:**
W. Jenkins, RAF	
W. Jenkins, WSY	
W.H. Lake, Dorset R	Charles Gulliver, RE, killed in action
F. Jenkins, MGC	Frank Shaw, Som LI, killed in action
C. Jordan, 1/5 Som L.I.	Albert Borrows 2nd C. of L killed in action
H.B. Jordan, 3rd Hants	Henry E. Brown, Som LI, died in hospital. India
L. King, ASCMT	Henry Scadding, QRWS Regt, died prisoner of war.
	Francis A.Hayman, 3rd Hamp Regt, killed in action

Wartime farming at Chipley.

children a book – Blair's *How can we help*, published by the London County Council. From the middle of the war the Parish Council supported better food production in the village by supplying seed potatoes.

Heywood Farm played a very particular part in the war, the Sanfords' agents reporting in 1917 that:

... a considerable portion of this farm was commandeered by the Government as a large mule depot, at which something like 20,000 mules were run during the early part of the war.

Mr Mortimer the farmer was thought to have benefited but the land suffered from an infestation of docks (from hay brought in from Sedgemoor) and serious poaching by animal feet in wet weather. It is said that many mules died and were buried on the farm, and that their bones appear from time to time.

THE SECOND WORLD WAR, 1939–45

Twenty years later Britain was drawn into a second war against Germany, the effects on Nynehead being different from those of the First World War. There is no official record in the village of how many from Nynehead served in the war but it is significant that all returned – there was no loss of life.

There was a direct physical impact in that the establishment of airfields on the Blackdowns required protective measures in the surrounding areas. In Nynehead searchlights were set up at Hornshay on the Poole side of the bridge in 1940, while the County Sites and Monuments Record lists a decoy near Higher Nynehead, although it is thought that this could have been at Luckham Farm, just outside the parish. American servicemen were temporarily based in the village, camping on the flood plain near Hornshay prior to the D-Day invasion, and it is said that their vehicles were parked in the avenue of trees along the coach road for camouflage. The Americans came to have their drink in the sitting-room behind the shop at The Bush in East

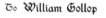

This Token
accompanied by a cheque from a fund subscribed by your friends of
Nynehead
is to greet and welcome you on your safe return from Service during the Great War—
1939 - 1944

The certificate given to William Gollop in recognition of his services in the Second World War.

Nynehead. Herbert Williams made the cider in a huge press in a shed to the left of house. Prisoners of war appeared on farms in the parish, cutting flax in the fields at Bickley and working at Chipley.

Nynehead had its Home Guard contingent which, in addition to its official activities, organised social events. On Friday 8 June 1942 a 'Home Guard Dance' was held in the schoolroom from 8p.m. to 1a.m. The music was provided by Gilbert Hussey's band and admission was 1s.3d. (1s. for members of HM Forces). This was one of several dances held at the school in that year and one of many activities to raise money for the war effort. The 'Wings for Victory' week in June 1943 was particularly successful, with £3,014.14s.0d. being attributed to Nynehead. On a lesser scale but also important was the sum of £2.17s.8d. collected by the schoolchildren in three months in 1944 for the Red Cross Rural Pennies scheme.

At the school the immediate response to the declaration of war by Germany on Poland at the end of August 1939 was its closure for 18 days, as required by the County Education Committee. It was reopened on the 18 September when 25 evacuees from St Paul's School, at Bow in East London, were received. They worked in the infants' classroom, with two certificated teachers, Mrs Parker and Miss Elwood, separately from the Nynehead children who were in the main classroom. Some of the evacuees were billeted in the village although they did not always find the wholesome food of the country to their taste. At Christmas 1939 they put on their own entertainment. The evacuees remained at the school until April 1942. In the meantime they had been visited by health visitors from the capital. More evacuees came for a short time in 1944, perhaps because of the V1 bombing raids. The first respirator drill at the school was held on 31 May 1940 followed by air-raid precautions in June (during the Battle of Britain). The windows of the school were covered with cellophane as a precaution.

Nynehead cannot have been in a particularly vulnerable area for air raids and in fact the one bomb that did fall on the village was dropped by a British aircraft. In about 1943/44 a bomb fell in the field next to the vicarage in Higher Nynehead. It did considerable damage to the roof and windows of the building and a lesser amount to Glebe Cottage on the other side of the field. The bomb was witnessed by John Sparks, then a boy living with his family at the cottage:

I well remember a winter's evening during the 1939–45 war when we were sitting around the living-room table. My sister had gone to bed. Reg Marks who lived in

Island Cottage was with us. I think my mother and father and Reg were probably playing cards when there was an almighty bang and I remember Reg shouting 'get under the table'. A bomb had dropped in the field between us and the vicarage.

It transpired it was dropped from an Allied plane which had a bomb jammed in the hold and had been instructed to try and release it over Langford Common. As the pilot described on visiting the village the following day he thought he was in fact over the common. The next day we found fragments of the bomb, one piece 15" long on the lawn in front of the house.

Joy Stone recalls the effect the war had on the village:

I remember the searchlights at Hornsey as they picked out a German plane droning above. The prisoners of war hand cutting the flax in the fields at Bickley Farm and the many evacuees who attended Nynehead school. The siren going when we had to cling under our desks and then the all clear. Several bombs were dropped, one at Bradford and one in the field by the old vicarage. It blew out the windows of the house all around. It was dropped by one of our planes because of terrible weather conditions that night.

The end of the war in 1945 was celebrated with enthusiasm in the village:

The day war was declared over [8 May 1945] Mum gave me and my two brothers a treat. We were allowed to stay up for the celebrations. This was held in the field next to Hornsey Farm up near the small copse. A fire was lit and someone gave barrels of drinks and local man Mr. Floyd played the violin. We all danced with joy. (Joy Stone)

In the Wellington area many villages put on events on behalf of their 'Welcome Home' funds. In Nynehead Tom Stevens junr organised two dances at the school which raised £14, while between 30 July and 6 August a week's skittling was held 'near the school', for which the prize was a live pig. More formally on 2 March 1947 a service of thanksgiving for the homecoming of servicemen and women was held at All Saints' Church. Because no one from the village was killed in the war the money collected for relatives was put towards the building of the village hall – known as the Memorial Hall – which is now officially registered as a war memorial.

The Nynehead branch of the British Legion was started in 1945 as a small sub-branch of Milverton until, in November 1951 with a membership of 72, it became a full branch. A new standard was purchased in April 1952 from voluntary contributions towards the cost from members of the branch. Edgar Poole the secretary recalls:

The total number of this sub branch to Milverton was 6 members and cash held £8. I accepted charge and in a

short while had enlarged the membership and encouraged outsiders to come to events arranged and using the school for a small charge. For about 18 months we attended Milverton branch meetings travelling there by coach and made many suggestions and contributed to the Mother or Father Branch.

We then concentrated on entertainments using the school, dances, plays, cabarets carried out by some members, also people I knew and managed to entice. It was so popular that in a short while we had 200-odd members and I and the committee arranged buses to bring those interested and who bought tickets to the events – Bus free!! It was a great success and some people I now meet remind me of the good old days at Nynehead.

With a greatly increased membership which had added a women's section there was the time to become a Full Branch and we did and obtained the Branch colours, and also had a special service at Nynehead church of dedication, the service conducted by the vicar of Wellington and Nynehead, the Rev. John Grinter.

I, with Committee's blessing, asked Capt. Sanford if he would become President which he did and we commenced Annual dinners at the Squirrel Hotel, Wellington. Sam Broom of Nynehead was our Chairman.

A total of 140 people attended the dedication and 'laying-up' of the new British Legion flag in Nynehead church in July 1952, which was followed by buffet tea in the Memorial Hall.

Form of Thanksgiving for the Home-Coming of Service Men and Women to Nynehead.

As sanctioned by the Lord Bishop of Bath and Wells, and held at

ALL SAINTS' CHURCH, NYNEHEAD.

SUNDAY, 2nd MARCH, 1947, at 6.30 p.m.

INTERIOR OF NYNEHEAD CHURCH

The following Men and Women have returned to Nynehead from Active Service during the World War 1939–1945 :—

Ernest Birch	Thomas Hayman	Raymond Winter
Claude Broom	Reginald Humphries	Alfred Williams
John Cornish	Douglas Parsons	Arthur Williams
James Elson	Martin Sanford	Norah Birch
Geoffrey Fletcher	W. C. Ayshford Sanford	Joan Lock
Frederick Gollop	Thomas Stevens	Margaret Macabe
William Gollop	Charles Waterhouse	Eileen Phillips
Frederick Hayes	Desmond Winter	Mary Waller

The three following served during the War, and are still away from home :—

Francis Bickerstaff.   Robert Elson.   Harold Lock.

Programme for the thanksgiving service held in Nynehead church in 1947.

Postscript
2003

In 1947 H.E. Bracey of the University of Bristol's Reconstruction Research Group carried out a survey of the social framework of rural society in Somerset. The return made on behalf of Nynehead showed a village with virtually no facilities or locally-based craftsmen. There was no playing-field and no utility services apart from an electricity supply to the church and school by the Wellington Electricity Co. Domestic waste was collected only once every 12 weeks and the bus service was limited to Wednesdays and Saturdays. There was a Post Office (but no shop) and a district nurse was resident in the village.

The school was the focus for social activities such as dances, sponsored by an Entertainment Committee and held at least once a month. The provision of a village hall was being actively investigated. There was an active cricket club and regular whist drives.

In the ensuing five-and-a-half decades Nynehead has changed significantly. There is no longer a Post Office but the village has acquired many of the facilities expected at the beginning of the twenty-first century. Mains electricity is universal, nearly all houses are on mains water and much of the village is served by mains drainage. Although many houses have been built the population has not increased significantly compared with the number living in the village 200 years ago. However, the majority of adults in Nynehead were probably not born here and for most people village life without the modern facilities expected by town and country dweller alike – such as televisions, telephones, cars and supermarkets – would be unimaginable.

Most people go out of the village to work and relatively few are still working on the land. Nevertheless, Nynehead remains an attractive rural parish whose environment is largely governed by the farmers and others who manage the land.

The beginning of 2003 was marked by a very successful pantomime put on by a new Nynehead Amateur Dramatics Society involving a large number of villagers, whether as performers or audience. This reflects the amount of social activity going on with as many organisations now as there were at the end of the nineteenth century. There is again an active and successful cricket club. Developments in nearby Wellington which could have an effect on Nynehead are being watched with interest, as are proposals to reinstate the Grand Western Canal. These would have major implications for the village and its environment.

In May 2003 a questionnaire survey was carried out in Nynehead under the Countryside Agency's Vital Villages initiative. At the time of writing the results of the survey, which had a response of over 70 per cent, are being awaited with interest.

Residents of the village in the millennium year.

Subscribers

Mrs J. Allgrove, Taunton

Jean and Dennis Almond, Nynehead, Somerset

Marjorie Baker, Rockwell Green

Josie, Paul, Keri and Jade Barnett, Nynehead, Somerset

Jane E. Barr, Nynehead, Somerset

Alison J. Barratt, Nynehead, Somerset

Martin and Zen Bellamy

Norah Birch, Nynehead, Somerset

Doreen E. Bird, Westford, Somerset

Annie Harriet Bone, Wellington, Somerset

Alison Boreham (née Clarke)

Shirley M. Boyes, Wellington, Somerset

Mike Briginshaw and Nancy Douglas, Nynehead

Stanley J. Broom, Rockwell Green, Wellington, Somerset

Mrs Susan E. Buckling, formerly of Nynehead

Phil and Sarah Bunker, Nynehead

Paul and Gill Carter and Family, Nynehead, Somerset

Mrs Rosemary Chorley, Cambridge

Anthony J.C. Clarke, Bristol

Mary Cook, Wenvoe, Cardiff

Brian A. Curran-Gollop, Wellington, Somerset

Hugh and Jann Dalzell, Wellington, Somerset

Joy E. Darby, Nynehead, Somerset

Robin and Carole Darby

Mr D.M. and Mrs B.M. Davies, Nynehead, Somerset

John Denham, Eton Wick, Windsor, Berkshire

Andy Denham, Wellington, Somerset

K.M. Dew, Taunton

Keith Dyer, Bradford-on-Tone

R.W. Dyke (née Greenslade), Nynehead. 4 August 1945

Mrs Jean V. Edwards, Wellington

Richard N. Emeny, Goathurst, Somerset

Mr Bryan Eveleigh, born Nynehead, of Plymouth, Devon

J.M. and F. Figg

Janet and Peter Fox

Robert and Kathleen Gibbs, Pershore

Brian D. Gill, Taunton, Somerset

Dorothy E.L. Gill, Rockwell Green/formerly of Lower Poole

Roger and Graham Gollop, formerly of Oakridge, Nynehead

Mr John W. Gollop, St Brelade, Jersey

Kevin J. Gollop, St Peter, Jersey

Advocate Julian C. Gollop, St Ouen, Jersey

Mrs Margaret Audrey Gollop, Guernsey, Channel Islands

Professor Peter Haggett, Chew Magna, Somerset

Vera Hake, Nynehead

Michael Hake, Corfe, Taunton

Revd Josie Harrison

Michael L. Hartnell, Nynehead

Louise and Keith Haslam, Nynehead

Edward Hawkins, Donyatt, Somerset

D.J. and T.M. Helps, Wellington

Kim E. Hewlett, St Brelade, Jersey

Steve and Sandy Higgs, The Old Vicarage, Nynehead

John and Marjorie Hill, Holywell Lake, Somerset

Doreen M. Hoeller, Nynehead, Somerset

The Hollingsworth Family, Court Cottages, Nynehead

Julian B. Hosking, Nynehead, Somerset

Ann Corsan Howe, Court Gardens Farm

Dr J.A. James, Bradford on Tone, Somerset

Mrs Margaret May Keates (née Goldsworthy), Nynehead

P. Alan Ketley

Muriel and David Kodritsch,

Douglas Lentell, Old Vicarage, Nynehead 1924–46

Capt. John Lloyd, Langford Budville, Somerset

Mr J.H.A. Lloyd, London

Rose Lomax (née Hawkins), Taunton, Somerset

Jan MacLaran (née Press), Nynehead

Denise Fredalyne Maynard, Nynehead, Somerset

James Methuen-Campbell, Corsham, Wiltshire

Cathleen M. Moon, Wellington, Somerset

Mr and Mrs J.K. Morrish, retired farmer, Ham Farm 1958–90

Angela, Rob and Georgina Néeds, Nynehead, Somerset

Jennifer Mary Newman, Wellington, Somerset

Nynehead Church of England Primary School

Peter and Geraldine Orr, East Nynehead, Somerset

David and Carolyn Palmer, East Nynehead

David Parry

R.C. and C.C. Pearson, Nynehead, Somerset

Denice and Mike Perrin, The Lynch 1989–2000

Mr Gerald H. Perry, late of Farthings Close, Nynehead, Somerset

Mike Perry, Wellington

Yvonne Phillips, Sheffield

Mr Edgar E. Poole, Wellington, Somerset

David J. Price, Roundoak Gardens, Nynehead

Mrs Dorothy M.S. Priddle, Taunton

Mr and Mrs D. Raybould, Nynehead, Somerset

Susan and Alec Reynolds, Nynehead, Somerset

Mark A. Reynolds, Cutcombe, Wheddon Cross

Paul D. Reynolds, Crouch End, London

Barbara Ridgley, Milverton, Somerset

Alan and Sheila Rogers, Wellington, Somerset

Elizabeth A. Russell (née Clarke), Wellington, Somerset

Edward Sanford, Chipley Park, Nynehead

M. Ayshford Sanford, Broadway, Worcestershire

Susanna Sanford, Chipley Park, Nynehead

William Sanford, Chipley Park, Nynehead

Mr Paul N. Ayshford Sanford, Evenlode, Gloucestershire

Marietta Ayshford Sanford

Mrs A. Sartain, Wellington, Somerset

Valerie E. Simpson, Ham, Nr Nynehead, Somerset

Mrs Mary A. Sparks, Nynehead

John R. Sparks, Nynehead, Somerset

Mr Gary J. Sparks, Nynehead

Betty Sparks, Nynehead, Somerset

Margaret J. Spurway, Wellington, Somerset

Anne M. Stack, Willand, Devon

Mrs Joy Stone (née Gollop), Trull, Somerset

Paul and Jill Swindale, Croscombe, Wells, Somerset

William Desmond Gollop Twose, Bristol

Captain Neville E. Upham of East Nynehead, and Mr Matthew R. Upham of London

H.J. Van De Hoef, Chipley, Somerset

Mrs C.M. Waller

John F.W. Walling, Newton Abbot, Devon

Janet and Chris Watson, Aysgarth, Nynehead

Sylvia Waymouth, Wellington, Somerset

Wellington Museum and Historical Society

Del Wiggins, Buckland St Mary

Roy and Bridget Wrenn, Wellington, Somerset

Community Histories

The Book of Addiscombe • Canning & Clyde Road Residents Association & Friends

The Book of Addiscombe, Vol. II • Canning & Clyde Road Residents Association & Friends

The Book of Axminster with Kilmington • Les Berry and Gerald Gosling

The Book of Bampton • Caroline Seward

The Book of Barnstaple • Avril Stone

The Book of Barnstaple, Vol. II • Avril Stone

The Book of The Bedwyns • The Bedwyn History Society

The Book of Bickington • Stuart Hands

Blandford Forum: A Millennium Portrait • Blandford Town Council

The Book of Bramford • Bramford Local History Group

The Book of Breage & Germoe • Stephen Polglase

The Book of Bridestowe • R. Cann

The Book of Bridport • Rodney Legg

The Book of Brixham • Frank Pearce

The Book of Buckfastleigh • Sandra Coleman

The Book of Buckland Monachorum & Yelverton • Hemery

The Book of Carharrack • Carharrack Old Cornwall Society

The Book of Carshalton • Stella Wilks and Gordon Rookledge

The Parish Book of Cerne Abbas • Vale and Vale

The Book of Chagford • Ian Rice

The Book of Chapel-en-le-Frith • Mike Smith

The Book of Chittlehamholt with Warkleigh & Satterleigh • Richard Lethbridge

The Book of Chittlehampton • Various

The Book of Colney Heath • Bryan Lilley

The Book of Constantine • Moore and Trethowan

The Book of Cornwood & Lutton • Compiled by the People of the Parish

The Book of Creech St Michael • June Small

The Book of Cullompton • Compiled by the People of the Parish

The Book of Dawlish • Frank Pearce

The Book of Dulverton, Brushford, Bury & Exebridge • Dulverton & District Civic Society

The Book of Dunster • Hilary Binding

The Book of Edale • Gordon Miller

The Ellacombe Book • Sydney R. Langmead

The Book of Exmouth • W.H. Pascoe

The Book of Grampound with Creed • Bane and Oliver

The Book of Hayling Island & Langstone • Rogers

The Book of Helston • Jenkin with Carter

The Book of Hemyock • Clist and Dracott

The Book of Herne Hill • Patricia Jenkyns

The Book of Hethersett • Hethersett Society Research Group

The Book of High Bickington • Avril Stone

The Book of Ilsington • Dick Wills

The Book of Kingskerswell • Carsewella Local History Group

The Book of Lamerton • Ann Cole & Friends

Lanner, A Cornish Mining Parish • Sharron Schwartz and Roger Parker

The Book of Leigh & Bransford • Malcolm Scott

The Book of Litcham with Lexham & Mileham • Litcham Historical & Amenity Society

The Book of Loddiswell • Reg and Betty Sampson

The New Book of Lostwithiel • Barbara Fraser

The Book of Lulworth • Rodney Legg

The Book of Lustleigh • Joe Crowdy

The Book of Lyme Regis • Rodney Legg

The Book of Manaton • Compiled by the People of the Parish

The Book of Markyate • Markyate Local History Society

The Book of Mawnan • Mawnan Local History Group

The Book of Meavy • Pauline Hemery

The Book of Minehead with Alcombe • Binding and Stevens

The Book of Morchard Bishop • Jeff Kingaby

The Book of Newdigate • John Callcut

The Book of Nidderdale • Nidderdale Musuem Society

The Book of Northlew with Ashbury • Northlew History Group

The Book of North Newton • Robins and Robins

The Book of North Tawton • Baker, Hoare and Shields

The Book of Nynehead • Nynehead & District History Society

The Book of Okehampton • Radford and Radford

The Book of Paignton • Frank Pearce

The Book of Penge, Anerley & Crystal Palace • Peter Abbott

The Book of Peter Tavy with Cudlipptown • Peter Tavy Heritage Group

The Book of Pimperne • Jean Coull

The Book of Plymtree • Tony Eames

The Book of Porlock • Denis Corner

Postbridge – The Heart of Dartmoor • Reg Bellamy

The Book of Priddy • Albert Thompson

The Book of Princetown • Dr Gardner-Thorpe

The Book of Rattery • By the People of the Parish

The Book of St Day • Joseph Mills and Paul Annear

The Book of Sampford Courtenay with Honeychurch • Stephanie Pouya

The Book of Sculthorpe • Gary Windeler

The Book of Seaton • Ted Gosling

The Book of Sidmouth • Ted Gosling and Sheila Luxton

The Book of Silverton • Silverton Local History Society

The Book of South Molton • Jonathan Edmunds

The Book of South Stoke with Midford • Edited by Robert Parfitt

South Tawton & South Zeal with Sticklepath • Radfords

The Book of Sparkwell with Hemerdon & Lee Mill • Pam James

The Book of Staverton • Pete Lavis

The Book of Stithians • Stithians Parish History Group

The Book of Stogumber, Monksilver, Nettlecombe & Elworthy • Maurice and Joyce Chidgey

The Book of Studland • Rodney Legg

The Book of Swanage • Rodney Legg

The Book of Tavistock • Gerry Woodcock

The Book of Thorley • Sylvia McDonald and Bill Hardy

The Book of Torbay • Frank Pearce

Uncle Tom Cobley & All: Widecombe-in-the-Moor • Stephen Woods

The Book of Watchet • Compiled by David Banks

The Book of West Huntspill • By the People of the Parish

Widecombe-in-the-Moor • Stephen Woods

The Book of Williton • Michael Williams

The Book of Witheridge • Peter and Freda Tout and John Usmar

The Book of Withycombe • Chris Boyles

Woodbury: The Twentieth Century Revisited • Roger Stokes

The Book of Woolmer Green • Compiled by the People of the Parish

For details of any of the above titles or if you are interested in writing your own history, please contact: Commissioning Editor Community Histories, Halsgrove House, Lower Moor Way, Tiverton Business Park, Tiverton, Devon EX16 6SS, England; tel: 01884 259636; email: katyc@halsgrove.com